An Alcoholic's
Collateral Damage

G. MICHAEL SANBORN

An Alcoholic's Collateral Damage

ReadersMagnet, LLC

In memory of my beloved sister, "Cilla,"
Priscilla Lee Sanborn Chase.

CONTENTS

INTRODUCTION

This is a retrospective accounting of the life my siblings and I endured at the loving hands of our alcoholic mother. Every family has its own idiosyncrasies. Most are trivial and benign. Others are overtly harmful and easier to expose. It is the subtle, persistent ones in an alcoholic family that takes a toll with long range, even lifetime consequences on the members of an alcoholic family. The effects are in our relationships within and outside the family. We may be stronger in some respects but it comes with a price to our confidence and esteem.

I describe the everyday interactions within my family. We descended from a very typical family in the 1950s to growing up in poverty as our mother's alcoholism overpower her and the effects it had on us. Survivor is a label often applied to us. I never liked the label since it implies a high mortality rate. There may be a slightly higher mortality rate due to the abuse and neglect, but it is difficult to isolate from other risk factors. We lived through it but not without a cost. The alcoholic suffers damage, emotionally and physically. Those hopelessly connected to the damaged alcoholic suffer collateral damage. In some ways, the damage is comparable to the alcoholic's damage. In many ways, it is significantly different. I refer to these differences as collateral damage. Like alcoholics who share characteristics with other alcoholics, we share some common characteristics and some unique to our personalities.

We vividly remember that which hurt or scares. We learn to avoid harmful things as a survival technique. Pleasant memories often involve feeling safe, comfortable, and satisfied, which are secondary to our immediate survival. This process becomes distorted in a family with an alcoholic. These intensive negative experiences related to immediate survival dominate memories overshadowing the few happy ones. Even the happy times are infused with intense sibling rivalry for an advantage in the daily struggles. I described how I felt and learned how to cope with my mother's inconsistent and often irrational parenting. I struggled from being a very dependent child through my developmental years and began asserting my own adult voice. This account ends when I become an adult. I address the life-long struggles in subsequent book, *"Recovery from an Alcoholic's Collateral Damage."*

Though unique for everyone, there are commonalities among families with an alcoholic. Like in other families, we encounter people in our lives that help us along the way. Some play a large role with prolonged guidance while some have a significant impact with brief involvement. There are those that could have helped but chose not to get involved. Sometimes a small action can have a profound effect. It can be the simple recognition, validation, or understanding of our situation. Lastly, there are those that make it harder for a child suffering with an alcoholic parent. It is the cumulative and exponential effects that help us develop into who we become. I wish to recognize some of these people and show my great appreciation even for those powerless to help. During the fifties and sixties, there was little general understanding about how to help families with an alcoholic. Television showed men in roles that solved all family problems. My dad was helpless against my mother's powerfully domineering personality and there was no one to help him. Instead, he was perceived as being weak and less of a man for not controlling his wife.

I divided the book into age clusters normally set apart by some rite of passage. After each section, I review the damage as it progresses through our lives. I also evaluate the impact of influences within and outside our family.

I hope to help others validate their feelings and begin to understand them. I hope so very much that I can positively influence alcoholics to understand, accept and to seek assistance to help their families. My readers can consider themselves survivors. I prefer to describe us as collaterals.

EARLIEST, PRESCHOOL YEARS

Mom told me that we lived at ten Douglas Street when I was born. The older, two-story home that was built on the hillside opposite to the Fellows Gear Shaper, the dominant employer in Springfield, Vermont. My paternal grandfather, George Henry Sanborn, was a mechanical engineer and a salesman for this company. He traveled all over the world; selling and setting up the machines they sold. I rarely saw him. My paternal grandmother, Effie Allison Sanborn, was around more but still infrequently.

My father, George Henry Sanborn JR., set out to follow in his father's footsteps. He attended college, studying engineering. He dropped out after one semester and took a job with Fellows Gear Shaper as a draftsman.

Typical of the times, Dad was the "bread winner," the family provider who worked all day. My mother, Lillian Mary (Blais) Sanborn, was a stay-at-home mom. Mom was proud to be the first one in her family to graduate from high school. She met and married my dad the year she graduated from high school, in nineteen fifty. Dad was two years older than she.

My older sister, Priscilla (Cilla), was born in nineteen fifty-one. I came along in nineteen fifty-two, followed by my brother, Gary, in nineteen fifty-four. It always frustrated me when people asked if we were twins. He was a year and a half younger than I was. It cheated me out of the respect commonly given to an older child. Debra was born in nineteen fifty-six.

I have no memory of living at ten Douglass Street. In what would be a recurring theme in my childhood, my parents felt that things will be better in the new, larger, or better home. We moved to one hundred sixty South Street just before my first birthday. It was a small, modern ranch style home with a large back yard. It was diagonally across the street from an elementary school with a playground.

My mother often boasted that my sister taught me how to walk. When I stood supported by a kitchen chair, Cilla pulled the chair causing me to take a step. Mom often reminded me of this as though I owed her something for her efforts. It felt like she wanted me to feel an obligation to her, which was successful. I sometimes wondered. Perhaps Cilla's intensions were more sinister. Perhaps she intended to deprive me of the support of the chair and wanted me to fall. Whatever her intensions, too much was projected onto my two-year-old sister. Much later, I began to realize that this was the first stages of parentifying my sister and later me. Mom and my father delegated many responsibilities upon the older children that parents should have retained.

Because I was just eighteen months old, I do not remember my brother's birth. I vaguely remember him as a baby. I was only aware of his presence and the attention given to him, leaving Cilla and I to entertain ourselves.

I remember strict guidelines on where we could play. Most limitations involved a small area on the living room floor in which we had to remain. We were expected to sit or crawl in this area and play with only the single toy that was given to us. Mom monitored our language with occasional threats to wash our mouths out with soap for using the wrong words or argued. If we misbehaved, we were told to kneel in the corner.

There was a card table set up in the living room near the kitchen door. That is where we ate and could color in our coloring books. I often played with a wooden train. It had a wooden track but the track fell apart or the train fell out of it most of the time. Pushing this wooden train around in circles on a track soon grew boring. I gave up on the track and pushed the train on the floor. Mom did not allow this so I did it when she was not watching. It was much more fun off the track. Discouragingly, it kept falling apart off the track. I played mostly with the engine and coal car and my imagination. I could imagine pulling and pushing large objects simulated by the pieces of track and the other cars. Within the restrictions of the small play area, I spent many hours in this imaginative play to escape boredom.

Cilla and I took baths together to save hot water. Mom controlled the temperature and the amount of water. It was only enough water to cover our butt and private parts. We were not allowed to touch these parts. They got cleaned by soaking them.

Aunt Billie, my father's aunt, occasionally babysat us when we were small. Things seemed odd when she was there. Though she seemed strict, she never punished us. We did not have to be so closely corralled on the floor. We could play in our rooms. With more freedom, I did not feel as secure and confident when she was around.

I remember one traumatic episode with Aunt Billie. I required a toilet seat insert and step stool when sitting on the toilet. I felt embarrassed asking for her assistance, so I thought that I could hold myself without the seat. Everything was going well until I tried to wipe myself. I placed one butt cheek on the edge of the toilet seat, leaned to my left and held myself with one hand. Almost immediately after releasing the other hand to reach for the toilet paper, I fell in. My butt felt the cold water. My knees were in my chest. I tried to lift myself out of the toilet, but I just could not get my butt high enough. I reluctantly called to Aunt Billie. She came to my rescue. She was so nice, telling me that I should have asked for her help. I do not understand why I did not trust her in the first place.

Uncle Bernie, my mother's brother who was nine years younger than her, babysat us sometimes. We had a fun relationship with him on the farm. We used to wait for him to get off the school bus and wrestle with him on the front lawn. He used to say, "Pull my finger." We refused at first, thinking it was a strange request. He insisted so I complied. He farted when I pulled, then blamed me for causing him to fart. I wanted him to fart more to understand this relationship. I struggled to get to his fingers he tried to keep away from me. When I finally got one and pulled, it did not work.

Uncle Bernie brought a plastic dart gun when he came to babysit one time. He showed me how to load it. I could barely push the dart in hard enough to get it to click. He cautioned me on how to not break things or leave marks on the wallpaper. The painted wooden doors worked best. When the darts would not stick, he said, "Come here, I'll show you." He spat into his hand and indicated that he wanted me to dip the dart in the puddle of spit in the palm of his hand. When I hesitated, he became more demanding. I thought it was gross and ran off. He called, "You little bastard," as he wiped his spit on his pant leg. His comment hurt, especially since it came from someone I admired. I put the gun away and played alone the remainder of the time he babysat.

I played alone with the gun when he was not around. I moistened the darts with my tongue. It worked well but I could only play with it when Mom was not around.

When Debra was born, I was four years old, Cilla was five, and Gary was two years old. We stayed with my maternal grandparents. We called my grandfather "Pop." My Uncle Bernie started calling him that instead of the standard French-Canadian "Pa-Pere." Pop liked this special title so we all used it. Grandma genuinely enjoyed having us in her home. They lived on "The Farm." My grandfather called himself a market gardener, selling vegetables to local markets and from his stand on the farm. Both grandparents were proud to call themselves Canuck that described their Canadian heritage.

My grandparents' farmhouse had little internal plumbing. They had a spring fed tank in the kitchen. The overflow drained from the house to the old horse trough under the barn. They had a shallow well in the basement that provided pressurized water to the kitchen sink, which was used sparingly. There were no inside bathrooms. The outhouse was in the back inside corner of the barn. It dropped expelled bodily functions eight feet into the old pig pen under the barn. We were much too small to use it. It was too high for us to climb. I certainly did not want to fall in like I did with Aunt Billie. We used a parlor pot in the house. Grandma just set it in the hall for us when we needed it. The boys were expected go outside to pee, behind the woodshed, garage, or barn. I was OK with it when the corn was tall. When the corn was short, the neighbors could see us. Even though they were eight hundred feet away, I felt self-conscious about exposing myself. Gary and I often had peeing for distance contests, which I always won. Once, Gary tried to humiliate me by calling out to everyone, "Michael is peeing." I retaliated by getting my best distance ever and peed on him. He shouted, "Hey," stopped, then ran off. It successfully stopped his attempts to humiliate me.

We washed our face and hands every night before bedtime at Grandma's. Baths were once a week, on Saturday evening. Grandma gave us our baths in the elongated porcelain kitchen sink. She got the warm water from the tank in wood-burning kitchen stove using a cooking pan. She held it with a potholder and a towel to prevent dripping on the floor. I remember being proud when I was big enough to jump onto the cabinet without her having to lift me. I always wore my underwear. Grandma did not wash the area it covered. When our baths were done, she used the same pan to fill the woodstove tank from the spring water tank beside the kitchen sink.

Pop did not shave every day, but always shaved before going to town. He used a straight razor that he sharpened with a leather strap. He lathered his face with a moistened brush and a bar of soap. We were fascinated with the swirling motions he made with the long-bristled brush against the soap, then on his face. It seemed scary watching him drag that straight, sharp razor across his face and neck. He dried his face with a towel, then poured some cologne on his hand and splashed it on his face when he finished.

We all climbed into my grandfather's nineteen fifty-one Internal Harvester flatbed truck to go visit my mother in the hospital. We were not allowed onto the maternity ward. I remember talking to my mother in the second-floor window from the parking lot. I stood beside my grandparents as my mother talked to them. She was giving them some information about when she would return home and when my father would come get us. I grew bored, anxiously pacing around my grandparents until we finally left.

Most of my early memories of my grandmother are her working in the kitchen while we played on the floor of the living room. Grandma saved empty thread spools. I could use them to build imaginary forts with imaginary attackers. I built walls, then knocked out the spools one-by-one until the wall collapsed. Grandma also showed us how to use a large button and thread to make a spinning toy. We started it by holding the thread with the button between our hands. By twirling the button in a circle, we were able to get the thread to twist. With enough twists, we could get the button to spin back and forth by pulling our hands apart, then relaxing to get the button to rewind itself. I could get it spinning so fast that it made a whirling sound. Eventually the friction wore through the thread and it broke. Usually, the thread entangled on the button but sometimes it took off like a wheel spinning and rolling across the floor until it crashed into something. I tried combining the spinning button and my play with the spools, but I could never find an interesting interaction. The spinning button made a noise against my spool fort, but it would not knock it down as I imagined my fictitious attackers did. I could swing the bottom like a wrecking ball, but it was too light to be effective.

Outside in the wintertime, I found small chunks of snow on the banks that I could bomb with snowballs. My goal was to make them fall from a castle wall in my private war against a king. I imagined that the snowbank was a wall that I could never penetrate. Attacking it and seeing parts crumble were satisfying.

At our South Street home, Dad built a fence around the back yard, a sandbox, and a swing set. We were not allowed outside while he built these. Afterwards, we were allowed in the sandbox and swing set but not near the fence. My brother and I got toy bulldozers. I liked to meticulously build a road in the sandbox. Gary liked to push his bulldozer at unrealistic speeds, wrecking most of what I did. Whenever I complained to my mother, she told me to "help him play" or to "play together." It meant to me that I needed to let Gary wreck my projects. I was learning that my efforts were of little concern to my mother who just did not want to be bothered. I tried to stay in one small area and let Gary have the rest of the sandbox but he would intrude just as I built something nice. Sometimes we used our bulldozers outside the sandbox and were told by either parent to stay in the sandbox. I got very frustrated with the bulldozer and played with it progressively less.

One day, Dad came home with three large balloons. My sister, brother and I were ecstatic. Dad warned us to keep them off the ground or they would pop. Cilla and I were having fun bouncing them into the air and carefully keeping them off the ground like Dad said. Gary allowed his to hit the ground and it burst. Dad left and returned with another one for him. We did not think that was fair. Gary was careless and should not be rewarded with a new balloon. I decided to burst mine. I let it hit the ground several times but it would not pop. I sat on it and still it did not pop. I sat on it and bounced until it finally broke. I brought it to my mother who said that Dad was not going to buy any more. I protested that it was not fair because Gary could have another. Mom replied that I needed to be more careful with it because I was older. I was angry with this growing double standard with me on the losing end.

Mom regularly sent us to bed at six-thirty. I protested that it was too early and that I was not tired. She told me to go lay in bed until I was tired. I had the top bunk. Gary and I often argued and Mom would yell at us, "Go to sleep." I could not command myself to sleep like Mom demanded. Instead, I started imagining myself as a cowboy or Indian in various circumstances that I saw in TV shows. My favorite fantasy was to be captured and raised by the Indians.

One night, Dad decided to mow the lawn outside our open bedroom window just as we went to bed. I felt how unreasonable it was to send us to sleep knowing the loud lawn mower would keep us awake. I remember one fall how my father debated whether he should rake the leaves before he mowed the lawn on one of these nights. He mowed the lawn first, explaining that there would be fewer leaves to rake because some would be ground small and settle into the grass. He started raking leaves a little each day but never finished before it snowed.

I began to realize the early bedtime was that Mom just wanted us "out of her hair" and "to have some peace and quiet." These were likely the times she could enjoy her beer more. I was aware that she drank something in the kitchen while we played but lacked the understanding of what it was. I have a vague memory of a glass on the end of the kitchen counter next to the refrigerator.

She often interrupted her cooking, cleaning, laundry, or ironing to drink from it.

We shared a tricycle. It had very narrow tires that did not roll easily in our crushed stone driveway. The front walkway was easier to pedal on but was short and narrow. Turning the tricycle around was difficult. The lawn formed a small bank near the entrance to the house. I used to pretend that I was driving my bulldozer and pressed hard on the pedals trying to climb it. I rocked back and forth to get some motion and extra pressure on the pedal. It was much too hard to pedal on the grass like Mom said, so I turned around and pedaled back down the walkway into the driveway.

Mom was talking to a neighbor in our driveway one day. She told us to play nearby. When we asked to go into the back yard, she told us to be quiet. The adults were talking, and kids were not allowed to interrupt. Telling us to be quiet and ignoring our request to play in the back yard meant that we had to stay with her. I rode the tricycle while I waited. I grew bored riding on the walkway and tried riding in the driveway. I came upon a rock that presented a similar barrier as the bank on the edge of the walkway. I pretended that I was driving the bulldozer that could climb the boulder. I tried the similar technique, rocking forward and back. I got part way up onto the rock, then rolled back. I tried rocking harder, with all my effort. I tipped too far forward and went over the handlebars. As I fell, I desperately maintained my tight grip on the handlebars. When my chin hit the driveway, I thought how I should have let go of the handlebars and place my hands in front of my face but instinctively maintained my grip on the handlebars. My chin hurt. It did not feel right. I touched it. It felt numb yet painful and there was blood on my hand when I took it away. I did as my mother had told me other times, leave it alone and it will stop bleeding.

My chin continued to hurt and feel numb at the same time. Mom was talking with the neighbor and I knew that she did not want me to interrupt. I walked around a little and felt my chin several times. It was still bleeding. I decided to show my mother. I walked up to her and called to her. She ignored me and continued talking. I tried a few more times and she continued to ignore me. I checked my chin and it was still bleeding and felt strange. I pulled on her dress several times, harder each time. Finally, she looked down at me and saw the blood. She stopped her conversation and brought me into the kitchen. She wet a washcloth and rubbed my chin. It hurt. She looked closer and decided that she needed to call my father at work. Dad came right away and brought me to the hospital.

What I remember most about the short ride to the hospital is how Dad gave me special attention. Dad assured me how he would stay with me while the doctor fixed my chin. He pretended it was an emergency and accelerated the car for a short distance, then returned to normal speed. He said that it was like riding in an ambulance. I felt safe with him and trusted his care.

Mom thought Dr. Bacon was a great doctor. He was a generalist providing family medicine and minor surgery. I learned later that he was a bit crude. He stitched my chin but it was not well done, leaving an annoying bump on one end. The scar was my visible badge of courage and strength.

I remember a routine visit to Dr. Bacon's office. We waited in the small waiting room, reading the children's books. Cilla and I were first. The nurse checked us and administered the vaccinations. We returned to the waiting room and Debra and Gary went it. After a short time, I heard Mom's voice trying to get Gary to cooperate as he screamed. She called out to me saying, "Stop him." I was confused until I saw Gary running out of the office. She was holding Debra and Gary took the opportunity to make his escape. Many conflicting thoughts ran simultaneously through my mind. Whenever I got physical with Gary at home, I got punished. I got punished much more severely if I did anything physical in public. I wanted to do as my mother asked and to stop Gary but did not want to get punished. I also felt a little sorry for my brother who was screaming in a panic. I stood by the door to the hallway and spread my arms like I did to help move the chickens back into my grandparents' chicken coop. I anticipated trying to catch Gary as he ran as fast as he could but did not expect that I could. He was running with all his strength and I was not that much bigger than he. I was much relieved when Gary diverted to the small table in the waiting room. He dropped to the floor and crawled under it. He turned onto his side and curled into a fetal position. I felt satisfied that I met my obligation and he was contained. Mom came out of the examination room and ordered him out from under the table. He refused, while crying and screaming. She tried to drag him out but he was too tightly wedged among the table legs and held onto them. Mom lifted the table off him. He laid there on the floor, fully exposed in his fetal position, and screaming. Mom grabbed his arm and dragged him back into the examination room. Gary screamed the whole time but still got his vaccination.

Dad spent some special time with me in the cellar letting me help him with things on his work bench. He had a short stool for me to stand on. One day, Mom allowed me to play downstairs while Dad was at work. I tried to get a screwdriver from its holder that was just out of my reach. I stretched hard, then the stool suddenly went out from under my feet. I fell with my groin hitting the edge of the bench. I felt a pain as I slid to the floor. When most of the pain started to subside, I felt an enduring pain in my upper left thigh. It was hard for me to walk but I managed to get up the stairs. I waited in the living room for a while, but the pain continued. I decided to tell Mom.

I walked into the kitchen and interrupted her as she worked at the kitchen counter. I told her that my upper leg hurt. She did not seem concerned and told me to rub it. It hurt to touch it and I felt a swollen area. I told her that rubbing did not help. She told me to sit and rub it some more. I followed her instructions and returned later, insisting that it still hurt and it was swelling more. Mom reluctantly stopped what she was doing an instructed me to pull my pants down. An area at the top of my left leg was swelling, making an oval bubble. Mom described it as the size of a goose egg. Mom told me to sit in the living room. She gave me a wet, warm wash cloth and told me to hold is on the swelling until it went down.

After a while, I called to Mom and told her that it was getting bigger and harder. She called Dad and he brought me to the doctor's office. Dr. Bacon said that I needed surgery and admitted me to the hospital. I had been to the hospital to have my tonsils removed, so I had an idea of what to expect. He operated the next morning. I remember the nurses placing a gas mask on my face. They told me to count backwards from ten. I tried but I knew they could not hear me through the mask, so I just moved my lips, making them think that I was counting. I fell asleep at seven. I saw a large array of key holes. There were rows and rows of them moving diagonally in front of me. I tried to look through them but could see only yellow light. They became annoying. I imagined having a machine gun and started shooting them. They just kept coming. I then imagined shooting through the key holes and wondering what I might be hitting on the other side.

The key holes stopped moving and went away. I opened my eyes and saw a nurse on the other side of the room with two other beds. She noticed me waking up right away and came to me. She asked me how I was feeling. I was very groggy and tried to figure out where I was and what was happening. I started to realize that I was in the hospital and tried to take a mental inventory of my body so that I could answer her question. I just could not gain my senses well enough to respond. She said some kind words assuring me that she was going to take good care of me. When she asked how my leg was feeling, I realized that it hurt worse than ever. She gave me a pill and assured me that it would help. It did not. I forced my mind to ignore the pain with little success. I was extremely uncomfortable.

Dr. Bacon came in a short while later. He was dressed in green clothes and had a face mask hanging from around his neck and a green cloth tied on his head. He assured me that I would be fine. He told the nurse that they could bring me to my room.

The nurses asked if I could climb onto the stretcher as they placed it beside my bed. I moved carefully onto the stretcher. I realized that I was wearing only a johnny and no underwear. I felt uncomfortably exposed. I felt vulnerable on the stretcher. I did not like relinquishing control over moving my body. Mom was standing by the window and watched as they rolled me in the hospital room. They placed the stretcher alongside of the bed. The nurse asked me if I could move into the bed, which I did. I got tangled in the blanket. The nurse took away the blanket, exposing my private parts. I tried to cover myself. She pulled my johnny into place, covering me properly. My leg hurt immensely but I tried extremely hard not to show it. Mom talked to me but I found it hard to focus on what she was saying. It seemed more like she was talking to the nurses than she was to me. I fell back to sleep. Mom was there when I woke. She said that I would have to stay in the hospital for a while. She stayed a little while longer, then left.

The nurses checked on me several times. As I grew more awake, I felt weird as my privates rubbed on the sheets. I also felt trapped in bed and vulnerable without underwear. I pulled the sheets tightly along my sides. A nurse demanded that I pee in a strange urinal. I was reluctant to expose myself but knew protesting would be futile. After I peed, she offered me some choices of things with which I could play. I chose dominoes. She showed me how I could set them up and have them knock themselves down. I played for a while. I had to stay in bed, had only a few dominos, and the table was wobbly, so it became frustrating. I fell back to sleep again.

When I woke up the next morning, my mother was there. She pointed to a box at the foot of my bed and said it was from Uncle Bernie. He came to visit while I was sleeping. It was a Mr. Potato Head. I opened it and she showed me how to make faces with the plastic potato. It was OK but did not allow for much creativity. I played with it mostly because she expected me to.

I was very bored. Somehow, I found a piece of string. I could try tying different knots. I could imagine rescuing people off the cliff edge of my bed, using the guard rails to bring them to safety. I could image a high wire performance on my string, putting it at fantastic angles and variations. I made a lasso and caught wild mustangs, buffalos, and renegade Indians. I wished that I had more interesting toys but the string was the best that I had while confined in this bed. Later, Mom joked that all she needed was to give me a piece of string and I could entertain myself for hours. I hated that comment but of course remained silent. I very much wanted better toys but the string and my imagination was all that I had.

Dr. Bacon came again. He removed the bandages and exposed a deep, open cut in my leg down the center of the goose egg. He squeezed some white paste from a tube into the deep cut. He taped a large piece of gauze on top of it. He told my mother to do this every day.

Mom described to people how fascinated she was to see the tissue grow in and the blood vessels developing. She often told me to open my pants to show people when they came to visit. I did not care to expose even my underwear but did as she told me. She eventually stopped telling me to do this. She explained that I embarrassed her because she wished that I had clean underwear on. I did not understand. I always bathed and changed my clothes as she told me. Still, I felt responsible for embarrassing her but did not know how to avoid doing so again. I did not know how to wear underwear and keep them clean. I did not even understand how they looked when they were dirty.

Cilla was entering the first grade. The school as diagonally across the street from us. Mom walked her to the playground and left her with the waiting teacher. She brought me to my first day of Kindergarten. I was neither excited nor worried. I knew that it was something that I must do and was unconcerned. Mom said that she would stay in the back of the room. I did not think it was necessary, knowing that I had to do this myself. The teacher told me to find the desk with my name on it. She told me to color the picture with the set of six crayons. I looked back several times and saw my mother talking with another mother. Each time I looked, I wondered why she had not said goodbye and left. Finally, I looked back and she was not there. I felt hurt that she did not say goodbye. From her point of view, she waited until I was sufficiently distracted so that she could sneak out and

I would not cry. I would not cry anyway, but I felt hurt that she did not say goodbye.

I finished the picture and was ready to turn it into the teacher. She told me to write my name on it. This put me in a difficult position. My name is George Michael Sanborn. My mother told me that Dad wanted my name to be George Henry Sanborn III. Mom wanted her first son to be named Michael. When I was with my dad, he called me George. When I was with my mother, she called me Michael, as did my maternal grandparents. Since I was last with Mom, I decided to write Michael. The problem was, I spelled it "MICHEAL." The teacher saw it and laughed, "Can't you spell your own name?" This hurt me deeply. No one taught me how to spell my name. I could spell George because I liked the symmetry of the name, "GE" twice and separated by "OR." It was almost musical when I spelled it with rhythm. In a short period of time, twice I was made to feel disparaged by adults, abandoned by my mother and ridicules by the teacher. Determined not to make the mistake again. I struggled to memorize the spelling of my name but was not confident. I made the connection that A came before the E, just as it did in the alphabet. Alas, I could confidently spell my name.

In our South Street home, we spent much of our play time together, on the floor in the living room. Debra was usually in the kitchen with Mom, in a highchair or walker. Cilla and I played well together. Gary was the disrupter. He often intruded in our play. It could be either with Cilla, me, or when we played together. Gary did not just join our play. He disrupted it by knocking over my toys, such as my dominos or the wooden train set. He took Cilla's doll clothes and tea set dishes from her. When we asked for Mom's help, she told us to get along saying, "Shut up and play with him" or "Let him play." She seemed to favor Gary because he was the youngest. She expected Cilla and I to correct his behavior. Mom's demands only gave Gary permission to continue his misbehavior. I was happy when he disrupted Cilla and left me alone. Eventually, he would take over my play. I found it easier to just give up and play something else. Unfortunately, Gary would follow. Sitting still, away from toys and ignoring him was the only way I could escape his disruptions. Eventually, we got terribly angry with him and would retaliate. Five and six-year-old children do not have many skills to control a three-year-old. Cilla especially started to slap him and eventually we punched him on the shoulder.

Gary protested and cried when we hit him. Mom would charge in from the kitchen. Due to her large size, there was a loud boom with each step she took. She leaned forward with her right hand ready to render discipline and demand what happened. She did not try to sort out our simultaneous crying, screaming, and attempts to explain. Her resolution was to slap the offender on the head. From her perspective, Cilla and I were the offenders for not getting alone with Gary. Our heads were the easiest for her to reach because we were expected to be kneeling or sitting on the floor when we played. She slapped us on our heads. The slap did not hurt that much but the strain on my neck hurt.

Other times, Mom detected the deteriorating interactions and warned us. This only encouraged Gary to continue because he learned that Cilla and I would be the ones to be punished. As Mom charged in, both Cilla and I said that it was Gary. Mom slapped all of us on the head. When Cilla and I protested, Mom's typical response was that she was being fair. I did not have the words to express it, but I knew it was not fair. I understood the concept that equal is not fair. Equal punishment to everyone for one person's actions is very unfair. I strongly resented Mom's methods of discipline. A telltale characteristic of my emotional status is in any pictures. I am the one who is never smiling.

Mom often threatened to wash our mouths out with soap if we said bad words or argued too much. One time, Mom charged in from the kitchen and grabbed Cilla and I by our wrists, half leading and half dragging us to the bathroom. She made it clear that she intended to follow through with her threat to wash our mouths out with soap because we would not stop arguing. We were crying and screaming loudly, mostly because we felt she was overreacting and acting unfairly. Gary was the greatest offender and the reason for our arguing but was not punished. Mom made Cilla sit on the toilet while I stood next to her. Mom ran the water and made suds with a washcloth and bar of Ivory soap. She turned to us, twisted the washcloth, and stuck it in my mouth. I immediately started gasping, struggled to breathe, and choking, then push past Cilla and vomited in the toilet. Later, when I asked her why she did it to only me, she laughed and said that my mouth was the widest as I screamed and it seemed like an easy target. I believe that she did not follow through with Cilla when she saw how badly I reacted to her abusive punishment.

When we were in public, Mom punished us by pulling hair and pinching instead of the overt head slapping. I so hated this punishment for my sibling's action that I would not let it bother me. I grew very bitter about being wrongfully punished. I wanted to insulate myself from the injustice. I had no power to resist Mom's brutal consequences, but I did gain power over how my body responded. I learned to turn off the feeling in my hair. I stopped feeling pain when anyone pulled my hair. I only felt a painless pull on my scalp. I never again felt pain by pulling my hair. However, I still felt the powerful whiplash in my neck. Having no pain when pulling my hair was one victory over my mother's brutal injustice. She could have lifted me by my hair and it would not have hurt.

Cilla and I spent summers with my grandparents on the farm. At first, it was for a few days at a time. Even at just five years old, my grandmother brought me with her when she did such things as weeding the garden. She helped me identify weeds and how best to grab them to pull the out by the roots. She taught me the names of weeds as she learned them in Canada. She called cow vetch alfalfa, hawkweed as Indian paint brush, and the almost impossible to kill purslane, red vine plant. There were two tall-growing weeds that she called pig weed. As the vegetables became ready, we picked some to sell at the stand and to eat. She taught me how to determine when the vegetables were ripe. I was not very proficient at it, but Grandma always appreciated anything I did. She showed me sweet clover and said it was edible. It tasted bitter. Regular, purple clover blossoms were much easier to eat. Grandma also liked to eat choke cherries. They numbed her mouth so that her lips puckered and slowed her speech, but she loved them. I found them too bitter to eat.

I enjoyed baking time with Grandma. She always mixed things by hand. I stood on a stool beside her and watched as the mixture became smooth and uniform. She would beat cakes with only a wooden spoon, frequently turning the bowl. She seemed to beat it far more than necessary, explaining that it required six hundred strokes to mix properly. My favorite part was when I got to clean the bowl and spoon when she finished.

When Grandma did not have cake or cookies for us, she made snacks with Saltine crackers. Sometimes we put a little butter on them. They were surprisingly better with cottages cheese and a little jam. Milk was always necessary with every snack. The milk was delivered to her house every week. It came in glass bottles with cardboard seals. It was hard to break the seal. Afterwards, we replaced the seal but it came out easier. The milkman was very friendly and they always chatted about their families, neighbors, and church. For the times she had to work in the fields, Grandma left a note and money for what she wanted in an insulated silver box on the front porch.

Grandma was meticulous about many things. Mondays were wash days. The wringer washer was the typical machine. Dryers were rare and considered wasteful. Grandma hung her laundry outside. Rainy days did not stop her. She hung the clothes on the porch. She even hung them in the winter, often finishing the drying in the cellar. It was odd helping her bringing in the stiff, frozen laundry.

Grandma dust mopped the entire house on laundry day. She did it again later in the week during the dusty summers. Meals were always on time and prepared by her. The table was always set. She had a knife with no handle. The handle had fallen off years ago. She said it was still useful and kept it in service as her own. It seemed to identify Grandma's conservative character.

When there was time, Grandma braided rugs. She got material from a variety of sources but mostly from the church. She stored it in barrels in the barn until she was ready. It was a great adventure to go with her as she selected the material she wanted for that day. I watched as she cut it into strips, folded it over and sewed it with her pedal driven Singer sewing machine. She sewed the strips end-to-end by hand and braided them together. She then carefully laced them into a circle or oval to form the rung. It was a slow process, often taking all winter.

Sometimes, Grandma found coats and sweaters that fit us. They were old and out of style, but still good. Cilla liked the sweaters and took most of them. Sometimes Grandma made clothes for us. I particularly liked the purple, long sleeve shirts that she made for Gary and me. The material felt scratchy but the shirt looked nice. I did not mind the scratchy feeling to have a nice-looking shirt. She made nightgowns for us. I liked having something to sleep in beside just my underwear. I turned a lot during my sleep and soon became tangled in it.

When there was something that she needed to do without me, she sent me under the barn to play. I brought the bulldozer that was not much fun in the sandbox at home. Under the barn, I had half the barn size of open dirt to play in regardless of the weather. My brother was not around to wreck my work. I built large roads with my bulldozer. There was also an old toy dump truck for me. It did not load well with a bulldozer but it made a great race truck on my road. I was particularly fascinated about how the dirt sprayed up from the front tires as I raced it through corners around my track. I moved through the dirt on my knees, getting my pants very dirty. When Grandma called me to supper, I was thoroughly dirt covered below my knees. I was worried that I would lose this unstructured playtime but the dirt did not bother Grandma like it did my mother. She just made me brush the dirt off on the porch and take my shoes off before coming in. Then she sent me to the sink to wash my hands.

Once, when Cilla and I were playing under the barn, we heard the barn door above us open. The closing of the door was followed by the thunderous footsteps across the barn floor above us. Our imaginations could have gone in many directions about monsters but our logic kept it real. It was Pop. We listened as his footsteps went across the barn above our heads to the outhouse in the back. The toilet opening in the weathered barn board-colored boards was covered with his white, ugly butt. We momentarily turned away but were drawn back with a roaring fart and falling turds. Each well-formed turd splattered flatly on top of the pile of previous events. The toilet paper drifted down less accurately. We wondered about what happens when the pile gets too big. Later, we asked Grandma. She said that Pop spread it in the field each fall. We watched him from a distance as he shoveled it onto the wagon that he towed with the tractor. It was the same trailer he used to harvest vegetables and we rode upon. He drove to a distant part of the farm where he shoveled it off the wagon and distributed.

When I grew bored with the bulldozer and dump truck, I entertained myself using my imagination. I could use clumps of soil in the plowed fields to bomb larger clumps that were imaginary buildings, just as I did in the winter with the snowbanks. Throwing the soil chunks made them explode like bombs in one of my favorite TV shows, *Combat*. I especially admired SGT "Chip" Saunders played by Vic Morrow.

I had fun catching grasshoppers. The big ones were hard to sneak up on and flew on wings several feet when they jumped. If I were persistent and could find where they landed, I could eventually get one before it took off again. Pulling the hind legs off kept it from getting away. They were fun to play with for a while. I put them in a can with some grass to climb on. Grasshoppers spit dark saliva on the grass that I fed to them. It fascinated me that they would eat when I held them. I was careful not to get any grasshopper spit on me because it stained my hands dark brown.

Pop encouraged me to look for tomato bugs. These were large caterpillars that ate the leaves on his tomato plants. He showed me the easiest way to spot these well camouflaged "worms." They left small, black nodules of poop on the ground. Finding a cluster of this poop indicated that there was a caterpillar above it in the branches. Leaves were missing where the caterpillar was. The caterpillars were ugly, large, soft and a little scary. They looked like they had eyes on both ends but one set was just coloring. Collecting them was more fun than playing with them. They did not move like the grasshoppers did. It made Pop happy, which made me feel good.

Pop also liked it when I found a mouse in his tomato field. I could find these by first finding a partially eaten tomato. Poking around the vines in the area, I could scare out a mouse. I then chased it and stomped on it. It was difficult to kill it in the soft soil. As I repeatedly stomped on the mouse, the soil packed enough so that the mouse eventually split open. The mouse burst. Its gut splattered with the insides of the tomato. I proudly displayed my mouse kills to Pop but he told me to just bury them in the field. The successful pursuit of the mouse was more rewarding than Pop's approval.

When we were all visiting at the farm, it was a great place to play hide and seek in and around the buildings. The woodshed, garage and barns provided many attractive places to hide. Pop had some large, heavy blankets he used in the fall to cover harvested vegetables and protect them from freezing. He stored them rolled up in the barn. It was a great place to hide, rolling oneself into one. Once, I found it more difficult to breathe and discovered that I was stuck. I barely was able to free myself. I realized then how dangerous these blankets could be and stayed out of them.

Pop liked to sing. He sometimes tried to get me to sit in his lap and sing a song with him. It was both strange and fun to listen to Pop sing silly songs. I let my siblings do the singing and sit in his lap. Pop still tried to get me to sing along with them, but I did not. I hated to sign.

Pop also joked about being a "Barr," which was a bear. Sometimes he pretended that he was a "Barr" and chased us short distances. It was easy to escape him because he let us. One Christmas, my cousin Victor was only three years old when he ventured into the dark front room where the Christmas tree was set up. He came running back screaming in panic, "Barr!" We were confused until we looked. The silhouette showed two top branches that appeared to be the raise front legs of a bear. Everyone thought it was funny but I felt sorry for my little cousin. I knew how intense fear felt and did not wish it upon anyone.

We often gave Aqua Velva after shave lotion to Pop for Christmas. He said it was his favorite and used it every time he shaved. One year, we decided to give him some shaving cream. He very much enjoyed it, too. What seemed strange to me is that he squirted it into his shaving brush and applied it to his face rather than with his fingers like Dad did.

Pop also liked to wrist wrestle, which is what he called arm wrestling. He called it wrist wrestling because dominance was in the wrist. He taught me how. He routinely challenged me to a match, which of course he always won. He completely controlled it to prolong the contest to make me stronger.

I found snakes in the sun in front of the barn. Catching one was challenging because they could quickly slip into the rock foundation of the barn. It was also challenging to hold the snake so that it could not coil around and poop on me. Their poop was liquid and smelled badly. I learned Grandma's feelings about snakes when I brought one in the house to show her. She said firmly, "Get that thing out of my house!" She did not like snakes and did not want any dirty animals in her house. I got a similar response once when I caught a sparrow that caught trapped in the chicken coop. Snakes and sparrows did no harm so I just released them. Capturing them without hurting them was the challenge that I enjoyed.

The vegetables stored in the woodshed and garage attracted lots of large flies. Sometimes we swatted many using fly swatters. I liked snapping them with a rubber band. I imagined that I was shooting them with a gun. When they got bad enough, Pop used a hand pump sprayer to kill them.

Woodchucks caused a lot of damage to the squashes and raccoons damaged the corn. Pop and Uncle Bernie filled a barrel on the back of the tractor with water when they found a woodchuck hole. By flooding the hole, they could cause the woodchuck to come out. They would then kill it using a shovel or axe handle. I saw one run out of the hole and Uncle Bernie speared it with the point of the shovel. He struck it several times until it stopped trying to escape, then buried it.

Pop made rounds in the mornings to check his raccoon traps. He also killed these with an axe handle. I often went with them. I was amazed at Pop's strength and accuracy with the axe handle as he killed these varmints with a single blow to the head. There was no need to waste the cost of a bullet. Later, Pop found it more efficient to kill the woodchucks using cyanide gas bombs. These were cylinders about the size of his fist. They came with a fuse taped to them. He poked a hole with his pocketknife where it was indicated on the bomb and inserted the fuse. He lit it with a match that he ignited by rapidly dragging it on the outside of his thigh. He quickly placed the bomb deep into the chuck hole, then placed some grass and weeds to keep the dirt from extinguishing the fuse, then shoveled dirt onto the hole. I could hear the bomb go off, producing a loud fizzing sound and a poof. Smoke seeped through the soil as Pop covered it with more soil and stepped on it, packing it. As Grandma used to say, we must constantly wage war against these varmints to save the crops.

Cilla and I played well when we were on the farm together. One of my fondest memories was on a spare bed in the corner of the "front room" which was more like a living room. We sang a song we learned in school. It was about being kind to a duck because it could be somebody's mother.

"Be kind to the duck,
"Because it may be somebody's mother.
"We're going to sing this again.
"But we're going to sing it louder."

We laid on our backs on this bed holding our feet high while pressing the soles together. As we sang, we alternated our feet back and forth. For the finale, we bumped our butts together. We made a mess of the linens and tried to help Grandma fix them but did not do it very well. Grandma never seemed to mind.

We went to church with Pop and Gram. We learned all the protocols of the Catholic Church, genuflecting, sign of the cross, kneeling for prayers, sitting, standing, and kneeling at the proper times during Mass. Pop often fell asleep during the sermon, which upset Grandma, especially when he snored. After the sermon, the priest performed the ritual before communion. The altar boys chimed the bells at the significant times. Grandma explained that it was in preparation for God's descension to the altar. I tried to imagine God coming down past the crucifix and statues behind the alter. I also wondered how the priest could summon God when he wanted. Grandma explained that priests had a special holiness.

There was a lot of structure and routine with Pop and Gram. We washed our hands before each meal. We washed our hands and face and brushed our teeth before bedtime. We were in bed by nine o'clock and got up at six o'clock. We worked in the fields after breakfast and came in for lunch. Pop always took a nap after lunch, which was free play time for us. After his nap, he called for us and we worked until supper time. After supper, we relaxed and watched TV.

We always ate together at the kitchen table with Pop and Grandma. Pop made us lift our chairs to avoid sliding and wearing out the linoleum. Grandma always used the knife with the missing handle. She would not throw it away because it could still be used. I marveled at watching Pop's large bicep flexing with every raising of his fork or spreading butter on bread that he ate with every meal. He always had two slices of bread and applied butter above his plate so any crumbs would fall onto his food. There was always conversation during meals. Pop often complained about neighbors, discussed plans for maintaining the garden, or stores to which he needed to deliver vegetables. Sometimes they switched to speaking French when they spoke about neighbors. I very much resented this and vowed to study French when I got to high school. After meals, Pop always used a toothpick on his teeth. He often carried the toothpick in his mouth after leaving the table. When he finished, he put the toothpick in the kitchen woodstove, whether it was burning or not.

Pop regularly went to his doctor. He ate a banana every day. It was to keep his potassium level up for his heart. He took blood pressure medicine. He always felt that he looked much younger for his age and attributed it to his hard work and healthy diet. He liked asking people to guess his age. Of course, they were kind and guessed about ten years younger than he was. He boasted that he would live to be a hundred. Pop never went to the dentist. His teeth were covered with such thick tartar that it was difficult to see the individual teeth. Grandma regularly went to the dentist but rarely to the doctor.

Grandma provided us with the intense moral guidance always defined it in terms of her faith. We memorized the ten commandments and several prayers. Grandma's guidance went far beyond these. During daily activities, Grandma cautioned us about things that were a sin and what we need to avoid. If we committed any of these sins, we could not get into heaven unless we confessed our sins and performed the penance prescribed by the priest. At our young age, the sin according to Grandma that we witnessed most were bad words spoken by many people. If these words were spoken in anger or directed at someone, the sin was much more severe. I asked her about the French words Pop said sometimes but she diverted from answering. When Pop was angry with someone, he said "Go to hell." He was confident that his damnation was effective. That person would go to hell. As we grew increasingly concerned about getting into heaven, I learned that priests were guaranteed admission to heaven. So, I decided that I would be a priest. This pleased Grandma.

We occasionally visited my Dad's mother, Grandma Sanborn in North Springfield. Dad used to mow her lawn for her. They had an interesting mower. Its handle pivoted over the engine so that it could be readily pushed back and forth in tight spaces.

Grandma S. was always very pleasant. Theirs was a nice, split level home. Grandma S. sometimes brought us to get an ice cream cone. She talked all the time. She also drove down the center of the road. She did not see anything wrong with using the whole road because she moved over when a car approached from the other direction.

My Grandpa Sanborn was rarely home, always off on business for Fellows Gear Shaper. One time, he taught me how to make an extraordinarily complex paper airplane. He made me promise to keep its technique as a family secret. I managed to amaze many people with a plane with real wings and a tail that could be modified with flaps and a rudder. The plane flew like an acrobatic plane, easily making loops and turns. I could make modifications to its tail and wings to vary its flight. Another time, Grandpa taught me how to play chess.

While I was on the farm one day, I started to not feel well. I told grandma and added that my chest was starting to hurt. She told me to go lay down on the bed in the front room and I would begin to feel better. Instead, I felt much worse. The pain in the lower part of my chest and back began to hurt intensely. I was in such pain that I arched my back, raising my butt off the bed. I started crying and calling loudly, "It hurts, it hurts, it hurts..."

My father came and brought me to the doctors. Dr. Bacon quickly diagnosed me with pneumonia and admitted me to the hospital. I laid in bed with an intravenous tube and penicillin injections. Soon the pain subsided but I was very exhausted. I mostly slept and just laid in bed. I had no interest in playing with anything like when I was in the hospital for my leg operation.

The next morning, I awoke and found my mother beside me. She directed my attention to the bed beside me and told me that my brother was going to get his tonsils out. There was a curtain drawn between us, but the top half was clear. Gary was jumping up and down and peering through the visible area in the top half of the curtain. He waved but I was in no mood to welcome him. I enjoyed my time at the farm without him. I came from the farm to the hospital, so his appearance seemed like an intrusion. I was so exhausted that I felt vulnerable to his presence. I went back to sleep, more to escape from him than to recover from my illness.

The times that my brother and I played reasonably well together were when Mom let us go to the school playground diagonally across the street. It was the summer before I entered first grade. Gary was not yet old enough to start kindergarten. Mom always gave us the warning to behave because she was watching. We played on the swings, teeter totter, merry go round, horizontal ladder, and monkey bars. Later, we convinced our mother to let us play in the bushes behind the school, out of her sight. We crawled under the sumac branches and found a partial clearing. He broke and bent branches back enough to create a clearing under the brush that we called our fort. It seemed like a special place that we could keep secret from the rest of the world.

One day, Gary and I were playing on the swings after Mom's usual stern warning that she would be watching us. We noticed an older boy walking by who kept looking at us. He looked both ways along the street then suddenly walked directly toward us. He sat on the swing beside us and asked how high we could go. He started swinging hard and high, much more than Mom would allow us to go, even if we wanted. He made the whole structure wiggled with his force. He seemed to be about 18 years old and we were impressed with his physical strength. I wondered about Mom's reaction since she was watching. In the past, Mom would open the kitchen door and call us home when she saw something she did not like. She did not come to the door, so I thought that she approved. We felt special because this much older boy paid attention to us.

He stopped swinging and started calling us "half inch." I wondered what he meant. It puzzled me and I struggled to determine why he called us that name. I kept checking and still

Mom was not at the door. His "half inch" calls continued. I began to wonder if he was referring to my zipper being partially down because he was looking at it more intently. I thought that this might be his way of telling us our zippers were part way down, which was common for Gary and me. It was a rather low personal priority, so we were used to being corrected.

I looked down and pulled my zipper up. It was already high enough. Then he said, "No, not here." I was puzzled again because we checked our zippers anywhere, even in church. Then he said, "You guys must have a fort or something around here." I felt some relief as he seemed to be getting off the half inch topic and into something more applicable. I was proud to let him know that we did. At his request, we lead him to our fort.

He struggled through the bushes that Gary and I easily crawled through. Immediately after he stood up in our fort, he took out what we called his tee-tee and started urinating. We were amazed at the size. I asked him how it got so big. He replied, "You got to stick things up your butt to make it bigger." Since we thought it was what was expected, Gary and I urinated. The boy said, "See, I told you that you only had a half inch." Now, I understood what he meant, though it made little sense to me why it was any interest to him.

After we finished urinating, Gary and I closed our pants. He started stroking his penis and it got even bigger. Gary and I were even more amazed. After stroking it a while, his penis spit. He wiped it on a branch in our fort. I asked him how he was able to spit out his tee-tee and he said that you got to swallow exactly right. I did not understand his strange advice; sticking things up your butt will make your tee-tee bigger and swallowing hard will make it spit. It all made me uncomfortable and I said that we had to go home. We never went back to our fort. It felt dirty to me now. A few days later, as Dad drove up South Street Hill, we saw this boy riding in the back of a pickup. Gary and I debated briefly about telling Mom about him. We decided not to tell her, believing that we would get in serious trouble for what we did not even understand. We never saw him again.

We often went for a car ride. Mom and Dad liked to drive. It got to be very boring for me. I just sat, looking out the window with no interest in anything. I would rest my head against the car door when I was tired. The vibration loosened the wax in my ears. Once, we drove through a construction site. We were delayed for several minutes. It was hot in the car with no ventilation just sitting in the sun. Mom and Dad drank beer to keep cool. They thought that it would be fun to offer a beer to the traffic controller. I was surprised that he accepted it.

Sometimes, we drove to Sunapee Beach. It was also a long ride but it was fun playing on the sandy beach and in the lake. We were not allowed to go beyond our knees unless Dad was with us. Even then, he would not take us past our waist. We had to swim towards land. We could only float. We moved by pushing on the bottom.

On the edges of the public beach, there were water plants. In these plants, sometimes there were ducks. I had fun trying to catch frogs. I could never get close to the minnows that swam quickly away.

We had to change out of our wet clothes before getting back into the car. The bath house was just a large room with a bench around the outer wall. I did not like changing in front of everyone, so I changed as quickly as I could.

After the long rides, it felt good to be home. Unfortunately, it was soon our bedtime. I was bored with the long rides only to be sent to bed when I was not tired. I listened to the sounds of my parents' loud voices, though I could not hear them well enough to determine what they were saying. Hearing their voices interfered with my preferred imaginary pastimes.

Collateral Damage in the Earliest, Preschool Early Years

I was conditioned to accept that children's needs and desires were subservient to adult interests. Adults did not want to be bothered with our needs and especially not our wants. We were never kissed or hugged. Only the most serious injury or concern would Mom place any priority on us. Fortunately, I got medical treatment in time so that there was no permanent injury.

Parentifying older children to care for the younger children is another way the adults lessened their responsibilities to care for the younger children by assigning many of these responsibilities on the older children. Cilla and I were already taking responsibility for the care of our younger siblings. We attempted to parent our younger siblings the way we were parented, with aggression. When we tried to enforce our responsibility, our younger siblings protested and we got punished instead. Mom neglected her parental responsibility to supervise us. Her warnings that she was watching us when we were not gave us a false sense of security. It made Gary and I dangerously vulnerable to a sexual predator.

I struggled to make sense of the world and develop mastery within in like any child. My world was distorted through the interpretations and demands of my mother. It seemed like I was making sense of nonsense. I grew very resentful of Mom's unfair corporal punishment. It was arbitrary and brutal. There was no avoiding it. I learned how best to defeat it by being tough and eventually turning off pain. It was my private way at retaliating. I learned to escape through imagination and controlling my body. I even turned off hair pulling pain to obtain mastery over some of the painful injustice inflicted upon me. It was noticeable that I never smiled in any pictures. People saw my sincere expressions without smiles as a personality defect rather than a constantly somber child who never expressed emotion. My mother was authoritarian. Demanding unquestioned compliance without any explanation of purpose. Obedience dominated any autonomy. Individuality was not allowed and mercilessly punished.

I escaped the nonsense and chaos in my real world with my own world of imaginary play where I could control the events and their outcomes. I trusted the real world only with my sister and grandmother. Grandma provided safe, reasonable guidance. She never provided kisses or hugs, expressing her affection by providing for our needs. Her guidance was in the strictest Catholic traditions.

CALIFORNIA, EARLY GRADE SCHOOL YEARS

My life was fully dominated by my mother until I started first grade. She maintained her overpowering control of my life by teaching me to reject what others did or said. She had strict rules about not telling peers about what we did at home; "It's none of their business." She quickly suppressed any changes in our behavior that she detected as being influenced by our social interactions; "That's not the way to live." Never did she explain her reasons and we were not allowed to question them. "Things will be better when" was a common theme throughout my childhood. If the better time ever arrived, any benefits gained were short lived as things became progressively worse.

A few days before school was to start, Mom and Dad told us that we were moving to California where things would be better. Dad got a drafting job for a rocket company and would make more money. Dad left and returned with a U-Haul hitched to the back of the Ford station wagon. I remember his many attempts to back it into the driveway as Mom tried to guide him. They settled for the trailer awkwardly parked partly on the lawn. We loaded things up, then said goodbye to Pop, Grandma, and Uncle Bernie. We were off.

It was a long, three-day ride. We sang songs and played a lot of I spy. A person stated the color of an object in sight. If someone guessed it before it went out of sight, he or she got to spy something. It was like an opposite game of tag. It was desirable to be "it." If no one guessed it, the person could choose another color. As things go with siblings, we became competitive and mean at times. My siblings and I sometimes chose a tiny spot on something to identify. Many times, Gary just made up a color that was not in view. When it became impossible to win and we grew too angry with each other, we decide not to participate and the game would end for a while.

Dad used to help me identify the makes of cars. I wiggled to the center of the back seat and leaned into the front seat next to Dad. I learned about distinctive things such as the shape of the grill, fined rear fenders, hood markers, and the three holes on the side of Buicks. I could identify the distinctive Edsel and Studebaker grills. Only he and I were interested in this activity. It ended when traffic got too heavy to keep up or he needed to stay focused on the changing route.

Mom and Dad drove day and night, rotating the driving. One slept in the passenger seat while the other drove. We slept in the back seat as best we could. During waking times, I wiggled onto the floor behind the front seat. There were no seat belt concerns. Cars did not even have them then. Debra rode standing in the front seat a lot of the time. This was often fatal even in minor crashes. No one believed it could happen to them since they were good drivers. To be fair, we older siblings could take turns in the front between Mom and Dad. It was uncomfortable crammed between them, so I mostly chose to stay in back. I liked going into the far back of the station wagon among our packed things to be alone. Soon, Gary decided that he wanted to join me in the back. He wiggled and constantly crowded my space. If I tried to stop him, he protested and Mom told me to let him in. If I pushed or punched him, I was punished by being told to sit quietly on the back seat and got slapped on my head as I moved there. I learned that I had no choice and endured Gary's antics for as long as I could and gave up, letting him have the back to himself. He did not stay there long. Gary could only entertain himself for short periods before intruding into whatever Cilla or I were doing.

Mom and Dad debated once about who should drive. Mom reluctantly agreed to sleep. She gave me firm instructions to watch Dad and make sure he did not drift off the road. It was terribly stressful for me to take such a responsibility. I watched intently. Dad did not want me correcting his minor deviations within the lane. I quietly gave up my job, retreating to sitting on the floor behind the driver's seat.

As we were driving through the desert, the gas tank fell off. Dad started walking for help and was picked up by another car. He returned in a pickup driven by a mechanic. The mechanic attributed the tank's falling to the improperly placed to trailer tow bar that clamped to the bumper. He strapped the tank back up and adjusted the drawbar. We were on the road again.

Our first destination was Aunt Alice's house. Mom's sister lived in Riverside California. Aunt Alice, Uncle Beau, and our younger cousins Benita and Joycelyn greeted us. We had spaghetti for dinner that night. I did not understand Uncle Beau's question to my mother, "Are your kids twirlers or slurpers?" We were neither because Mom always broke spaghetti in short pieces as she added it to the pot. All we had to do was scoop it with our forks. When Aunt Allice served the long spaghetti pieces, Mom told us to cut it with our forks. I learned about twirling spaghetti by watching Uncle Beau.

Aunt Alice and Uncle Beau helped us find a house in a neighborhood not too far from Dad's work. It was a ranch style home with no basement and a one-car garage. The backyard was small.

Sometimes, Cilla and I played hopscotch on the concrete driveway. Cilla was much better than I at getting the stone to land on the correct square. We played mostly in the vacant lot next to us. We tried to build a cabin but lacked materials to construct more than a single wall. I liked climbing in the apricot trees. We were used to apples, plums, and cherries in our grandfather's orchard. Apricots were new and fascinating. No one tended to these trees and the grass grew tall under them. When the fruit was ripe, we could pick it off the trees. I was surprised when Mom made apricot jam. I did not know that she could make such a thing. It tasted great. We loved it.

Mom and Dad bought a bicycle for us. Dad put training wheels on it and we were instructed to stay in the driveway. The driveway was much too short. I could hardly get started then had to stop. Riding on the lawn was too difficult. After a while, Dad decided that he would help me along the road. Eventually the training wheels came off and he ran along beside me, holding the back of the seat. It was not long before he tired and let go and I was on my own.

Cilla was not interested in riding the bike and Gary was too small. Mom allowed me to ride along the street within certain limits. It was a quiet street, so I improved my skills. I liked making sharp turnarounds. Unfortunately, I made one of these quick turns into the path of a car. The driver stopped quickly but her daughter, who was standing beside the driver like so many others, crashed into the dash. I could see her nose or mouth bleeding. The squealing tires got Mom's attention. I lost bike privileges for an awfully long time. Dad chained it in the garage. I spent many hours sitting on this chained bike, pretending to ride it. When I finally got privileges to ride it again, I was not allowed to leave the driveway. I soon lost interest in riding it.

We used to go for car rides a lot, looking for movie stars and stopping at A&W Drive-Ins. My favorite shows were the *Lone Ranger, The Rifleman,* and *Superman.* We saw the Rifleman, Clint Walker, loading things on top of his van. I was amazed about how tall he was compared to the van. Abbott and Costello were our favorite comedians. Bud Costello's brother lived in our neighborhood but we never saw him.

I was puzzled one day when Mom said that Superman shot himself. I did not think anything of it at first. Superman got shot in almost every show. The bullets just bounced off him. She added that he was dead. I asked "How? He's Superman." She explained that he was just an actor, an ordinary man. I thought about it for a while then accepted her explanation. Of course, he was a real person. I was sad that he was dead.

We also visited my father's brother, Uncle Frank. He had a nice house high on the bank overlooking a bay. It was a surreal watching the waves coming to shore so far below us. I marveled at how the waves came to shore at an angle, then turned straight towards the beach. I thought that they always came straight in from the ocean. Uncle Frank pointed out some boats to me and told me about them, their type and how fast they could go. He tried to help me understand how sail boats were able to control their speed and direction.

It was not long until we moved to a better house. It was on Mulholland Drive, where many actors loved, though we never saw any. Mom said it was because we lived at the opposite end of the street.

Our driveway was steep. We had milk delivered here, like my grandmother did on the farm. I liked watching the truck driver as he cautiously backed up our steep driveway. I had firm instructions from Mom to sit on the steps while he backed up. I made a sign with start on stop on opposite sides and held with a clothes pin. I tried guiding the driver but only mimicked his actions, turning it back and forth as he started and stopped as he maneuvered up the driveway. Mom would put money in a small manila envelope with instructions on what to leave. He took the empty milk jars. I watched as he filled the order. He never said anything to me, as though I was not even there.

The side yard was bigger than the back yard. There were several bushes where I used to try to catch lizards. They were mostly too fast for me. We had an enclosed patio with sliding doors to the backyard, which was enclosed in a high fence. Whenever we played in this yard, the neighbors large dog barked and growled at us. We did not feel safe and avoided playing in it.

I attended first grade at Saint Mary's School. During recess, we were encouraged to play with friends. I mostly stood around. I did not understand the games the various small groups were playing and I did not feel welcome. Sister Theresa connected me with Patrick and suggested that we play together. Patrick hardly spoke. He liked to just walk the perimeter of the playground. I walked slightly behind him. He walked fast and I struggled to keep up. There was something about him I liked and wanted to be like him. His front teeth stuck out, so I tried to keep mine sticking out, too. Sister Theresa had good intentions but did not realize that two kids with no social skills were not going to magically attain these skills without some help.

At home, Mom spent a lot of time in the kitchen. Like on South Street, my siblings and I mostly played in the living room. Debra was older now, so Mom sent her to play with us, letting her concentrate on her kitchen duties. Our play area extended onto an enclosed patio. We had a rabbit named Pete that did not like being held. Sometimes, Mom got tired and went to take a nap, leaving Cilla and I to watch Gary and Debra. Cilla was eight and I was seven years old. We watched Gary who was five and Debra who was three years old.

Mom told us not to let Debra grab Pete's ears. Fortunately, she was not nearly as fast as the rabbit, but she was relentless and sometimes managed to corner it. She was too young to understand. We tried our best to please Mom but sometimes Debra could not be redirected. Admittedly, we liked to catch the rabbit, too. Debra tried grabbing its ears because they were the easiest for her to hold. Once, she grabbed Pete's tail and dragged him out from under the patio furniture. Pete struggled to escape and his tail came off. There was a little blood where the tail used to be. We knew we would be in a lot of trouble if Mom found out, so we hid the tail under the patio furniture and did not tell her.

Very much like any family in the nineteen fifties, Dad sat in the living room after work while Mom prepared dinner. He was the bread winner and Mom was the home keeper. We were interested in what she was making. She diverted us once by joking, "Go tell Dad to wiggle his ears like a jackass." This seemed strange to me to compare Dad to a jackass, a word I heard used negatively about people. I questioned her and she repeated it, assuring me that Dad would not care. Wiggling ears was an animal trait, not one for humans. It also bothered me that she so readily expected me to compare my father to a jackass. I expected it would make him angry. Nonetheless, I went to Dad who was sitting on the couch. Not wanting to take full responsibility for my request, I said, "Mom told us to ask you to wiggle your ears like a jackass." Much to my surprise, he complied without protest. I was amazed. For several months, I worked with him until I could also wiggle my ears. I was proud to share this silly connection with my father.

Dad also could talk like Donald Duck. He was happy to explain how he was able to do it. I practiced with him and other times on my own. Eventually I was almost as good as he. No one else in the family could do it. This was another silly trait I was proud to share with my dad.

Dad, Gary, and I had butch haircuts. Dad used Brylcreem and a soft-bristled brush to get the hair on top of his head to stand up so that the top was perfectly flat. I wanted my hair to look like his but, no matter how hard I tried, I could not get all my hair to stand up.

I got a toy tank. I could wind it up and make it climb over a book I placed on the floor. I used to have it climb a staircase I made from books. It was not overly exciting, but it was a good diversion from playing with tinker toys all the time. When I was riding with Dad once, he let the back seat of the station wagon down so that I could play with my tank as he drove. When I stopped playing with the tank and joined him in the front seat, he showed me how to tune the AM radio to another station as we lost signal. The song *Giant Purple People Eater* started to play. He encouraged me to sing it with him. Neither of us sang well but we had fun. I enjoyed his special attention the most.

Much of the time we played in the living room and on the patio, while Mom was busy in the kitchen. She baked a cake one time that she boasted was made with beer. She said that it was good but regretted that she could not repeat her success. I was puzzled about why she could not do the same thing as before. One day, as I was playing with my tank, Mom came out of the kitchen. Cilla and I immediately noticed something were wrong. Mom was leaning against the side of the doorway and appeared to be trying to see into the living room. She walked, leaning hard against the wall. There was a half-wall, then the hallway to the bedrooms. She placed her hands with great force on the top of this half-wall. Our TV was on a stand next to this half-wall. As she passed, she knocked it backwards, partial off the stand and against the wall. We asked her if she was alright. She just waved her hand for us to get away from her. She continued into the bedroom hallway and into the main bedroom on the left. She staggered and fell onto the bed. Again, we asked her if she was sick. She told us to close the door and "Wait until your father comes home." I did not know it then. Those naps Mom took in the afternoon was to sleep off the effects of alcohol before Dad got home.

Cilla and I were concerned about the TV in its awkward position. We tried to get it back up properly on its stand, but it was too heavy even for the both of us. We resumed our play and supervision of our little sister. Gary returned from his observing the events to playing with the tinker toys. We checked on Mom a few times. She was lying on her side and snoring loudly. We called softly but she did not answer.

We were glad to see Dad come into the kitchen when he returned from work. We went to him right away and told him Mom was sick. We led him to the bedroom and opened the door. Mom was lying on her side, breathing, and snoring hard. We did not think this was right. Dad assured us that she was fine and closed the door. We showed him the TV. He picked it up and placed it on the stand. I was amazed by his strength as he did this so easily. He went to the kitchen and we watched him prepare dinner for us. After dinner we watched TV until bath and bedtime.

The next day, Mom was fine, and we were relieved. Dad started arguing with her. Mom sent us into the backyard to go play. The neighbor's dog started barking and growling at us. We were afraid that it might crash through the fence and get us, but Mom would not let us back in. We tried to be quiet in the yard, so the dog would stop barking. Mom and Dad were arguing loudly. I worried that we did something wrong to make Mom so angry. Things eventually returned to normal.

We used to go to the beach sometimes. We drove on the freeway, then descended a long, steep bank with the road turning back and forth. The sharp turns were scary, and the steep drop off stressed my fear of heights. Dad was a good driver and I had confidence in him. I just did not look over the bank beside the car. Once we parked the car, we still had a long walk down the steep bank to the beach. We were barefoot and the sand was hot.

It was a big sandy beach with huge rocks dividing it. This was the first time we were able to see the waves up close. Their rhythmic behavior was fascinating and alluring. I cautiously walked closer to the wave. The texture of the sand changed dramatically from soft and rough to the hard, smooth area wetted by the waves. The frothy wave tingled on my toes and feet. It delivered fine, sharp grains of sand that settled between my toes. It was fun to follow a wave as it went out, then run back in ahead of the next wave.

We mostly built sandcastles and dug deep holes in the sand with our hands. I liked digging holes so deep and narrow that it was hard to back out of it. If I dug deep enough, it would fill with water. Mom could not swim and mostly sat on the beach. Once, Dad brought us to where the surf hit the large rocks and sprayed high in the air. It was loud with the awesome sprays. We ran around the large rock in between the waves. We had to be quick. It was exciting and fun.

Dad brought us into the water and showed us how to body surf. Mom never went far into the water, barely getting her feet wet. She could not swim and feared the waves and potential for undertow. Dad helped me learn how to swim. We found that it was easier to swim across the waves rather than with or against them. We went to where the waves came up to my chest. He stood about five feet away from me and told me to swim to him. I timed it so that the wave was exactly right and pushed off towards him. I could not swim on top of the water like he showed me but I could swim under water well. It made him laugh that I was better at swimming under water. He frustrated me because I wanted to be able to swim to him, but he backed up when I got close. I asked him to stay still so I could get to him. He said that he wanted me to go as far as I could. I felt cheated out of a success that I could have attained and never achieved it because he kept moving.

After swimming, we tried to build sandcastles. Dad showed us how wet sand worked best. Unfortunately, the sand dried and crumbled before we finished. We tried to keep it moist like Dad said, but we only washed away portions of our castle. We found seaweed on the beach. It was fun to pop the flotation nodes. Sometimes, we could find crabs, seashells, and jellyfish. Jelly fish felt weird, hard, and rubbery. We found a live one once and it released dark ink into the sand as it pulsed its body. Crabs were funny because they ran sideways. We did not risk getting pinched by the claws.

Christmas did not seem right in California. We were used to the cold and snow. Our tree was small and thin. We got a few presents: the operation game, coloring books and clothes. Cilla,

Gary, and I played operation. It had tweezers on a wire and holes in a man with parts to be removed. We drew cards with instructions on what we were supposed to remove. If you touched the sides, a buzzer sounded, and the patient's red nose lit up. Gary was too clumsy to do it. Cilla was too good and always won.

We moved again in the spring. This house was much smaller. The front and side yards were only about five feet wide and not much fun. The most exciting thing I could do with Mom's restrictions was to catch lizards. There was also a steep bank with a sandy path behind the house. It was so steep that we could slide down it like a playground slide. Mom forbid us from doing this because we dragged sand down and Dad would have to shovel it back up.

Mom sent us into the yard to play a lot, so she could do housework with us out of her way. We could climb on the bank. But not on the sandy path. We got too bored and the temptation was too great. We eventually started sliding down the bank and having a blast. Suddenly, Mom appeared from the side door holding a broom. She was furious and waving the broom at us, motioning us into the house, yelling at us for making extra work for Dad. Her favorite punishment was to make us kneel. As we ran into the house, she waved the broom and told us to kneel around the old wringer washer in the entryway. She hit us on the buttocks with the bristles of the broom as we passed. We were all crying and screaming as we held the washer as our familiar penance. Mom was angrier than I had ever seen her. She seemed most angry at me, I should know better, though we all knew what we were doing. She waved the broom handle at me as she yelled. With one quick strike, she hit me across the top of my head with the broom handle. I heard the loud crack as the handle struck me across the top of my head. I felt the force drive my head down onto my neck and shoulders. Suddenly, my vision got very narrow, dark, and tunnel-like and everything started spinning. Everything became quiet. I tried but could not cry. I realized that my head was hanging to my right and I could not pick it up. My whole body was limp and leaned to my right. My hands maintained an unconsciously firm grip on the lip of the washer. I realized that this was the only reason I did not fall on the floor. As the muffled sounds returned, I began to realize that Mom was yelling, "Get up." I tried my hardest, but I could not pull myself up. My fingers remained in their tight grasp but my arms just would not respond to my efforts nor would my neck pull my head back up. It felt strange to have no control over my hands that also prevented me from falling to the floor. Mom kept yelling at me to get up.

Finally, I regained some control over my body. My neck seemed to hurt as I struggled to right my head. I pulled hard with my hands and finally managed to get back into the proper kneeling position. I could hear my siblings' cries and screams coming back. My vision still was not right. Everything was blurred. I could barely make out images. Mom continued yelling as she came into clearer focus. I tried to comply as best I could when she yelled, "Look at me." Suddenly, she stared at me and just stopped yelling. She looked at me for a few seconds then said, "Kneel there for an hour," then turned and left. My siblings screamed and cried for a while longer. I could only cry quietly. I could feel the dent the broom handle left across my skull, which remained permanently.

We soon moved again. This time it was to the caretaker's house on the convent grounds. The nuns who served at Saint Mary's Church and taught at my school lived here. Mom said that it was a good arrangement because Dad worked on the grounds in exchange for rent. He also continued his job at the rocket factory.

There was a long dirt driveway to the house. The house was narrow and long. A bit small for us. The yard was fenced and a good size for us to play. There was a garage with a row of doors. It was converted from old horse stalls from the time before cars. There were a lot of things stored in there. We were not allowed to play in it.

The dirt driveway extended past the house on the opposite side of the fenced yard. From this side, there was a path and stairway that led up to the convent. Beside the convent was a pool. The sisters allowed us to use it at specified times. My father again amazed me when he jumped in at one end and swam the whole distance of the pool under water. I asked that he help me learn how to swim. He did the same as we did in the ocean for a while, then he said, "You don't need me. Just stay in the shallow." It was difficult to learn with my three siblings mostly in the way. I gave up trying to learn how to swim more than a few feet underwater even though I very much wanted to learn to swim so that I could go in the deep end.

The times in the Nuns' pool were rare treats. Most of the time, we had a small plastic pool in the yard. Mom sent us to the pool in our underwear as a substitute for baths. The little pool was too small to have fun. I got the requisite wetness to avoid taking a bath.

The nuns suggested that I consider being an altar boy. Mass was conducted in Latin. They gave me a Missal. It had the Mass prayers with the altar boy responses in bold. It was in Latin and had the English translation. I felt an immense privilege and power now that I understood what the priests and altar boys were saying during Mass. The nuns told me to memorize the Latin responses and the proper time for them during the Mass. When I was confident, they would bring me to the priest to be tested. I studied hard and memorized the additional prayers the nuns told me to learn in both English and Latin. I told Mom when I felt ready, but I was never tested.

The driveway on the opposite side of the house was a great place to explore for animals. There were a lot of lizards. When I could find one in the open, I tried to catch it. Though it was fast at first, if I were persistent, I could eventually catch it when it tired. Stink bugs were the worse. When I startled one, it would raise its rear and make a chirping sound, then I would release the awful odor. Toads were fun and easy to catch. I saw snakes and even rattle snakes but stayed clear of them as my mother instructed. It was the same with scorpions, though I liked watching them. They moved slowly and, when they saw me, they turned towards me and held their tail stinger over their head. If I poked them with a stick, they would walk off. I sometimes saw a jack rabbit in the field behind the house. They were huge with their exceptionally long ears compared to rabbits I knew. They stood up on their hind legs, looked at me, then ran off.

One day, I found a dead rattle snake in the driveway. It was still coiled up like it tried to protect itself from whatever crushed it. I brought it home and showed Mom. She took it and curled it up on the hood of the car. She said, "Watch your father when he sees this." We waited in the yard for Dad to come out of the house. He walked through the yard and opened the gate and closed it behind him. He opened the driver's door, then suddenly ran back towards the house, jumping over the gate. Mom, who was watching from inside the house, was laughing loudly. She came out and took the snake off the car. Dad was obviously angry as he got in the car and drove away. I could not hear what he was saying to Mom. I heard her call him a prick as he drove away.

This was the first time I learned that Dad was afraid of snakes. I did not understand why Mom would purposely scare my father or find pleasure in it. I wondered why she called him a name when it was her that caused the unpleasant encounter. My siblings argued and punched each other's shoulder, but never did we consider causing such terror for each other.

They were building a new school on the church compound near our house. We liked to explore the construction site in the evenings and days that they were not working. It was fun climbing on the scaffolding like a jungle gym. We brought home scraps of lumber and bent nails for projects. I remember Pop had a pail of bent nails on his farm. He collected used crates from the back of stores to use for his vegetables. He repaired the broken crates with parts from crates in worse condition. He did not believe in spending money on anything when it still could be used. So, what we found seemed like a treasure. I used Dad's tools to cut the wood. I had to straighten the nails before I could drive them in. I made simple things, often not knowing what I would end up with at the start of the project. Much of what I made fell apart.

It was a combination play and bath as we played with water the pool tub in the yard. Mom had us do this to cool off when temperatures reached one hundred degrees or more. She remained inside, watching us through the window. She often drank from a tall bottle of beer. We could not see her with the sun so bright but felt she watched us constantly. It was confirmed occasionally when she yelled at us for arguing with each other.

We got a German Shepard puppy. We all wanted to name it but Mom said that she and Dad would. A while later, while playing in the yard with the dog, Mom announced the dog's name, "Chino." Cilla dominated the time with Chino. I went about playing by myself, exploring nature and trying to build things.

Mom told us that we had to move again. She did it with her usual announcement out the window as we played in the yard. Mother Mary Teresa, the head of the convent, wanted us to leave. Mom seemed angry about it. I enjoyed playing with the lizards and toads and would miss them. Moving again did not seem so bad when Mom said that we were going back home to Vermont. We packed up the station wagon and another U-Haul trailer. Dad called the trailer a "you haul it."

Collateral Damage in the California, Early Grade School Years

Very gradually and subtly, I was assuming parent-like responsibility for my younger brother. Cilla was developing the same for Debra. I realized that it was pointless to complain when Gary intruded on my play and that it was best to accommodate him. It did not prevent me from giving him a good punch to the shoulder if he destroyed my project, even when I would suffer the consequences if Mom heard. Sometimes, I could get away with it even when Gary protested. I did not realize it then but Mom's response was related to her level of intoxication. The more she drank, the freer I was.

It was easier to give up my desires than to fight for them. I learned that I always lost the fight anyway. I gave up when my brother intruded into my play and let him have what he wanted. I gave up trying to swim, becoming an altar boy, and trying to make friends. I craved guidance and encouragement from adults and rarely received it.

We were also accepting social isolation. I changed schools a lot and never developed friends. The one friend I had was someone who I followed around the playground with no real interaction. I became overly infatuated with him for the extraordinarily little attention I got in return. We never had friends come to our house. We did not have birthday parties or any activities to invite friends.

We humans seek order in our lives to make sense and find security of our world. We thrive on routine and rituals. Our Catholic religion has centuries old rituals, which appealed to me. It was also a sure means to get into heaven. I memorized prayers in both English and Latin and repeated these prayers at every bedtime. I believed that this dedication would protect me. School was another structured and ordered place for me. I tried to bring order to my time at home. It was dominated by the unpredictability of my brother's interference and my mother's demands.

I was developing coping skills in and increasingly mixed-up world. I increasingly retreated to introverted, solitary, imaginative play. I created scenes and heroes in various situations. I also found satisfaction with nature. I found places in the yard where my brother would not go. These are the places where I found the snakes and scorpions. Gary responded to and may have acquired my mother's fear of them, giving me some respite from him.

The 1950s household concept of the father as the bread winner and disciplinarian with the mother as the home keeper contributed to our social isolation. We were hardly aware that Dad tried to divert my mother from her excessive drinking but was powerless. There were no socially accepted supports. Even worse, to ask for help was interpreted as weakness, especially for men. My dad did not know how to deal with my mother's emerging and powerful addiction. No one did then. My mother fully exploited this situation. Sometimes it was subtle, like wiggling his ears like a jackass. Other times, it was outright cruel, such as scaring him with a dead snake.

My right eyelid drooped. A condition called ptosis. Mom said that I was born that way and said I got it from my father. His left eyelid drooped more slightly than my right eye drooped. However, our eyes worked together. My eyes began to work separately with the vision in my right eye deteriorating. It got progressively worse throughout my life. I have seen many professionals and all believe it is likely from a brain injury. It was my mother's angry strike to my head from her broom, which has also left its mark as a dent across the top of my skull.

RETURN TO VERMONT, MIDDLE GRADE SCHOOL YEARS

It was a long ride home. We tried playing some of the games like I spy, but they did not last. We complained about getting into each other's space and drew imaginary lines on the seat to define limits. We complained, "Mom, he's on my side," or "He's touching me" for which Mom replied, "Shut up or I'll touch you and you won't like." It was her threat of a spanking, typically a single, strong strike to the body part closest to her. Once spanked and we cried, we heard, "Shut up or I'll give you something to cry about." Debra was lucky. She could ride in front. When we complained that it was not fair, we each got a short time riding in front. We climbed over seats of the moving car. I found an uncomfortable spot in the things packed in the back of the station wagon where I spent some time alone. When Gary intruded, I let him have the space, I sat on the floor between the front and back seats. It seemed to be the one place that I could find peace.

Four days later, we arrived at the farm. My grandparents were excited to see us. Grandma explained that it was the worst day of her life when we left and the best day when we returned.

She quickly got busy in her kitchen to feed us. She had cookies and cake already prepared, making her home smell good. It felt good to relax in my grandparents' home. It was the safest and most stable place I knew.

Pop and Grandma were in the middle of renovations. Gerry Beaudry was building new kitchen cabinets with a modern sink. He also installed a bathroom. They now had a regular toilet and bathtub. Boys were still expected to pee outside, but we did not mind.

Dad unloaded the trailer into the barn and returned it to the U-Haul dealer. In the next few days, he searched for work and a place to live while we stayed on the farm. Pop sent Cilla and I to work in the fields. He and Grandma had lots of pride in their work and thought everyone shared their concept. It is how they established a person's value, by their work ethic. No one should just sit around and do nothing. Pop and Grandma complimented Cilla and I for our hard work, which kept us motivated.

Grandma said that her little dog, "Cheeta," was a toy fox terrier. It did not want anything to do with playing with us and it remained close to her most of the time. Cheeta ran under the kitchen woodstove to get away from us. I crawled in after her. The few times I was able to corner her, she peed on the floor. Grandma knew we scared her dog when she found the puddles of pee. She was not happy about it but soon forgave us. We were fascinated how Cheeta did not like getting her feet wet in the dew-covered grass. She walked on her front feet with her back feet high in the air. In the evening, when Grandma finally sat down to watch TV, Cheeta jumped in her lap where Grandma would pat her. This was the only time we could pat the dog that still did not care for our touch.

Dad went to look for work while Mom helped Pop on the farm. It seemed strange to watch my mother work so hard at something she did as a child. Cilla and I helped the best we could. We were still learning what were vegetables and what were weeds. Pop and Mom boasted how Mom could lift a hundred-pound grain bag in each arm when she was a girl. We could not even get one to budge. Pop always pushed us beyond our limits, telling us that it would make us strong. He saw breathing hard as a sign of weakness.

I liked collecting the chicken eggs, as did Cilla and Gary. We used to race to the barn when Grandma told us to collect the eggs. Gary was too small and slow to compete. I usually beat Cilla but not by much. We had to go into the chicken coup slowly, not to excite the birds. The roosters often attacked us but Grandma showed us how to stop them by pushing them away. Grandma showed us how to collect eggs from under a setting hen. They were Rock Island Reds; big birds that could defend themselves. If we did not do it right, we got a painful reminder with the hen's peck. We had to approach low and slow, gently reaching under the bird. It felt weird under her warm feathers. We could feel around and find the eggs. Some had chicken manure on them. I tried to discourage Gary from coming to check for eggs by telling him about rooster attacks. I wanted to collect the eggs without him. My warnings were ineffective. Gary cautiously came into the coop. He moved quickly, disturbing the birds. Once collected, we proudly presented them to Grandma in her kitchen. Sometimes we found a wild bird that got into the chicken coop and was trapped inside. I brought the first one that I caught to Grandma in the house. She remined me that she did not want dirty wild things in her house. I studied their eyes, feathers, wings, and legs. I held the birds after that for a while, then let them go.

We had chicken for supper a few days later. Mom said that they did not have any roosters now. I asked, "So they will have no more eggs?" Mom replied, "No, stupid. Hens still lay eggs." She paused then continued, "There just won't be any chicks inside them." I had some difficulties processing this. For someone who claimed to be a world authority on sex, Mom shared little knowledge with us. By her tone and calling me stupid, I knew that she did not want any further discussion and I was left to process this information on my own. I was confused. She had assured me that a woman could not have a baby until she was married. I made the logical transfer of this knowledge to animals and coming into "heat" to be ready for mating. Mom likely never understood variations among farm and wild animals' mating cycles.

Dad found a job with Young's Propane. I did not understand why he did not go back to Fellows Gear Shaper and do drafting. Mom said that the job was too stressful. I was not sure what he did for the gas company, but I knew he drove a red pickup truck with utility body and silver gas cylinders in the back.

Mom told us that we would be moving into a house just down the road. It was the large, old farmhouse nearest the Cheshire Toll Bridge, near the bank of the Connecticut River. It had a large yard and a small garage. The farmland around it had long been sold to build other homes. Mom and Dad had a bedroom upstairs. Cilla and Debra shared a bedroom also upstairs. Gary and I had a small room downstairs, off the living room and next to the bathroom. We had bunk beds. I always had the top. Because our bedroom was so small, we spent most of our indoor time in the living room next to our bedroom.

There was a small vegetable garden in the backyard. Mom explained that it belonged to the previous tenant with the last name Lucas. Mom explained that Lucas was not happy that we got this house. She would tend to her garden for the remainder of the year. One day, we came home to a window screen with multiple cuts in it. It was the window that Mrs. Lucas walked by to get to the garden. Mom blamed her for the damage but did not pursue it.

We played games that we learned in school such as red-light, green-light. We lined up a distance from the person who was it. Like I spy, being it was desirable. The person who was it turned her or his back to the others and announced "green-light." WE COULD ADVANCE ON THE PERSON WHO WAS IT DURING A GREEN LIGHT. After a short period, the person announced "red-light" and turned quickly around. If she or he caught any of us moving, we were sent back to the starting line. I often made several big steps before my siblings said red light. I started as my sibling turned her or his back and before she or he called "green-light." I became frustrated that one turned to see me move before calling red-light. As we got closer, a sibling would falsely accuse us as moving and send us back to the starting line. The game descended into arguing and was no longer fun.

We also played hide and seek. There were few places to hide. We could hide behind the two large Maple trees in the front yard or in the shrubs on the bank around our yard. We were not allowed in the garage because there were bats in there. Mom believed the old superstition that bats could get stuck in our hair. I marveled at the many bats fluttering around at dusk. I remember Dad trying to shoot one in flight with his twenty-two-caliber revolver. Mom sent us inside. We tried to watch through the kitchen window. I hoped Dad would kill one so that I could see a bat up close. Mom sent us to the other side of the house where it was safer. Though he fired many times, he never hit one.

I started third grade that fall. I rode the bus to school for the first time. Like in California, I could make no friends. I brought a lunch pail. Those who brought their lunch could sit on the playground with it during lunch. There were no places for sitting. I made the mistake of sitting on a swing. Two much older girls told me that it was theirs and told me to leave. No boy would risk getting beat up by a girl, so I moved. I sat alone on the steps. There was another, older boy who sat on the steps opposite me as we ate. We seldom spoke. I noticed a white line around his lips at the edge of his milk carton when he drank from it. I tried to copy this but spilled the milk, causing it to run down my face and onto my shirt.

Some older high school boys harassed me on the bus to and from school. They called me names such as girl, sissy, and stinky boy. When I told Mom, she dismissed it. "Ignore them. High school boys are mean." They continued to harass me but I ignored them like my mother told me. Riding the school bus was miserable for me. I tried to understand Mom's explanation that high school boys are mean. There were others on the bus that just rode quietly. I also wondered what was in store for me when I got to high school. Would I be mean? Would younger kids fear me?

Once, the bus driver started yelling at two of these older boys. Suddenly, he stopped the bus, got off, then returned with a two-by-four with a nail sticking out of on end, which he held high. The driver said, "Get off!" several times. The boys got off. The driver closed the doors and drove on. I did not know what provoked such a response from the bus driver but expelling these boys seemed like justice for me.

On the playground, there was a larger boy who kept trying to pick a fight with me. He called me names such as sissy, girl, dummy, and weakling. He kept chanting, "Georgy Porgy kissed the girls and made them cry." He criticized my mother and how she made me such a sissy. After consulting Mom about the bus, I knew that it was pointless to ask for her help with this boy. Finally, I accepted his challenge to fight. It was very brief. I returned his punches but neither of us were effective at it. I did what I often did with my brother, only harder. I pushed him into the side of the building. He crashed into the bricks hard enough that he lost interest in continuing the fight. For fighting, the teacher kept me inside during recess. I was perfectly content with this. I helped her do things for the class or sat and colored. I did not care much for trying to color in the boring lines, so I constructed my own designs outside the limits of the drawing. I liked making geometric shapes, especially triangles and arches.

There was a hurricane predicted. Uncle Bernie came to stay with us during the storm to help protect us. The wind was blowing loudly, and it was getting dark outside. We were worried that the two large maple trees in the front yard would fall on the house. Uncle Bernie assured us that the house was strong enough. It had survived the 1938 hurricane that came right up the Connecticut River Valley and hit this house directly. It was the year before Uncle Bernie was born. My mother was nine years old. It both assured me and worried me. We were only 100 feet from the river. My grandparents' farm is similarly on the river. Uncle Bernie reminded me of the story Pop said many times. The storm blew open his barn doors. While the eye of the hurricane passed, Pop went to re-secure the large doors because the open doors made the barn vulnerable to channeling the wind into the barn and blowing the roof off. The house and all the farm buildings made it through the 1938 hurricane. The center of the hurricane passed by without directly hitting us, but it was still a very scary time. Losing power was not so worrisome. Everyone hand hurricane lamps that used kerosene. I had to be close to the light to read.

Mom told us to keep books far away from the flame, too far to read. We just sat in the living room and listened to the wind. At bedtime we laid in our beds and listened to the wind and the small things blown against the side of the house. Eventually, we fell asleep. The next morning, we found several broken branches from the maple and other trees around our house. We dragged them to the riverbank.

My parents decided that things will be better in an apartment closer to town. Before the end of the school year, we moved to Southview. Southview is a large housing complex that is only a few yards from our previous home at 160 South Street. They were blocks of four apartments. Ours was apartment number two, the second one on the left from the beginning of the complex. It was the worst maintained and lowest class place that we ever lived. It had a small kitchen and living room downstairs and three bedrooms upstairs. It was a sharp contrast from the ranch style home at One-Sixty South Street, which was around the corner from our new home. We had traveled across the country to return to the same neighborhood. It was a short distance from where we started but a significant regression is social status.

The backyard was small especially since Mom restricted us to the space immediately behind our apartment. The yard descended into a valley with pathways. There was a lot of trash over this bank, so we were not allowed there at first. Over time, Mom let us go into this area. We could climb among the trees and establish an area we defined as our fort.

We were required to come in when Dad came home from work. Mom made supper. After supper, we took baths and then had to sit on the floor in the small living room. The living room had only two stuffed chairs for Mom and Dad. Cilla and Debra sat on the small sofa but it did not have a good view of the TV.

Gary and I could sit in the stuffed chairs but had to immediately vacate them when either parent walked into the room. Since there were four of us and only two chairs, we competed intensely for a chair. When Mom heard us fighting over the chairs, we were denied using them. Still, we competed for them, only more quietly, so Mom could not hear us from the kitchen.

Mom and Dad seem to feel some satisfaction when sitting in their chairs while the four of us sat on the floor by their feet as we all watched TV. We watched *Leave it to Beaver*, *The Rifleman*, and *Ozzie and Harriet*. I liked *Candid Camera* the best. I liked the *Ed Sullivan Show* the least. We sat on the floor, cross-legged or leaning back on our arms. Sitting cross-legged was too uncomfortable for me so I mostly sat with my legs outstretched and leaning back on my arms. After a while, my wrists hurt, so I leaned back on my elbows. This brought an immediate order from my mother to sit up straight. I suffered with painful wrists.

One evening, Dad invited me to sit in his lap. I was thrilled with the special attention and the opportunity to get off the floor. After a couple of minutes, Dad started to remark about much I had grown and I felt proud. He had me shift my weight in his lap because it was making him feel uncomfortable. Then he told me to sit on the floor and invited Gary into his lap. Dad remarked how much better that was because Gary was smaller and he allowed Gary to sit in his lap until bedtime. I felt rejected. Gary had yet again managed to displace me from my place.

It was fun to play checkers, chess, and cribbage with Dad. I liked the strategy of planning several moves ahead, especially in chess. He praised me as I got better. I felt that he was genuinely trying when I beat him. I also liked adding scores in cribbage. Dad challenged us to add quickly and accurately while seeing all the possible combinations to make the best scores. He was good at it. I liked competing with him to find all the combinations before he could. Dad made the math fun.

We sometimes went to Sunapee Beach as a family. The water was cold and we were not allowed to go past our waists, which made it less fun. It was hard to learn how to swim with my legs dragging and hitting the bottom with my hands. Dad sometimes brought me deeper to practice swimming to him like we did in the ocean in California. Just like in California, he backed up so that I never caught him. I felt the same feeling of being robbed of success as I did in California. We built sandcastles like we did on the California beaches but the sand was not as good. I liked going to the edge of the swimming area and catch frogs and chase tadpoles and minnows.

Other times, we went to Lake Mascoma. It was a longer ride but the water was warmer. It was shallow much further from shore. It had algae floating in the swim area and tangling in it was very unpleasant. The bottom was mucky and squished between our toes and onto our feet. The water and beaches were not as pristine as Sunapee.

Sometimes, when Dad was working, Mom brought us to the town pool. It was a nice place to swim but was very crowded. I could barely get started with swimming and either had to make a sharp turn or stop to avoid running into someone. Mom stopped bringing us to the pool when we got impetigo on our legs that she said was from the pool.

Dad asked me if I would like to join the cub scouts. He explained it some, then got a book about it. I read through the book, looking at the interesting things cub scouts did and how they earned badges. Dad explained that I had to memorize the oath. The scout master owned the neighborhood store. When I learned the oath and the three-finger hand signal, Dad brought me to the store. I recited it to the scout master and he agreed that I was worthy of joining the cub scout pack.

Dad got the uniform and neckerchief. He helped me dress with the neckerchief clasp and brought me to the first meeting. It was in a small family home around the corner from where we lived. The den mother seemed nice. Dad left me there and went home.

The den mother brought me to the enclosed patio in the rear of the house. There were other boys there and an older boy scout. Cub scouts wore blue uniforms while boy scouts wore green ones. The den mother had prepared several crafts for us. I chose to glue walnut shells onto green felt turtle outlines. The finished product created a turtle with a walnut half shell. It looked neat, but I quickly grew bored.

We had these cub scout meetings every week. Dad stopped bringing me because it was close enough to walk. Mom gave me two dimes every week before I went to the meeting. It was the dues. The older boy scout showed me a shortcut through the woods and up the bank behind my house. It was much quicker than walking the long way on the street.

One week, the den mother was a little late and the boy scout started the meeting. He was being much stricter than the den mother and seemed mean. I resisted doing what he told me to do. He led me to the backyard and told me to run circles around a pole. I complied but he wanted me to run faster. I complained that the ground was wet and that I would slip and fall. He angrily insisted that I run faster and threatened to kick my ass. I tried running faster but slipped and fell on the wet ground. My cub scout uniform was now soaked with water and mud. I knew this would make Mom angry. I started to cry, and he ridiculed me, calling me a cry baby. I walked home and never returned. It was just one more thing that was easier to quit. There was no value and only hardship in continuing with it.

We watched Captain Kangaroo on TV before school started. I did not realize that Mr. Green Jeans wore green jeans with our black and white TV. When the show ended, it was time to walk to school. The same school where we played when we lived at One-Sixty South Street. It was called Southview School. I was in the third grade, Cilla in the fourth and Gary in first grade. Debra was in kindergarten; the same one in the center of town that I attended. The entrance to the third grade was through the back door. The bushes where Gary and I had our fort were across from this entrance. I felt a strange connection but no desire to enter our former fort. The cafeteria was in the center of the school. As always, I brought my lunch in a pail. This time, I struck up a friendship with Michael Dubanovich. We had the same birthday, which made us sort of twins. He and I ate together and usually played together during recess.

When winter came, we built a snow fort and had a snowball fight during recess. We had a lot of fun climbing around our combination igloo and fort when a boy, who was not playing with us, threw a snowball at me. I could not duck in time and it hit me in the face. It had a large chunk of ice in the purposefully placed middle of it. It hurt much more than an ordinary snowball and caused my nose to bleed. I ran to him and punched him several times, wanting to cause his nose to bleed. A teacher stopped me and brought us inside the school. She brought me to the cafeteria sink where she helped me stop the nosebleed and to clean up. She told me the large clump of blood that came from my nose was called a clot. She then brought me to my classroom.

My teacher brought me and the other boy to the outside, through the entrance of our classroom. She made us stand on the small porch, facing each other. She commanded us to apologize to each other. I had never heard the word apologize but surmised that she wanted me to say I was sorry. I was not sorry. She insisted that we apologize and it was obvious that I had no other option. Since I did not know for sure that saying I apologize meant that I was sorry, I said, "I apologize." The other boy said the same. The teacher was happy, and we went back inside. I felt true to myself because I did not say that I was sorry when I was not.

Sylvia Freitas was our babysitter when Mom and Dad went out. She was a typical high school girl who was nice to us. We liked her because the rules seemed to be relaxed and she played with us. We wanted to stay up late but she sent us to bed on time. We used to sneak to the top of the stairs and peek around the corner as she watched TV. We tossed some things into the living room. She brought them back and told us very nicely to stop doing it. We probably were a little mischief but we also liked to interact with her too. Once, I threw my pillow downstairs. She did not return it as I expected. I got very worried that she would tell Mom and I would get in a lot of trouble. When I woke the next morning, my pillow was next to me. Mom never said anything. Sylvia likely waited until we fell asleep before she returned the pillow.

One night, I awoke with intense pain in my right ear. I cried louder and louder and Mom finally came. She told me to go back to sleep with my ear against the pillow. Putting my ear against the pillow did not help. I thought that maybe another position might help. I tried several positions, but the pain grew worse. I cried some more, and Mom returned with a warm washcloth and told me told hold it against my ear. I found it pointless to cry anymore because nothing Mom did helped. I dozed off for a short while but mostly could not sleep.

That morning, I felt a sudden sharp pain and yellow liquid came out of my ear and onto the washcloth. I called to Mom. She came and said that my ear abscess had finally burst and that I would be fine. She let me stay home from school that day so that I could catch up on my rest. It left a scar on my eardrum that doctors have noticed with every physical exam I have received. I am extraordinarily lucky that I did not suffer hearing loss.

We were becoming settled into a routine as springtime came. The backyard was still too muddy for playing so we played in the front yard. We had an exceedingly small front yard, even smaller than our small living room, so we mostly played in the street. Mom made us stay near the edge of the street. The street turned sharply in front of our house, so cars had to go slowly. One day, a car came by with its engine roaring and driving too fast. We got out of the way, but our neighbor's dog named George did not. It was a short-legged, brown hound and always moved slowly. The car hit the dog, sending it flying to the edge of the street. The car kept going. The dog screamed and howled horribly upsetting sounds as it thrashed around rolling back and forth in the street. The kids who owned the dog went running to it but stepped back as George thrashed and bit at the air around him. Mom came to the door and called us in. I walked slowly, watching as George's thrashing diminished. He slowly stopped moving and making those horrible sounds. He was dead. Mom would not let us play in the street anymore. If we were in the front, we had to stay on the short walkway or small yard. I was a bit ashamed of our front yard. The grass was long and it embarrassed me. I tried cutting it with grass shears, but my hand got tired too quickly to be effective.

We visited Pop and Grandma on the farm every Sunday afternoon. Sometimes, Uncle Bernie played with us. We played catch and wrestled with him. He tried to pin all four of us, which was not that hard for him because we were so small. His tickling was often extreme, to the point it hurt. We pleaded with him to stop. He responded with, "Why are you laughing if it hurts?" and tickled us more. I calculated my wrestling attack to disrupt his ticking of Cilla when she asked for him to stop. I let Gary suffer longer. Even though Uncle Bernie was somewhat sadistic, it was still fun playing rough with him.

Uncle Bernie taught me how to "Indian dance." He showed me how to raise one knee high, then shuffled forward on the other foot, then exchanging the raised foot, repeating the sliding motion with the other foot. He directed me to dance in a circle. When I accomplished the technique, he told me to tap my mouth with an open hand while doing the Indian chant, "woo, woo, woo." He convinced me that, if I did it long and intensely enough, I could cause it to rain. I liked *The Lone Ranger* show with Clayton Moore. I greatly admired his Indian companion, Tonto, played by Jay Silverheels. I respected his practical wisdom. I felt that knowing how to Indian dance honored him.

Uncle Bernie worried me once when he called my attention to the skin that was peeling on my ears due to minor sunburn. He said that it needed to be treated by cauterizing it. I asked him what that was and he explained that in involved a needle and cutting deep into my ears. I wanted no part of it and concealed my ears from him. I did not understand why Mom or Grandma seemed unconcerned and why Uncle Bernie was so serious. I remained confused with these conflicting interpretations. I did not yet realize the differences between Uncle Bernie and Grandma. Uncle Bernie was subtle in his prejudices. He spoke of Native and African Americans as being inferior. I was aware that Uncle Bernie could not read and the family's disappointment when he dropped out of school in his senior year. Grandma respected everyone and prayed for anyone who suffered any harm or injustice.

I thought that my nightmares were normal. Like others, I awoke with a sensation of falling due to my fear of heights. It also seemed normal that running from a monster chasing me was difficult. I could not raise my legs. I thought that it was because I slept on my stomach and attempts to raise my legs only pressed them into the mattress. I had Superman's power of flight in my dreams but my fear of heights prevented me from flying too high. What seemed to be unique about dreams is that the monster from which I fled was always at my grandparents' farm, between the house and the woodshed. The monster came from south side of the farmhouse, the very place where Uncle Bernie told me about cauterizing my ears. Though I never had a clear vision of the monster chasing me, I felt that it was a form of my uncle. I tried to redirect my dreams to something more positive. We watched a lot of westerns like *Wagon Train* when settlers battled Indians. I dreamt of being captured and raised by Indians like I saw on one of the shows. Sleeping in a teepee and struggling to understand what my captors wanted from me seemed more pleasant than my present daily experiences. My dreams were my private space and a place I could go even while awake.

Cilla and I spent most of the summer on the farm, helping in the fields. Pop always wore bib overalls, a white T-shirt, ankle high leather shoes, and a plain brown baseball cap. Pop had distinct tan lines. Pop had a deep, dark tan contrasted with the snow-white tan line across his forehead and upper arms. When it was cold, Pop wore a denim jacket that he called a barn coat. Grandma wore a dress or jeans and a collared shirt, tennis shoes, and a straw hat.

It was still hard to feel relaxed on the farm. Pop and Grandma had a lot of overly strict rules. Tools such as the hoes had to be put in their proper places. We had to take our shoes off before entering the house. We had to lift our chairs as we sat closer to the kitchen table so not to wear the linoleum with sliding chairs. Pop had his special chair. We could sit in it but had to get out as soon as he entered the room. We had to wash our hands before meals and wash our face, arms, and feet before bed. Bedtimes were strict. If we got up too early, Grandma sent us back to bed. Despite all these and many more strict rules, the farm was a nice, clean, safe place with consistent rules.

We were growing older and could work more independently now. We served customers at the farm stand. The vegetables had the prices marked. There was a hanging scale for vegetables that were sold by the pound. There was a pad of paper and pencil if we needed it to add up the sales. I could do the addition in my head. I only used the paper to demonstrate to a customer that I was correct when they challenged me.

When a vegetable was close to selling out, I would go to the fields with the wheelbarrow and pick more. It was an old-fashioned, wooden wheelbarrow with removable sideboards. Sometimes, when Pop felt playful, he would give us a ride on it. I enjoyed the ride and the special attention he gave to me. It was even more fun with him when I did not have to meet his often unachievably high or changing standards.

Pop demanded a hard day's work. It was engrained in his character and expected nothing less in his descendants. He was a perfectionist. He strived to have a weed free garden, all twenty acres of it. He expected things to be done his way. He had learned how to do things most efficiently over his many years. Many times, he was correct. Sometimes it made no sense, especially when it contradicted his earlier expectations and instructions.

Weeding was on a schedule. The fields were divided by the crop. He seldom went two weeks without weeding a section. When he went to town to deliver his vegetables, he gave an assignment to Cilla and me. He always inspected our work. Most of the time he was critical. On a rare occasion, he told us that we did a good job.

When Pop was not pleased with our work, he ranted for long periods of time on how useless we were. He often commented about my father and how he did not know how to do hard work. He believed that he had to remain hard on me so that I would grow up to be like him and not my father. These comments hurt. I could not turn off this pain like I did with Mom's hair pulling. I developed a sense of defiance. The more he criticized my father, the more I sought a valued part of me that was from my dad and was not recognized by Pop. Dad was great at math and a good swimmer. He played intellectual games with us. He encouraged me to try, to do better next time. Dad accepted less than perfection while assuring me that I will be able to do better with practice.

Pop expected a quantity of work that was difficult to achieve. Cilla and I tried hard, but sometimes made mistakes. For instance, if I accidentally hoed up a stalk of corn, I buried it so that Pop would not find it. I would hear all day and many times into the next about how much money he lost because that stalk could no longer produce the two ears of corn he expected.

Pop worked a full schedule. We got up early and often worked in the fields while Grandma prepared breakfast. After breakfast, we returned to the fields until lunch. When Grandma was caught up with her household chores, she would join us. She had to leave early to prepare the next meal. We got a reprieve after lunch when Pop took his nap. We could "go play," but there was little to entertain us. We had to stay close so he could call us back to work. When we got behind in our weeding, we worked after supper until dusk. The sun was intense in the fields. Pop said his hat kept him cooler. A hat made me feel hotter, so I did not wear one. Pop said that I would lose my hair early if I did not wear a hat. Grandma wore a straw hat mostly because she was fairer skinned and would sunburn. Never did we take breaks or bring extra water with us. We drank three to four glasses of water from a shared cup or from the garden hose when we came in for meals.

Grandma took care of everything in and around the house, including the mowing. Pop worked the fields and barns. I started helping Grandma mow the lawn. She supervised me closely. They had two working mowers. Grandma made me follow her through the orchard. She insisted on using only half the width of the mower to be certain the grass cut well. We mowed two times around each section blowing the grass inward, so that it would not go into the driveway. She thought grass in the driveway looked sloppy. We turned around afterwards. When the mower's grass chute clogged with wet grass, Grandma showed me how to make the mower bounce by pressing the handlebar to the ground, raising the front wheels, then sharply raising the handlebar so that the front wheels slammed to the ground. Repeating this action until the clog dislodged.

Grandma watched me closely when I started mowing by myself. I was not allowed to mow in front of the barn due to the steep hill. She thought that I was not yet strong enough. One day, Grandma asked Uncle Bernie to mow the front of the barn before he left. He complained that he did not have time and convinced Grandma that I could do it. He told me to let the mower go if I slipped so that my foot would not go under it. It was extremely hard pushing the mower up the hill and hard to hold it back going downhill, but I did it. I was enormously proud of this grown-up accomplishment at ten years old.

Pop decided that I could operate the front tine rototiller. He called it the putt-putt because its small engine made a rhythmic sound. I was proud to have this increased responsibility and enjoyed operating machines of any type. This rototiller was hard to handle with its occasional lunges. Pop required close tilling of the vegetable but had no toleration for damage done to any vegetable plants. I would be subject to the long-lasting barrage of belittling language illustrating my incompetence and how much I cost him, which was perhaps five cents.

Pop talked about farming with horses in a team of two. He hated them because they were hard to handle, not like the machines. He often spoke about how the team would work slowly as they pulled the equipment away from the barn and quicker on the return trips. The horses hoped each return would be the last and they could go back to the barn. Half his farm and more than half his time was dedicated to caring for them. Caring for them over the winter was a lot of work with no immediate return, though sometimes they used the horses to pull logs out of the woods. He spoke about how dangerous a horse could be. During cold winter mornings, Pop often brought heated water with molasses in it to help the horses resist the cold temperatures.

The steam from the heated water startled the horse. It reared up and kicked him in the chest, nearly killing him. He was glad when he could buy his first Ford tractor in nineteen fifty-one.

When he had babies, Pop got a cow to provide milk for them. It made me think about just how much he raised everything he needed to care for his family. Grandma canned and pickled vegetables. She still had her old butter churn. Pop got ice from the river and covered it with sawdust under the barn. It was called an ice chest, not a refrigerator. I knew only of Grandma's old Frigidaire with a pull handle to unlatch the door.

Pop had a part time worker at that time. The farm hand was paid with room and board and some shares of the crop. Pop laughed at a story he repeated many times. He told the farmhand that the stool goes beside the cow and not behind it. I did not see the humor. Of course, it goes beside the cow when you milk it. If you sit behind the cow, you could get peed or pooped upon. You also could not reach the udder or get seriously hurt or killed by the cow's kick. Later, I realized the joke. A stool was placed behind the cow when someone committed bestiality with the beast. I still did not think it was that funny.

Pop sometimes briefly spoke about his father. His father had married twice. Pop was the eldest of twenty children. Two died young. Pop worked his father's farm with him until he could buy his own farm. He borrowed three thousand dollars from his father and paid him back in three years. One thing Pop repeated about his father is how he could empty a pint of whiskey without even swallowing.

Harvesting the vegetables was fun when Pop was in a good mood. He seemed proud of his efforts that produced the best vegetables around. He could always sell everything to the local markets. His mood also seemed to be driven by having the revenue coming in. I was fascinated with the tractors. I rode with Pop a lot throughout the summer as he tilled his garden. My first time driving the tractor was when I was eight years old. We picked squash like a fireman's bucket brigade. Pop picked them and handed them to Cilla, who handed them to Gary, then Grandma, then Debra, then me. I was taller than Grandma and could place them carefully into the crates on the trailer towed by the Ford tractor. Pop closely supervised us to be sure we did not damage the stem connection or the blossom bud, which would cause it to rot and spoil the ones next to it in storage. Despite his constant reminders, I felt it was fun. As we got older, Pop and I picked squash alone. He tossed them to me "like playing football." Pop was good at throwing the squash so that I could catch them without damaging them. He threw them hard and I had to slow them as I caught them. He praised me for the good catches, saying that I would someday be a good football player.

We were getting ahead of where the tractor and trailer were parked. He told me to pull it ahead. I was thrilled. He talked me through turning on the key, setting the throttle, stepping on the clutch, and pressing the start button. I had to stand to fully depress the clutch, which the Ford Model Eight N allowed. He then told me to put it in gear. I asked him "Which gear?" I had studied the numbers on the gear box with my many hours of sitting on the idle tractor and imagining driving it. He said, "Any of them." I chose the largest number, four. He told me to let up easy on the clutch. I reached the friction point and the tractor sputtered and stalled, moving only a couple of feet. Pop told me to try again and to be slower on the clutch. I pressed the started button then raised my foot even more slowly. Again, the tractor sputtered and stalled, moving a few feet. I tried twice more, then Pop said the tractor was moved enough. When we got back to the house, he said that he figured out why I had so much trouble getting it to move. He told me that I should have chosen second or third gear. In hindsight, a novice tractor driver should start in the lowest gear until he gets used to the clutch.

At the end of the summer, Pop gave Mom $100, $50 each for Cilla and me. This was used to buy our school clothes. The money also was used to buy school clothes for Gary and Debra. I took little notice of this, happy to get new sneakers, three pairs of pants, three shirts and new underwear. Cilla felt slighted that she had to give her hard-earned share to Debra, who did nothing to earn it. I was more submissive to injustices, knowing how futile it was to resist.

In the fall, Pop brought home loads of slab wood he got from the sawmill. He had a cordwood saw driven by his tractor. Pop ran the saw. Grandma grabbed the pieces as they were cut and tossed them into the woodshed. Cilla and I dragged the slabs to Pop. We had to keep up with him. He wanted a slab ready at his hand when he reached for it. The saw made a high pitched, loud sound as it cut through the wood. Our ears hurt after a few hours. Pop told us to "Be tough."

The piles of wood had to be stacked in the shed to conserve space. Pop was very fussy about how to stack wood so that it would not fall. It was extremely hard to make him happy. I struggled trying to place each piece to his satisfaction. I was amazed at how he could so accurately place several pieces at once. He seemed to just toss them into position. No matter how carefully I tried to place just one, it was never to his satisfaction.

Pop tried to teach me how to recognize kindling wood, but I made many mistakes. He was obviously frustrated that I could not understand his explanation. Pop also taught me how to split the kindling with an axe. I liked splitting the wood. He made certain that I followed his technique to split it safely. I appreciated his formation of a special connection with me as he tried to teach me what he learned. He started calling me "Tichael" instead of Michael. I was already conflicted with being called George or Michael at different times. I did not like being called Mike. It just added one more deviation of my name. I hated it when Pop called me "Tichael" but it was his way of having a special connection with me. I was learning at an early age how important one's name was to one's identity or sense of self. I did not like being called Mike and certainly not Mikey. I was troubled enough with being called by my legal first name, George. I wanted to be called Michael, the name my mother and grandmother called me. It was from Michael, the Arch Angel, God's defender warrior.

Pop always framed his instruction as 'the trick to" doing something. His were techniques that he had developed over many years. He sometimes frustrated me, especially on his hoeing techniques. Sometimes we were not allowed to bury the weeds. Their roots had to be removed from the soil. Other times, it was OK to cut the top off the weed and other times we were expected to bury the tiny weeds. I learned to ask how to best do the hoeing to be sure that I was doing it correctly. If I did it wrong, it would be a long, very unpleasant day of verbal barrages about how stupid I was not knowing how to even hoe the weeds. Unfortunately, just asking was often met with a response reminding how stupid I was for not being able to remember.

I could not sweep the barn properly. Pop demonstrated how to sweep the dirt, leaving lines between strokes, and doubling back after each sweeping action to get the dirt left behind. It angered me that Pop would not let me accomplish the task my own way if I could meet his standards. I not only had to meet his standards, but I also had to do it his way. Sometimes, he called me stupid for having to ask how to do something so simple. Pop often criticized me for not wearing a hat in the hot sun, reminding me that I would lose my hair when I got older. I did not trust his warning because his hair as very thin. I especially did not want his very distinctive tan line across his forehead. As Pop delivered these verbal barrages, he always brought in how useless my father was and how I was going to be just like him. After a while, I began to realize that half of me came from my father and I wanted to prove that I was capable. Comments about my father hurt me more as I grew older. As an adult, I began to realize that Pop needed to feel superiority to dominate his family. It is easier to be superior by tearing down the opposition rather than to rise above it on one's own merits.

I started the fourth grade, the highest grade at Southview School. Cilla took the bus to another school. I was quiet and responsible so that the teacher took notice and made me a crossing guard. I got a yellow harness to lead a group of kids across the street and to the street corner after school. I had the authority to stop traffic to allow kids to cross the street. I was immensely proud of this honor. Mom thought that it was good but did not share my excitement. She just seemed to expect it of me. Nonetheless, I was proud each time to wind the belt up after taking it off like the teacher showed me and again when unwinding and putting it on.

Schools had fallout shelter signs on them. It indicated that these were good places to go in case the Soviets attacked us with nuclear missiles. We also did nuclear attack drills. We curled up under our desks. It seemed scary to us but we trusted the adults who assured us we would be safe by following their instructions.

My siblings and I were unaware of our parents' deteriorating relationship. The arguing seemed normal. We became suddenly aware that something was not normal as Mom prepared dinner one evening. Dad went into the kitchen instead of waiting in the living room with us. They were talking normally at first, then their voices got louder. I paid little attention to what they were saying as I watched TV. I heard Mom yell, "You son of a bitch," follow by a loud crash and a metal cooking pot's twang as it fell on the floor. Mom came rapidly out of the kitchen, making thunderous steps around us in our usual spots on the floor. She went upstairs to her bedroom. The house was suddenly quiet. When we did not see Dad, we cautiously approached the kitchen. Looking around the corner, I saw Dad face down on the floor. Spaghetti and water were all over the floor and the pot was on the floor beside Dad. We were scared. We could not figure out what happened.

We called to Dad and he did not answer. He laid motionless on the floor. He finally started to move and slowly got up. We knew better than to ask what happened. Dad slowly cleaned up the mess, then cooked some more spaghetti for us. We spent the evening with Dad, but no one said anything about Mom, who remained upstairs the remainder of the evening. Days later Mom showed us the dent in her cooking pot. She said that Dad had said Gary looked more like the milkman than he. Years later, I began to think Dad was trying to address her excessive drinking. This makes more sense to me because she went to bed and remained there, which is what she did when she had been drinking. We did not make the connection to the time in California when she staggered to bed, pushing the TV out of place.

We used to go to the races in Claremont on some Saturday nights in the summer. Mom lied about our ages, so we got it at a cheaper rate. I was proud of my status afforded to my age, which was disregarded with Mom's lie. We sat on benches on the side of the bank. There were a lot of benches and many people filled them. Mom made us stay close. We could only leave to go to the bathroom. The bathroom smelled awful. There was a trough to pee in. I could barely reach it. Several people peeing the same time made a little river that flowed to a drain on one end. I felt intimidated by the lack of privacy and hated going, so I went only when I absolutely had to go and in danger of wetting my pants.

We enjoyed watching the cars around the dirt track. Dirt sprayed off their tires as they went around the corners. I enjoyed the crashes the most. One exciting crash was when a car went off the banked corner and into the trees. It seemed to fly into the trees, then dropped out of sight.

Cilla and I had a favorite car in the fully modified class, Number 311. It was a white car with red numbers. The engine and front suspension were exposed, showing the dirt sprays even more. It was a nice-looking car and it often won, which is why it was our favorite.

Second to my favorite race car, I liked watching the grader and water truck restore the track between races. The grader went faster than any grader I saw working along the highway. He brought the dirt that had migrated to the outside of the track back towards the center. All those cars that spun up the dirt had an accumulative effect of pushing it to the outside. When the grader made a pass across the top, the water truck followed, spraying water on the newly graded surface.

This was the time that long lines formed at the concession stand and the bathroom. We did not notice much about how people would drink beer and bring in their own food and drink. We brought a cooler. We enjoyed some snacks, usually Necco wafers or licorice. For a rare treat, we got a bottle of root beer. Dad carried the cooler to and from the car. Sometimes it was a long walk and he had to set it down to catch his breath. It was common for people to bring beer. When the flagger made an unpopular call, people threw beer bottles at him. There was a fence to protect him. Bottles getting on the track interrupted the races, which angered the whole crowd, calming the bottle chuckers.

Demolition Derbies were the most fun. These old, junk cars were restricted to the center of the track. The last car running was the winner. They crashed into each other, sometimes several at a time. Some would try to get some speed going backwards to ram the front of their opponent. It got boring as the cars conked out, leaving only a few. Some lost only because they were trapped between two broken down cars.

Mom and Dad often argued while we rode back home from the racetrack. Mom was the loudest. She said mean things to Dad, calling him useless, not a man, and a prick. The intensity of the arguments was frightening. Adding to the fear was, as the intensity of the argument grew, Mom would strike Dad. Especially when Mom drove while arguing, the car often drifted or moved suddenly into on-coming traffic or towards the ditch, requiring quick corrections. Sometimes, during the most intense arguments, Mom threatened to drive the car into a tree or a bridge and "kill us all." This was especially scary when she identified a specific tree or bridge and swerved towards it, causing us all to scream loudly. After she drove by it, she said that she would drive into the next one. As we approached the next lethal structure, she identified it as her target and swerved the car towards it, narrowly missing it. When my siblings and I screamed and cried, we were told to "shut up." It was difficult to tell whether the drifting into on-coming traffic or the ditch was intentional. I wondered whether she would suddenly correct the car's direction or purposefully drive it into another car, truck, or a tree.

These times remain the scariest in my life. The fear while riding with my arguing, intoxicated parents as they fought physically overwhelmed me. When Mom and Dad got this way, I found solus by resolving that we were going to die. Cars did not have seatbelts back then. I had only the arm rest on the car door to hold, which I knew was insufficient. I thought that maybe I could somehow hold myself against the front seat. Then I realized that I could crouch onto the floor between the front and rear seats to where I retreated other times. When Mom and Dad fought like this and when Mom started to threaten to kill us all, I crouched my body as tight as I could onto the floor between the seats. I held my arms over my head. I tuned out the arguing as much as I could. I was helpless to do anything and this was my best recourse. Here, I felt a little safer and more in control of my life. I listened to my siblings' screams as they moved about, trying to get my parents to stop fighting. From this position, I could not see the on-coming hazards but listened intently, viewing everything in my mind as my sibling's screams intensified and abated. I thought about how I might be the only survivor of a crash. I might be in the hospital with serious injuries for a long time. Nurses would care for me. When I got better, I would go live with Pop and Grandma. It would not be so bad.

Dad was driving home from the races one of these nights when Mom and he were fighting. We drove down Route 12 and turned right onto Lovers' Lane. The front right tire blew out just after the turn. Dad pulled over. We were in the front of someone's house. It was a nice, newer home with a nice front yard.

After pulling over, Dad just sat in the driver's seat while Mom continued calling him names and telling him that he was not a man. He finally got out and went to the trunk. Mom was quiet for a few minutes, telling us to stop crying or she would give us something to cry about. Dad managed to get the bumper jack and jacked the front of the car. We felt each little jolt as the car rose with each movement of the lever. As Dad worked on the front right tire, Mom was able to continue her argument with him out the car window. I worried that she was getting too loud for the people living in the house. Dad responded now and then, but I could not hear what he said from the opposite side of the car where I was sitting. She said, "I don't give a shit about them." Dad must have warned her about alerting the people in the house. Then he apparently said something that made Mom very mad and she started throwing empty beer bottles at him. She grabbed them with her left hand from the floor, transferred them to her right hand, then threw them as hard as she could at Dad. He was an easy, vulnerable target outside her window. She called him names, including "prick" and "son of a bitch." Dad held his hand up as she threw several bottles while he tried to change the tire. She ran out of empty bottles and started throwing full ones. I heard the thud as one that struck him hard. Mom started yelling, "Get up. Get up and fix the tire."

I got worried, wondering why Mom was telling Dad to get up. I stood up and leaned over my siblings. I saw Dad lying face down on the ground by the front tire. I asked Mom why he was not moving. Mom said, "He's faking." She remained quiet for a while. My sisters and brother were crying hard, trying to avoid being too loud. Eventually, Dad moved his leg. He finally bent his leg and put his knee under him. He slowly went back to changing the tire. When he finished, he put the flat tire and the jack in the trunk. Mom slid across the seat and said that she was going to drive, insisting that he was too drunk.

As we drove, the fight resumed and got louder. Mom started punching Dad as she drove, the car violently swerved each time. They only took a time out from fighting as we passed the toll booth for the Cheshire Toll Bridge crossing the Connecticut

River between Charlestown, New Hampshire and Springfield, Vermont. The fight intensified with more punches and threats to drive into the tree or bridge as they appeared before us, threatening to kill us all. Mom had to readjust her position behind the steering wheel several times. When she did this, she wiggled her butt cheeks one at a time. As she did this, she jerked the steering wheel, causing the car to swerve back and forth again violently with each shuffle of her butt. All the time, she was yelling and punching at Dad. I resolved to the possibility of dying as I took my safe place on the floor between the seats. I tried unsuccessfully to block the sounds by covering my ears.

I recognized that we were on Clinton Street in Springfield and knew we were getting closer to home. I would be glad to be at home and get into my bed, where I would finally be safe. There was a concrete traffic island at the turn to go up South Street Hill from Clinton Street to our home. Mom was yelling and striking at Dad while she was making this turn. She jerked the wheel as she threw a punch and crashed into the island. This blew out the front left tire. Dad criticized her driving, telling her that we had no other spare tire. Mom told him to shut up and continued driving. She drove slowly on the flat tire that made a lot of noise. I was concerned, of course, about whether we would make it home, almost a mile away. The tire's noise was so loud that even by shouting, my parents could barely hear each other. The competing concerns of whether we would make it home and the violent fighting seemed to be lessened by the noise of the flat tire. Somewhat reassuring was that Mom had to drive slowly, giving me an odd sense of worrisome relief. We made it home and got into bed. Mom and Dad continued their fighting. Somehow, I drifted off to sleep.

The next day, Dad carried one flat tire to a garage to get it fixed. He changed the tire and drove the car to the garage to get the other tire repaired.

My parents decided that things will be better in Claremont. A few weeks into school, Mom said that we were moving to Claremont. We would have a house of our own, on Mulberry Street, across from the cemetery. It had two floors, but we were not allowed upstairs. Mom said it was not safe. The floor could collapse. Gary and I went up there when Mom did not see us. We walked onto the floor in the first bedroom. It seemed fine until we tried to bounce it up and down. It did wiggle some, so we left quickly.

This house had a small, dark kitchen. The living room was a reasonable size but Mom and Dad had their bed in it. Cilla and Debra had the best bedroom. Gary and I had a small room between the girls' room and the bathroom.

Mom made us take baths together. She said that it was to save hot water. The amount that we were allowed did not even cover our legs. We could only draw enough water to soak our private parts. We were not allowed to touch even our own private parts. They were to get clean by "soaking in the tub." Cilla and I took baths together for years, but Mom would not let us at this house. She said that we were getting too old. I did not like taking a bath with Gary. He wiggled around too much. He did not do it on purpose but while wiggling around, his foot often went into my groin. Sometimes he pressed against my delicate parts and it hurt. He kept doing this despite my protests. I complained to Mom, but she would not do anything about it. I nagged her to take a bath with Cilla again, but she said no. Eventually, she let me take a bath alone.

We liked watching Saturday morning cartoons on TV. It was a way of escaping reality and finding comfort in an imaginary world. We watched Mighty Mouse, Bugs Bunny, Tom and Jerry, Woody Woodpecker, Yogi Bear, Quick Draw McGraw, The Jetsons, Space Ghost, and the Flintstones. Our reception was poor and required frequent adjustments to the antenna. The television was getting old and the vertical hold was weak, which caused the picture to roll. We tried to adjust it but our attempts did not last long. I once convinced Cilla that I could cause it to roll by rolling my eyes up. When the picture started to roll and I said it was because I caused it, Cilla got terribly angry with me. Of course, I had no such power but enjoyed deceiving Cilla. Watching TV was often very frustrating.

We had a small back yard and lots of bushes. The cleared area was not large enough for any activities. We made paths through the thicker shrubs much like the fort we had on South Street. It was fun chasing each other through the paths we made in the shrubs. We had to get down on our hands and knees in some places. Once, a sharp twig pierced my eyebrow. It bled a lot but eventually stopped. I told Mom later that day. She looked at it and said I would be OK. It healed with a significant scar, so it probably should have been stitched.

Cilla showed me that we had new neighbors just down the hill from our house. Two blond-haired boys a little younger than us were playing in the back yard. Cilla said, "Watch this." She asked, "What's your name?" The older boy responded, "Mind your own beeswax, huh." It was a strange, southern accent that we found fascinating. I asked for his name and got the same, immediate response, almost robotically. We had fun asking a couple more times and got the same, immediate response. We decided to stop asking, not wanting to be mean. We thought that they were a little stupid by consistently acting this way. Perhaps they were subjected to intense parental control, which we could understand and did not want to cause any hardships.

I attended fourth grade at Saint Mary's School. This was the furthest I ever walked to school, about a half a mile. I carried my lunch pail and placed it on the floor in the back of the classroom with the others. Sister Theresa was proud of her tough reputation. She sometimes held her right arm up as if to show her bicep. I thought this was strange since she was covered completely by her tunic and habit. Only her face showed. She had a yard stick leaning against the blackboard behind her desk in the front of the room. Sister Theresa often warned us that she would use it to enforce discipline. She did use the yardstick on some students, but never on me. I would never do anything to upset her. Being hit with the yardstick was inconsequential to me. I was more afraid of what my mother would do to me if I were so bad that a nun had to punish me.

I was mostly bored at school. The math was too easy and always the same. I did not like reading history or memorizing religious passages. I watched the clock for recess, lunch, and dismissal times. The playground was filled with kids riding on the swings, playing ball, tag, red-light green-light, and hopscotch. One group of boys gathered at the far end of the playground and were mean to anyone who approached them. Sometimes, they roamed the playground terrorizing younger kids. There was little to no adult supervision to stop them.

Bobby Dupont was the primary leader of the gang. He gained fame by bragging that his dad was a boxer and he learned to box from him. He and his gang patrolled the playground during recess, commanding others to get out of his way. I stood my ground one day and refused to be intimidated by him. He had his gang of followers in a semi-circle behind him. He decided that he wanted to fight me after school. I accepted his challenge. I waited at the agreed location, but Bobby did not show up. Finally, one of his followers came and said that Bobby had to stay after for the teacher. He did not attempt to reschedule our fight. I expected to lose the fight but apparently my determination to avoid being bullied prevailed.

I did not like going onto the playground with so many bullies and no friends. I could work for the sisters, cleaning the kitchen in the convent or working in the yard. They gave me an apple for my efforts. I did not care for the apple. I was only glad to have a place to go other than the playground.

Cilla slipped on ice in the playground and hit her head. She could not continue so her teacher sent her home. We did not have phone so Mom was not aware. Luckily, Mom saw Cilla as she walked past the house in a stupor. Mom called to her and she came in. Mom treated Cilla with a wet cloth and bedrest, never bringing her to the doctor to treat her concussion.

One day, a student in the back of the classroom reported that someone's milk had leaked all over the floor. I sat near the front and mostly ignored the report. Sister Theresa went to the back and located the offending lunch box, held it up and asked who owned it. I was devasted to learn that it was mine. She then moved the other lunch boxes out of the way and told me to clean it up. I had no idea how to do it. I wanted to disappear. She seemed very mean about it as she called me to her location in the back of the classroom. She showed me the puddle of milk. The glass liner in my thermos was broken. The only way this could have happened was for someone to have kicked it. I argued that the responsibility to clean up the milk was not mine. It was for the person who kicked it. I got no sympathy, only her demand that it was my responsibility because it was my thermos. She placed my lunch box in the sink in the back of the classroom, then she brought me to the closet and showed me a mop and pail. I did my best to clean it. I was very awkward, never having any experience using a mop and pail. I fought back tears unsuccessfully as I worked. I not only suffered with a wet lunch; I could not focus on school for the remainder of the day. I also worried about what Mom would do. I told her that I did not want a thermos with my lunch anymore. She let me buy a two-cent carton of milk available at school.

Sister Theresa was working at her desk as we worked on our assignment. She held up a piece of paper and called my name. This school knew me as George because Dad registered me. Mom registered me at the other schools that called me Michael. As she held the paper up, she said that I needed to tell my parents to pay their bill. I had no idea what she was talking about. She went on saying that they owed the school ten dollars. I thought hard about why they would owe the school money. Sister told me to let them know that they had to pay right away. I told Mom when I got home. She explained that we had to pay because Saint Mary's is a private school. She said that she would let Dad know because it was his fault that the bill was not paid. Mom assured me that I would be able to continue attending the school.

Mom wanted Gary and I to take guitar lessons because she liked the guitar. She found an instructor who was blind. We went to his house every week. I hated the guitar but Gary loved it. I kept telling Mom that I wanted to quit. She demanded that I continue because she wanted me to be able to play the guitar for her. I finally convinced her to let me quit. Gary continued and played well enough to make her happy, especially when she was drinking beer.

Mom told me that I should start doing pushups. She said that it would make me stronger. She said that it would make my chest muscles bigger. She liked actors with big chest muscles. I was happy to follow her suggestion. Every boy wants to be strong. Pop's emphasis was on bicep muscles. He gauged the development of my biceps by squeezing them.

My parents determined things will be better if we moved to Charlestown. Mom thought that it was a particularly good move because we were going to live on a farm. We were going to have a lot more room with neighbors at a distance. It was the old Bemis Farm. We liked it much better. It had a large, eat-in kitchen, a large living room, a front room, one bedroom was downstairs and two upstairs. It had one bathroom with two doors. One door to the kitchen and the other door to the living room. There was a large, enclosed porch and the barn was connected to the house.

Cilla and Debra used the upstairs bedroom in the front of the house. Gary and I got the smaller room upstairs in the back. Mom and Dad used the bedroom downstairs. The kitchen had a combination kerosene and gas stove. It looked a lot like my grandmother's wood-fired kitchen range but smaller. There was a woodstove in the living room. This is how the whole house was heated. There was an exceedingly small, dirt floor cellar that was very creepy with the many spider webs, so we did not go there very often.

The yard was large and plenty of woodlands around it. There was an active dairy farm across and down the road from us. They pastured cows beside and behind us. It was neat to watch them and especially their routine of returning to their barn at milking times. Farmer Simmons put up signs while he and his wife held flags to stop cars while the cows crossed the road.

We could have pets. Mom got a male cat and a female dog. Cilla named the cat Zippers. She said that the name applies well because it would zip around the house and purr. Mom named the dog Chino, again, because she liked that name. We freely let them out of the house. Chino stayed with us in the yard, but Zippers was gone sometimes for days. When he came back, he often had scratches around his face. Some were infected and swollen. Mom did not like the cat because he peed on a house plant and killed it.

Cilla, Gary, and I explored the barn. There were cow stanchions in the lowest level. It was fun looking at some of the old milking supplies, hoses and teat cups that attached to the cow. The old stanchions had water troughs and feed bins. The water troughs were a small bowl with a lever in the bottom. When the cow pressed her nose into it, the lever let water flow in. There was a separate dug well behind the barn that was connected to the barn. Water for the house came from a spring further up the hill.

Upstairs, the barn was a lot like my grandfather's barn. It had a large open area with a calf pen on the right side. On the left, there were two enclosed stalls that were likely used for horses. One had a door with top part half that could open separately while the bottom half could remain closed. We called it the horse stall. It looked like chickens were kept in the other stall, so we called it the chicken coop. The back part of the second level was open but it had some stored construction materials. The loft was empty. In the back of the barn, there was a window with a view of the neighbors, fields, and hills to the north. Almost directly across the Connecticut River was my grandparents' farm. We could not see the farm but the mountain behind the farm was very prominent.

Something we enjoyed together without fighting was catching lightning bugs. At first, we tried to catch them flying at night. Their intermittent flashing made it hard to track them and remain focused on one. As we waited for the next flash, another bug was flashing nearby. We tried to fashion a net made from a pillowcase, but it did not work. Eventually, we realized that there were bugs on the ground that were flashing. These were easy to catch and put in a jar. It was odd to see up close their abdomen's light up and glow. Some even flashed while we held them. We hoped to make a biological lantern with several in a jar but they were inconsistent with their flashing and eventually stopped flashing.

We found a baseball and bat in the shed connecting the house and the barn. Cilla, Gary, Debra, and I tried to play baseball. We were terrible at pitching and hitting the ball was nearly impossible. We decided that it was best to just toss it up and hit it on the way back down. We did not have enough players for someone to be on the bases.

Frustrated with trying to play baseball and gain cooperation from my siblings, I found fun by batting the ball along the ground. It was almost like golf as I selected a target and tried to see how few hits it took to bounce the ball off my target. Targets could be a tree, rock, bush, or anything lying around. It was a solo game but Gary sometimes insisted on joining. He just hit the ball indiscriminately, at nothing. His purpose seemed to be to deny me my time to play. When I told Gary that I wanted to play alone, he interfered however he could. Often, he stood between me and my target. I would simply select a different target. This worked only on my first hit as he would then identify my new target and interfered, again. Sometimes, he threw rocks at me to interfere. Normally, it was easy to dodge his rocks, but one bounced unexpectedly and hit me in the head. It hurt and I wanted retaliation. I picked up his rock and chased after him. I could easily outrun Gary but as I closed in, he often dropped to his knees, laid on his side and tried to trip me. This time, I backed up, aimed for his right thigh facing me and threw with all my might. Just as I released the rock, Gary rolled onto his back. It was not my intention to hit him in the groin but the rock was already in flight. I could not recall it. It seemed to fly in slow motion as it perfectly hit him where it hurts most, even more than the head strike I suffered from him.

Gary hurt so badly that he could not cry, or even breathe for a few seconds. He eventually started to cry. I watched until I was satisfied that I had delivered vengeance even greater than I intended. Gary slowly got up, held his groin as if his precious parts would fall off if he let go, and staggered into the house. Mom came back out and called me in. As I walked past her in the doorway, she hit me hard enough on the back of my head to cause me to stagger, nearly falling faceward onto the floor. She directed me to kneel in the corner of the kitchen next to the wringer washing machine, her favorite torture-like punishment. This reminded me of the blow to my head that she delivered in California while I knelt by this washer. For several long minutes, she yelled at me. She told me how terrible I was that I would do such a thing, "You can kill someone that way." I had learned that trying to explain my different intentions or behavior was futile and more likely to increase and extend my punishment. I spent most of the afternoon kneeling in that corner. We had to "kneel up straight" and not sit back on our heels. She frequently checked for compliance. She claimed to have a special mother's sense and could tell when we were lying or otherwise not in compliance with her demands even when she could not see us. She occasionally yelled, "Kneel up straight," while she sat watching TV in the living room. I knew her claim to a special mother's sense was invalid because I was already kneeling up straight. I shifted weight from knee to knee but I was determined to be stronger than her punishment. Each time Mom came to the nearby fridge to get a beer, I had to listen to Mom's renewed verbal barrage that hurt more than the physical assaults. I would rather just get a physical beating than hear these insults on my character. Cilla and I spoke of these and agreed. A physical beating is brief and over within a short period of time. Verbal assaults were relentless and hurt more, tearing deep into our being. If Mom did not like my reaction to her verbal assault, she either slapped me on the head or pulled my hair or both. I so much wanted to overcome and be stronger than these treatments. The slap to the head strained my neck, so I stiffened as best I could. I managed to desensitize the pulling of my hair by turning off that pain. No longer does pulling my hair hurt. However, the hard pull on my hair still strained my neck.

We had few toys. There were some things with which we could play. On one corner of the house, there was a large cluster of knotweeds. I had never seen this plant before. We called it bamboo. We used this bamboo for spears and swords, though it was not strong. Mullein stalks stood out in the field. They were like wood and much stronger. Getting them out of the ground and breaking the roots off was challenging.

Japanese beetles ate big holes in the knotweed leaves. Dad said that he would give us 5 cents for every beetle we caught, then went into the house. Cilla and I thought this were a great opportunity to make some profit. Gary soon joined us. When I had collected more than two dollars' worth, I went to Dad with my catch. He peered into the can, then said that he did not have the money, explaining that he did not expect us to catch so many. He gave a little assurance that he would get some and pay us later, which he never did. We were getting used to broken promises, but we were still extremely disappointed. Sadly, this was one of many times we got excited with a promise, only to be disappointed.

Dad came home from work one day and suggested that I join little league baseball. I agreed. He brought me into the yard to practice throwing. We threw the ball a few times. I did not do very well so Dad had to chase after some. He got tired of this and set up a bushel basket against the barn door and told me to practice throwing the ball into it. He said that I could learn to be the pitcher this way. That was the extent of my preparation for membership on the baseball team. I had no practice with the team for the first game. I was assigned center field. I missed all the balls that came to me. I was not prepared to intercept a ball that bounced off the ground unpredictable. I chased the ball and got it when it hit the fence. Batters got several bases and sometimes homeruns as I tried to get the ball back to the infield.

During one game, the catcher got hurt and could not play. From the outfield, I saw Dad talking with the coach. Soon, he called me in and told me to put on the catcher's gear. I struggled getting it on. It restricted my movements and the mask made it extremely hard to see. I did not like it but wanted to please my dad. I was a horrible catcher. Almost every ball got by me. The pitcher and coach told me that I had to stop the ball from getting by me. I tried as hard as I could, but I had no experience to prepare me for this awkward equipment. As runners stole bases each time that I missed the ball, I noticed the pitcher was starting to cry. After this game, I told Dad that I did not want to play baseball. Again, it was easier to quit than continue.

My favorite evening television shows were *Lost in Space* and *Voyage to the Bottom of the Sea*. I noticed that the sea monsters in the *Voyage to the Bottom of the Sea* sometimes resembled the space monsters on the earlier *Lost in Space* show. My favorite Saturday morning show was *Johnny Quest*. These shows did not have superheroes or people with extraordinary skills like *Superman* and *The Rifleman* and *Gunsmoke*. Their success was from their intelligence and cleverness.

Mom and Dad still argued a lot. Some nights he came home late and eventually there were nights that he did not come home at all. Mom was poised to argue as he walked in. It was horrible to hear the arguing and Mom sometimes hit Dad and threw things at him. We went outside or in the barn so that we did not have to hear it.

Collateral damage during the return to Vermont, early grade school years.

We could see that our parents drank beer and thought little of it. Though their fighting caused us great anxiety but it was mostly fear for our own safety, especially the fighting while driving. We were much too socially isolated to see this was abnormal. We never had friends to our house nor did we go to theirs. We moved much too often to develop meaningful relationships outside our immediate family.

We also did not notice the regression in our financial status. I was embarrassed and confused when Sister Theresa called me out in class for the unpaid bill. I thought it was only careless oversight by my parents. My parents owned our first few homes. Now, we were renting properties. By the time I was nine years old we had moved seven times and attended five different schools in four years. With all these changes, my parents always said that "things will be better." Being better depended on external influences.

Moving to another home brought unfulfilled expectations and broken promises. We could not move away from our problems.

Medical care was also lacking. Mom brought us for vaccinations that were required to attend school. It had to be an obvious emergency to go to the doctors. My ear abscess and eyebrow laceration went untreated. Cilla's concussion was similarly treated by Mom. This practice extended to our pets though Mom seemed to favor the animals' care over us. She explained that they were helpless and we could take care of ourselves better than they could. They were never neutered or spayed. If they got seriously sick or injured, Mom put them out of their misery. She drowned them by placing a rock with them in a grain bag, tying it off and throwing them into the river.

I wanted a friend but did not know how to connect. I only tried to copy their behavior to fit in. I was ill prepared for cub scouts and baseball. Any chance to build a relationship was severed with the next move.

Parental guidance was dependent upon physical punishment. We behaved to avoid punishment. There was never a reward for good behavior nor for completing chores unless you consider that the absence of punishment is your reward. The cruel corporal enforcement dominated our sibling relationships. We were becoming increasingly competitive and violent for our limited resources. Being parentified, Cilla and I were expected to concede our claim to any resources to favor Gary and Debra. Cilla and I did the chores and worked on the farm while Gary and Debra enjoyed lower expectations.

At this time, I could not understand how much Dad tried and why he failed. His father was away on business most of his childhood, so he lacked a good role model. Dad's mother was very loving and kind. He was not prepared for my mother's dominance and alcoholism. Society's concept of a perfect family required a father as the bread winner and Mom as the homemaker. Alcoholism was only in the drunken bums on the street, the hobos. Treatment was not even considered an option for these societal outcasts. The effects upon the family were not well known. There was no one at school or society in general to recognize our plight. Even if there were, it was generally understood to stay out of family business. The father was expected to be the all-knowing head of the family and control such things. There was even a television show called *"Father Knows Best"* to reinforce this concept. There was no one to support my father.

Dad tried to form a relationship with us with limited success. Societal expectations were mothers cared for the children until they were older when fathers started teaching his moral guidance. I felt some rejection as my younger brother, Gary, gained favoritism. I had not yet learned that I felt this way because I had become parentified and responsible for Gary's misbehaviors. The time Dad rejected me from his lap and accepted Gary hurt me deeply.

There were some good times with Dad. I enjoyed the card games and times in the car with him. Unknowingly, he sharpened my natural math ability with speed and accuracy, especially while playing cribbage. I found my math skills useful while serving customers at my grandfather's vegetable stand. He and Grandma needed a pad and pencil for what I could do in my head.

There was much denial of its existence let alone the effects of alcoholism on the individual and no recognition of the effects on the family. I see now that alcoholism skips generations. My maternal grandfather's boasting of his father's downing a pint without swallowing shows that he was an accomplished alcoholic. Pop took a shot of brandy when it was cold and Grandma took a sip of sherry but rarely. A bottle lasted for months, maybe more than a year. Grandma's vice was the lemon lime Squirt soda. A bottle lasted her for weeks, even when she shared it with us. Alcoholism reemerged with my mother. Children of alcoholics develop some common characteristics. One is an expectation of unachievable perfectionism trying to meet the elusive standards. Abusive and demeaning language and corporal punishment is intended to motivate children but it destroys their self-esteem. Its purpose is to protect the alcoholic and child of an alcoholic's self-esteem, keeping the child submissive. No one could be better than the adult alcoholic. We victims develop coping strategies. Mine was passive resistance, turning off pain and tuning out the verbal assaults as best I could. My fort building was intensified to construct my own safe space. I also daydreamed a lot, escaping the unpleasant reality. These were places where adults could never intrude because they did not know of their existence. My quiet space, though I could use them rarely and for short periods.

LATER GRADE SCHOOL YEARS

C illa and I were beginning to compare our lives with that of our peers. Our discontent increased as we were able to evaluate our condition. Mom kept us in check by refusing to let us go with friends. She consistently reminded us that we were different than others, who were from rich families.

I started fifth grade at Farwell School in North Charlestown. It was a stone building with two classrooms for six grades. For the first time, we were all in the same school. Cilla and I had Mrs. Minnie Smith. She taught grades 4, 5 and 6. Our day always began with a pledge of allegiance to the flag. She rotated the lead among the students. I normally did not like speaking in front of the class but did not mind leading the pledge.

Mrs. Smith structured the day that was coordinated among the three grades. As she presented a lesson to one class, she had the others doing work on other topics. I hated English and history. I loved math with its systems and structure. I could easily get the right answer. English and history did not have clear answers like math. Though Mrs. Smith insisted that we were not supposed to be distracted when she presented lessons to other classes, I could not resist listening to her as she presented math to the sixth grade. I had mastered the multiplication and division for the fifth grade and found the challenge of the sixth-grade fractions far more interesting. I hurried through my assigned work and did the sixth-grade work, too. I just did not hand in the sixth-grade work.

Mrs. Smith was short and a bit round. Long periods on her feet were difficult for her. She liked to have tea sometimes. When she had an opportunity to get off her feet to sit at her desk in the front of the classroom, she backed up to her wooden swivel chair with wheels. Her legs were too short, so she had to sort of jump and fall into the chair. This always gave the chair some rearward motion that crashed into the bookcase behind her desk. She then wiggled and pulled herself to her desk. Some kids thought that this was funny and giggled. I felt sorry for her. She may have been strict, but she was fair and praised me for my math skills.

Mr. Bryce came once a week to teach us music. He taught us songs and how to keep rhythm by tapping our toe. Sometimes he brought and played an instrument for us. It seemed silly and awkward to me to tap my toe as he taught us the rhythm of the song. I hated music and usually just moved my lips to appear that I was singing.

Recess was much more enjoyable at Farwell than my previous schools. Teachers made sure that the swings, teeter totters, and monkey bars were shared. Sometimes, a baseball game was organized. My only worry was a large girl in my class. Beverly was known to beat up boys. She had stayed back several years and was physically more developed. Getting beat up by a girl was any boy's worst nightmare. It would cause irreversible harm to his ego. I was not immune from Beverly's threats and attempts to catch me. Fortunately, she was quite overweight and easy to outrun. She had large breasts for a fifth grader. When she ran, all the lose flab and boobs bounced in different directions. Mrs. Smith eventually stopped Beverly from playing baseball because she "bounced too much." Cilla explained to me that Beverly refused to wear a bra, which made the motion her breasts too prominent when she ran.

I found many keys in the barn next to our house and decided to collect keys. Family and others gave me keys when they no longer knew what lock they fit. I had collected more than fifty keys of many types. I tried them on locks and became aware of the different styles of keys. One day, Mrs. Smith announce to the class that the key to the hand towels in the rest room was missing. She asked if anyone knew where it was or if we had one that would fit it. It was a round key. I knew that I had two that Uncle Bernie had given to me and volunteered to bring them in tomorrow. One of the keys fit. I was so happy to have helped. My happiness quickly dissipated when Mrs. Smith implied that I stole it in the first place. I tried to explain that it was from my collection and my uncle gave me the keys but she was not convinced. It bothered me to be so wrongfully and arrogantly accused of theft. I lost all interest in collecting keys.

Dad started coming home less. Mom said that he stayed with his friend in South Charlestown. She implied their relationship was getting worse. Once, when she had been drinking, she said they "suck each other" when he stayed with his friend. I was not sure what this meant but I could not imagine my father doing anything "sick" like my mother accused him. I did not understand and did not put any further effort into trying to understand it. Eventually, Dad stopped coming home.

There was another time Dad tried to move back home. He started visiting. As we waited in the yard for him on one of his expected visits, he drove into the yard much quicker than usual. The car slid sideways a bit as he rounded the corner into the driveway. He drove quickly past the house with us standing on the lawn and parked the car opposite the barn, facing away from the house. He got out of the car and ran down the driveway towards the Simmons Farm. I never saw my dad run and he ran surprisingly fast. We thought that there must have been an accident and Dad was going to help.

Mom came out of the house. She asked, "What's going on?" We showed her the unusual way Dad parked the car and that he ran down the road towards the Simmons Farm. She said angrily, "What has he done, now?" As we approached the car, we saw cow manure on its side and the cracks in the windshield. Mom said, "Oh my God! I can't look," and covered her face with her hands, crying. I looked at the front of the car. It was caved in significantly. Mom pulled her hands down from her eyes and looked at the front of the car. She cried hysterically, saying, "That son of a bitch!" Cilla and Gary came closer. Mom ordered them away. She walked briskly away, stomping, and saying, "That prick hit a cow." She walked back into the house repeating, "That son of a bitch, that prick." I realized then that Mom had been drinking. I did not notice earlier because we were outside, waiting for Dad. When she is sober, she is emotionally strong. When she drinks, she becomes irrationally sensitive to animals' needs and less aware of our needs. She went back into the house, crying. We could hear her crying and screaming the same things about Dad through the open windows.

I looked closer at the car and the amount of damage. I was puzzled about the cow manure on the front, side, and windshield. I wondered if the cow was broken open. I realized that the hard impact to the cow must have forced the manure out of its anus.

Eventually, Dad returned home. He walked slowly and I could tell that he was sad. We stayed outside while Dad was inside with

Mom. I could only hear her yelling at him. After a while, Dad came out and examined the car damage more closely. He spoke extraordinarily little. He decided that it was not road worthy and walked down the driveway and towards town. Mom called us into the house.

Mom said that Dad went to live with his mother. Grandma was living in Florida, now. Mom went to the welfare and applied for assistance. She got $350 per month. Rent was $50 per month. We also got food each month. We called it "surplus food." We went to the town hall where they had it sorted for us to pick up. We got several sacks of flour, rice, oatmeal, cornmeal, powdered milk, and powdered eggs. We also got a big block of cheese, canned meat, and bricks of lard. Sometimes we got bricks of butter. I did not like either the cheese or the meat. The meat tasted slightly better when it was fried. Lots of mustard helped make the meat barely palatable. Sometimes, Mom made macaroni and cheese, which was better than the plain cheese. Mom made bread and cornmeal bread sometimes. I liked both but she did not make them often. Sometimes, I made the corn bread. We ate pancakes and mush. The mush was always watery and did not taste good. Grandma's was firm and sweet. I usually made mush when Mom stayed in bed and there was no cold cereal. I cooked it firmer and it tasted better. We made milk from the powdered milk in the surplus food when the money ran out. We only had a bowl to mix it and kept the bowl in the fridge. We poured milk sparingly on our cereal. Partly because Mom commanded us not to pour too much and use it all up. Mostly, it was because she made us drink any remaining milk from the bowl. I did not like it flavored by the cereal. The worst was when we used the powdered milk, which did not taste good in any form. Oatmeal and mush were better because the milk mixed thoroughly, so there was none left over.

Mom did less housekeeping over time. Dirty clothes and dishes accumulated. Cilla and I often did the cooking. The worst part of cooking was to find and wash the dirty dishes we needed. We washed only the dishes we needed. Gary and Debra could wash their own. Mom made us wash one for her. Rarely did we use a knife to cut our food. We had to struggle with the edge of the fork to cut meat.

We stopped cleaning the house and even removing the trash. It was often left where we used it, often discarded on the floor. Trash collected on the floor to the point where the floor was no longer visible.

Our vegetables mostly came from the farm. They were never first or second grade because Pop could sell these. We got the odd, small, and damaged vegetables. Grandma gave to us her canned and frozen vegetables over the winter. Even with the summer vegetables, Mom over cooked them until they were soggy and tasteless. The boiled potatoes were also soggy. Mom used a lot of butter or margarine in everything she cooked. She liked it but I did not like so much margarine. She bought four pounds of Blue Bonnet margarine every week. Blue Bonnet was the cheapest. That is almost a pound for each of us. Because I tried to avoid margarine as much as possible, there was more for others.

When Mom cooked, she dished out the portions. If we protested about not wanting so much or complained about the taste, she usually hit us on the head with the serving spoon and said, "Eat it. It is good food. People in Africa are starving and would be happy to have what you have." I found it gross to be fed by a spoon that had just wacked my sibling's dirty head. I made the mistake of offering my food to the Africans only once. Besides a second whack on the head, I had to listen for hours about how terrible her childhood was and how much she was giving up being burdened with four children and no father to help.

Tang was a popular drink marketed as the drink preferred by astronauts. The ads showed astronauts drinking from pouches in a space capsule. Mom got Tang for us sometimes. She always mixed it with twice the water recommended in the directions "to make it go farther." It tasted sour and weak. I did not care for it so rarely drank it. She did the same with frozen orange juice. I only drank it when she made us, "It keeps you from catching a cold." Once, Cilla and I mixed the Tang according to directions and liked the taste. We felt so guilty about violating Mom's rules and did not do it again.

For a while, Mom decided that we needed to take Milk of Magnesia every day, "to keep us regular." I did not notice any change in my bowel movements. Since she dispensed these tablets before bedtime, it was often neglected when she was drinking. There were times she administered it twice when she was drinking despite our protests. There was an even shorter period that she demanded that we take Geritol, the liquid vitamin supplement. She did not like its cost. There was not "enough money to go around." When she was drinking, she blamed my father for not providing for his family as a real man should. "He's not a man" was her frequent putdown.

We had no toaster and toasted our bread on top of the kerosene stove that was intended to heat the kitchen in the wintertime though it was inadequate. We monitored the bread until it was sufficiently browned and turned it overusing a butter knife. Because the day-old bread Pop gave us was old and stiff, we often had to press on it so that the entire slice contacted the stove top. The process was slow. In our haste, we pressed hard to flatten the bread, as flat as the Eucharist at church. It tasted better. When we did this for Mom once. She immediately rejected it, telling us to bring her toast done right. We were only mildly disappointed and ate it ourselves.

We used Miracle Whip instead of mayonnaise. Mom said it was cheaper and just as good, even better. We did not have a special margarine dish. We used a small side plate. Since the house was cold, the margarine was hard, so it was necessary to scrape off margarine thin enough to spread it. We carefully avoided the crumbs left behind in the margarine, so the most unappealing margarine collected around the edges. Mom placed another stick of margarine on top of the contaminated margarine, so the margarine plate was never emptied and cleaned. It was gross, so I avoided using margarine as much as possible.

Mom often prepared spaghetti for dinner. We never had any meat with it. Mom liked Ragu spaghetti sauce. It was cheaper and as usual, she said it was better. There were times we had no spaghetti sauce, only margarine on it. We called it white spaghetti. I liked it better than with the spaghetti sauce. We often ate elbow macaroni the same way. If we had hamburger, we had goulash made with the elbow macaroni, spaghetti sauce, and hamburger.

Mom taught us to make dip with cottage cheese, shredded cheese, sour cream, onion soup mix and canned clams when she had them. She loved clams. I hated them. This made a lot of dip which was eaten buy scooping large amounts with potato chips. We always competed to get our fair share and ate it all.

Mom taught us to pop popcorn. She placed the popcorn in a saucepan, covering the bottom. Then she added cooking oil to cover the popcorn kernels. Popcorn popped best when it was evenly heated around the entire kernel. It was necessary to shake the pan back and forth while holding the cover on it. When the popping stopped, she dumped the pan into a large bowl. She made two batches then melted an entire stick of butter and spread it over the popcorn. There was so much butter on the popcorn that much of it was soggy. These were Mom's favorites. I could only eat a little before I could no longer tolerate so much butter.

Once, Mom told me to boil some eggs. After a few minutes, she told me to go peel them. They were not cooked enough. I told her that they were coming apart and sticking to the shells. She was focusing on her soap opera on television and told me to keep at it and do my best. I wasted about half of the uncooked eggs. I presented her with the bowl of partially cooked eggs, saying, "I managed to save this much." She called me stupid for not boiling the eggs some more. I protested that I tried to explain to her and asked her what to do but she did not listen to me. She paid no attention to my words as she continued her verbal assault on my ego while still trying to watch her television.

One day, Uncle Bernie dropped off two dead racoons. Mom showed me how to skin and clean them, then she cooked them in the oven with barbeque sauce on them. When I grew older, she encouraged me to shoot squirrels and we ate those. I did not care much for racoon but squirrels tasted alright. Mom would not eat the dead woodchucks the dog brought home. She said it was because she did not know how long it was dead.

We collected milkweed and dandelions. We boiled these and ate them. The milkweed was OK but the dandelions tasted bitter. As usual, if we complained, Mom spewed a barrage of demeaning language about not appreciating her efforts to raise four children without a father. We were lucky and should be thankful that she was keeping us from going to some awful foster home.

Watching Mom eat was somewhat repulsive. Her plate was always rounded to the fullest with food portions on top of each other. She justified her extra food because she was "big boned."

She heaped her fork with portions of meat, vegetable, and potato as much as possible on one utensil. She opened her mouth wide to fit it in. Her cheeks puffed out as she chewed. She often encouraged us to do the same as we picked about the tasteless food. She was careless about serving us in her haste and foods often got mixed. We wanted our foods to be separate but got no sympathy. She commented, "It all ends up in the same place," adding that it tastes better together. I sometimes responded, "Ya, it ends up in the toilet."

Mom was already grotesquely obese as we watched her shovel these heaping forkfuls from heaping platefuls of food into her mouth. The extreme calorie intake of beer and alcohol-fueled appetite was having a profound impact on her physical abilities. She justified her physique explaining that Cilla's body size was another example of being big boned and Gary was skinny, like Dad. He could not keep his pants up because he had no hips. She also explained much of Gary's poor judgement, clumsiness and behavior as being "like your father." Every time he fell, he landed on his head. He cannot do anything right. Gary would probably have kept his pants up better if we had properly fitting clothes and a belt.

Mom often corrected our posture, warning us that bad posture would permanently misshape our body. Sit up straight, walk straight, pick up your feet, and keep your feet straight were her most common commands. Gary's and my left foot turned in a little. Mom often corrected us to keep it straight. I forced myself but Gary continued. His was a little worse and twisted some with each step. He wore through shoes much quicker that I did.

Mom often corrected us for biting our fingernails. Again, I forced myself to stop biting them. The downside was that we did not have fingernail clippers. When my finger and toenails got too long, I tore them off. Often the tear went too deep, causing pain and sometimes they bled.

It was rare to have dessert. Cilla or I sometimes baked a cake but it did not last long. There was also fierce competition among us about portion sizes of the cake we made. On rare occasions, we had ice cream. Mom had a heaping bowl, so we did, too.

Cilla and I made donuts. We rolled out the dough and cut it with a donut and cookie cutter with a removable center. We carefully transferred the raw dough into a frying pan with hot lard we got from the surplus food. Most were misshaped. We flipped them over with a fork. We cooked the donut holes. It was hard to convince these to turn over, so one side was cooked more than the other. They were always lopsided with an annoying light spot. Like the cake, donuts were eaten quickly with everyone competing to get her or his fair share plus a little more.

We scrambled eggs. We whipped the eggs with a fork and added a little milk. I marveled at how the eggs coagulated on the bottom of the pan and easily formed into soft chunks. We made French toast sometimes. The recipe was the same as scrambled eggs. We coated bread in the egg mixture by dipping the slices in the bowl. Mom made us remove the bread quickly to avoid getting the bread too soggy and making the batter go further. "Go further" was Mom's favorite term that meant feeding us cheaply. The powdered eggs from the surplus food tasted badly, so we used it when there were no other eggs.

We saved the grease the few times when we cooked bacon. Mom liked its flavor and used it when frying eggs and other things. We kept it in a can on the corner of the stove. It looked gross in the can, streaks of brown and white paste. We scooped some out and melted it in the frying pan. Once melted, it seemed fine.

Mom taught us to boil hot dogs. It was easy. When their natural casing split, they we cooked. We never had hot dog rolls. That was for rich people who waisted their money. We wrapped our hot dog in a slice of bread. I put my hot dog diagonally across the bread to better simulate a hot dog roll.

When there was no dessert, I tried to save the best tasting food for last. With my favorite food, fried chicken, I saved the coated skin for last. We made our own bread coating with the flour and cornmeal we got with the surplus food distributed to those receiving welfare and added poultry seasoning. We cooked it in the lard also from the surplus food. We saved the lard for the next time we cooked chicken. Mom kept it in a can on the back of the stove. Once I was sitting next to Mom while eating my fried chicken in the living room. Just as I was getting to finishing the meal and anticipating the delicious finish with the skin that I set to the side of my plate, she grabbed the chicken skin and ate it as quickly as a dog might. I protested and she said, "It did not look like you were going to eat it." I know Mom knew that it was not true. We had told her of our practice of saving the best things as dessert. She did not bother to ask me for it because she knew that I would say that I wanted it. I felt cheated out of my delayed reward to motivate me to eat the tasteless food. I did not want to finish my meal but knew that I would be punished and berated for hours if I did not.

Mom's selfish act of taking my preferred food hurt me in several ways. Depriving me of an earned replacement for dessert hurt the least. Intruding into my space and taking my things as if they were her own hurt most. My feelings and efforts did not matter to her. Mom was grossly obese and gaining weight rapidly. She found some comfort in food but this was at my expense. When she had beer, she consumed even more food. When she said that she went without as a child, I knew that it was not a lack of food as Pop and Grandma grew and raised plenty of vegetables, eggs, and meat.

When I spent summers on the farm, I liked going with Pop when he delivered his vegetables to markets in Claremont, NH and Springfield, VT. He drove at a painfully slow speed. He said that he saw no reason why anyone would want to go more than thirty-five miles per hour. A line of cars always formed behind them. He said that they needed to learn to slow down. I remembered that Pop started with horses. He delivered vegetables house to house in Springfield using his horse. He then used a Ford Model T. It allowed him the reach the Claremont markets.

Pop got what he called day old bread and rejects from Holsum Company, the commercial bakery in Claremont. I went with him sometimes when he picked up two or three cardboard barrels full of old bread returned from the stores and loaves that got crushed during processing. He often found loaves that he retrieved for us to eat because there was nothing wrong with them even though some loaves were crushed and deformed. Pop fed the other bread to his pigs. Grandma would never use this bread. She baked her own. Grandma tended to overbake her bread and cakes, making them dry.

Pop also picked up discarded produce from the grocery stores that bought his vegetables. Pop fed this old, discarded produce to his pigs. Pop often recovered bananas and other fruit like he did with the bread. The fruit was overripe or bruised. If it was only a little brown, we were expected to eat it. If it had rotten parts, we could cut out the bad parts and ate what was still good. He picked up discarded crates and banana boxes to package his corn, tomatoes, squash, and cucumbers for market.

Pop pulled some tall pig weeds and brought them to his pigs. They loved them and ate them right up. We now realized why Grandma called them pig weeds. Sometimes, Pop had me cut old corn stalks with a sickle and feed them to the pigs. They liked the corn with less enthusiasm than the pig weeds. We were discouraged from getting in the pigpen. Pigs bite. They do not bite straight at you like a dog. They bite with the side of their mouth, where their strong grinding teeth are. Pigs are very capable of eating meat. Farmers know not to keep chickens beside them. If they can catch one, they will eat it. They often ate any rats that entered their pen.

Pop could not kill the pigs. When they were big and fat to his liking, he sent them to a butcher who returned the cleaned carcass cut in half lengthwise. It was weird to see the pigs cut perfectly in half. They also got the heart, liver, and kidneys. Pop and Grandma did the remainder of the cutting. The house smelled like urine when Grandma cooked the kidneys. I remember Grandma making head cheese. I was surprised that there was no cheese. It was the facial muscles and fat. It was most often eaten on toast. My grandparents also did not trim the fat off the meat. The fat was eaten with the meal. I remember Grandma talking about how the fat helped provide enough calories to stay warm during the winter months. The only fat I liked was on the porkchops.

Mom was more aggressive at recovering discarded food than Pop was. If the bread started to mold, we could just scrape off the moldy part and eat it. If an apple was mostly rotten, it still had a part that was good to eat. We were expected to eat the fat on meat. It was good food. Mom seemed to enjoy the chunks of fat and gobs of butter on her food but I did not.

Mom also scrounged food from grocery stores, looking for a deal. She begged sympathy for being a divorced mother burdened with four kids. We ate tongue and heart because it was cheaper. I did not mind the dense, leathery texture of low-quality meat. She managed to get storekeepers to give to her the ends of the bologna. We carefully tried cutting off pieces to put in a sandwich. I liked the bologna better when we fried it. Mom sometimes got a special deal on a ham. I complained that it tasted funny, but Mom was unsympathetic and demanded that I eat it. She lectured about kids in Africa would be happy to have what she got for us and that I should be ashamed for complaining. When I got sick a few hours later, she said that I was already coming down with the flu. My preadolescent cognition was so distorted by her that I felt that ham was a good indicator to warn of impending flu. It never occurred to me that I was suffering from food poisoning. Finding worms in our stool was not unusual. Mother expressed disgust but reluctantly brought us to the doctor. A small purple pill solved the problem. I asked Mom once about why the nurse told us to drink plenty of water when we were sick. I got the answer that I expected when Mom snapped, "To flush out the germs." I did not know then that people often got dehydrated when they were sick, which was the reason for this advice.

Mom also liked making Shepard's pie. She made it by combining hamburger on the bottom of her cast iron frying pan, a layer of corn and topped with mashed potato. It fit perfectly with the way she liked eating food, all combined and heaped on her fork. I hated it but, of course, was forced to eat it. Mom refused to separate out anything or ever doing something special for someone. "You're going to eat it and be thankful you have food." It was not possible to skip a meal. A beating and verbal condemnation was assured if we tried. Like the ham that made me sick, the hamburger often tasted odd. I did not get sick from it, though I felt odd after forcing it down.

With no central heat, we endured the winter with a woodstove in the living room and the little heat from the kerosene kitchen stove. Our beds were tightly arranged for everyone to fit in the living room. Mom taught me how to make a fire in the woodstove and it became my job to keep the fire going. I was expected to get up early and start the fire to add some warmth before everyone else got up. Mom expected me to build a hot fire. She was only satisfied when she saw the red glow in the sides of the woodstove and the stove pipe.

In these close quarters, one fart made it unpleasant for everyone. Farting was not allowed. Mom pressed, "Who did it?" Her tone was such that the guilty person was compelled to confess. Our penance was to go sit on the toilet until we had a bowel movement. She checked for the evidence of compliance before we could leave the toilet. I spent some extended times on the toilet. Soon, I learned to lie. My little sister, Debra, was the chief investigator. She went around smelling butts to identify the source. Mom never discouraged this practice. I so much wanted to let one loose just as she pressed her nose into my butt but was never able to coordinate it. Mom was not constrained by her own rules and sometimes let loose great rumbling farts, especially when she was drinking beer.

I wanted to know what a fart looked like. I imagined it to be a brown bubble. I tried watching in the mirror but the mirror was too high for me to see. I enlisted my little brother into an experiment. I would fart and he would watch to see what it looked like. He would then do the same for me. He agreed. I dropped my pants, bent over, and spread my butt cheeks. Gary fell over laughing hysterically immediately after I farted. He ignored my demands that he made good his agreement. He continued rolling around and laughing. When I insisted, he refused. I demanded,

"What did it look like?" He said, "Nothing." I did not accept this refusal to report and demanded again, "What did it look like?" He elaborated, "Nothing. Your butt just opened and closed and there was nothing there." I felt that he was avoiding my question and that I would not get any satisfaction from him. It was years later, while I was walking behind some cows that I saw a cow fart and defecate. I then understood what Gary had accurately described.

Mom said that she had the power of a mother and could tell when we were lying by looking into our eyes. I was often wrongfully blamed. I decided to test her superpowers once when I was guilty. She told me to come to her once when I blamed my brother, Gary, for taking a piece of cake without permission. She told me to stand in front of her and look at her eyes. She stared into my eyes, making me uncomfortable, then told me, "OK, you're telling the truth." I scored a major victory over her super mom powers. My sense of individuality benefitted at my brother's expense. He had to suffer Mom's berating while I got away with the misdeed. It felt like pay back for all the times I was punished for things he did.

Mom also treated us as an extension of herself in other ways. She often pulled a tissue from her pocket to wipe our faces. The tissue Mom carried was a few sheets of toilet paper she rolled and kept in her house coat, a large shirt with two waist level front pockets. It was the same tissue she used to blow her nose and clear her throat. Mom did a deep, disgusting, guttural clearing of her throat. Just hearing her do it made me feel nauseous. When we protested, she insisted that she was using the part that was not used. This was not true as sometimes I felt gooey moisture. I avoided her wiping my face at all costs, which was exceedingly difficult. The location of the tissues in pockets so close to her hands, her attacks on my dignity were stealthy, rapid, and powerful.

Mom closely monitored our use of toilet paper. She told us three sheets were enough to wipe ourselves. If we ran out, we would have to use a rag and wash it out after we used it. It is a difficult thing to do when there was no water during the winter when the spring froze. We hated doing it and often did not wipe.

We were not allowed to use toilet paper for our runny noses. We had handkerchiefs, like my grandfather. Unlike my grandfather's, Mom did not wash ours frequently. The snot collected and dried in our handkerchiefs. It scratched my face each time I tried to use it. It became so encrusted that it would not soak up any more snot. We were not allowed to pick our nose. Mom snapped, "Use a handkerchief" if she saw us picking our nose. Once, while sitting barefoot beside her, I noticed Mom make a quick pick into her nose. The worse part was that she discretely flicked it and it landed on my bare foot. It was gross. I felt betrayed by her hypocrisy but also belittled in that she did not care that her booger landed on me.

Mom used a lot of Vicks. Especially when she was drinking, she loaded her nose with it to the point that it dangled out. She also used it for her chapped lips. She pressed this practice upon us. Like her wet tissues, I hated the Vicks bottle contaminated by her snotty fingers. She spread lots of baby oil on her lower legs and feet. The more she drank, the more grotesque these things appeared. The more she drank, the more she had to go to the bathroom. She felt no obligation to respect our privacy if we were in the bathroom when she wanted it. She barged in and used the toilet in front of us. During intense intoxication, she became even less modest, sometimes leaving the bathroom still pulling down her dress over her naked butt.

Mom had a curious habit of puckering her lips towards one side of her mouth. She often pressed these lips sideways with her index and middle fingers. She did it watching TV, driving the car, or doing crossword puzzles. She did it whether drunk or sober but more when she was drinking. I once asked her when she was sober why she does it. She simply said, "It feels good." I tried it and found no pleasure, only strain.

Mom often sought sympathy for being burdened with four children and no one to help her. Her body suffered bearing four kids. She spoke of economic hardships and the amount of work it was to raise four kids. She complained mostly when she was drinking beer. Her self-pity increased with her intoxication. I could not understand what harm bearing children did to a female body but accepted it must be significant. However, it appeared to me that her extreme obesity was obviously harmful. I could not understand how it was so hard for her to raise us when we did most of the work.

She looked for ways to save money. One summer, she bought flip flops for us. They cost twenty-nine cents for a pair. She boasted how she got summer shoes for all of us for just over a dollar. I did not like them. They were unstable and flew off if I ran. The straps pulled free from the sole on rough terrain or when I pushed or pulled things. Very soon, I had blisters between my toes caused by the strap. When I complained, Mom told me that I would get used to it and to stop complaining. The blisters got worse and started to bleed, making it exceedingly difficult to move. Mom's angry response was, "Then go barefoot!" She added that she always went barefoot on the farm when she was a child. She liked going barefoot most of the time. She had large, ugly callouses on her feet. She could walk across the sharp stones and feel no pain. She insisted we could do the same if we toughened our feet. I began to develop a greater hatred towards her beer drinking as I realized that she drank away the money that could buy shoes for us. I wore my sneakers with their soles nearly falling off with each step. They were called laughing shoes because the front part of the sole dropped open wide like the mouth of someone laughing loudly. I dealt with scooping things into my shoes as I walked. I scooped a lot of dirt when I worked on the farm.

Mom rarely did anything fun with us. Sometimes, she brought us to the Little Sugar River in North Charlestown. It was a brook but was steady and wide. It was also very cold. Mom waited in the car, doing crossword puzzles while we climbed down the long steep bank to the brook. It was so cold that our legs were soon numb. It was so cold that my testicles hurt. We were ready to go home.

Sometimes, we got a picture puzzle to work on. Though we could do it together, it soon got to be competitive. My siblings would pull pieces closer to them and cover them. Some had missing pieces. The fun dissipated quickly.

Mom liked the James Bond movies and especially Sean Connery. We went to all of them in the Magnet Theater in Claremont. Mom lied about our ages so that we got in at the cheaper rate. Like most kids, I was proud of my age and did not like representing myself as anything less than my actual age. I was very resentful when people asked if Gary and I were twins. Another of Mom's annoying practices was always leaving shows early. We never saw the end so that she could get ahead of the crowd. If we complained, she said, "You can figure it out." We always left events early, including the races, fireworks, and even church when we went.

Mom began talking about finding another man to take care of the family. She went several times to a farmer's house on the River Road in Claremont. She made us wait in the car while she went in the house to visit. Mom said he was rich. He eventually sold his farm and Tambrands built a factory on it. We did not see the farmer after that sale. She started looking for another. She used her big boobs as bait to attract them. There were no takers.

Our cars were always old, used, and unreliable. A good day was when the car started. Freezing temperatures contributed to the challenge. If the temperature was below ten degrees, there was little point in trying to start it. If we needed to go somewhere, Mom sent me out to start the car. I pumped the gas twice as she said, then turned the key. I let the starter turn for a few seconds. I could try it three times, then had to give up. We had no telephone. If the car did not start, we were isolated. Mom did no maintenance on the car. She always bought gas two dollars at a time, about eight gallons.

Sometimes we brought our dog with us. Chino liked to hang her head out the window. Animals had privileges over us and we had to let her either stand on us or move out of her way. As we drove across Dean Flats in North Charlestown at fifty miles per hour one day, Chino jumped out the window. We all panicked. Mom said her usual, "Oh my God!" She did not want to turn around at first, expecting the worst but did. Chino was just standing in the middle of the road looking at us. She jumped back in the car and we continued our journey to Claremont.

Pop had helped us buy the car for fifty dollars. It was an old Plymouth that he said was a good deal. We always worried about whether our car would pass inspection. Sometimes it needed a tire. Sometimes brakes. Mom went to Pop who would often help pay for these repairs. Mom never maintained the car beyond adding oil occasionally when it was low. Eventually it broke down in West Claremont on our way to the farm. It was near a garage. The mechanic said that it was the oil pump. He said that when an oil pump goes, other parts of the engine go later. It was likely just a clogged oil filter. They replaced the engine, for which Pop paid.

We did not have a kitchen table. I decided to build one from the building materials that I found in the barn. I used tongue and grove boards for the top, but all I had was a hardwood plank for the legs. It took a lot of effort to cut these with a hand saw. I finally got it done and Mom helped me move it into the kitchen. It was a little too tall to sit at comfortably. I did not have the energy to cut the legs again, so it remained in the corner and collected stuff. We continued eating on trays in the living room where we could watch TV.

The laundry collected in the bathtub. I hated taking a bath. I had to take everyone's dirty clothes out. The worst part was putting the dirty clothes back in the tub after I was clean. Another thing I hated was that Mom always barged in when I took a bath. It was gross when she used the toilet next to me as I tried to cover myself with the washcloth. I asked her to wait for me to finish but she replied, "I'm your mother. You don't have anything I haven't already seen." We took fewer baths. After a while, we did not have toothpaste, so we stopped brushing our teeth. I felt the roughness on my teeth and did not want my teeth to look like Pop's. I used my fingernail to scrape my teeth. I had to do it without my mother noticing, otherwise she accused me of biting my fingernails. Oddly, I was the only one who did not bite my fingernails.

Cilla and I became increasingly more aware of Mom's beer drinking and how it affected us. She drank sixteen-ounce bottles of Black Label beer. We could see her mood change as she drank. We became exceptionally good at gauging her mood by how much she drank. When she was on her first six pack, she was happy, pleasant, and generous. As she progressed into her second six pack, she became demanding, telling us to do things around the house as she sat in front of the TV. One task was to get her another beer. For a reward, one could drink the first swallow. I did not like it. I also did not want to contribute to her getting any drunker, so I let my siblings bring the beer to her. When she reached her third six pack, she was outright mean. She sought an opportunity to fight with us. These were the times to stay clear. Even going outside and away from the house did not work. She called us in to fight. Of course, these fights were irrational, loud, and potentially violent. Most often she accused us of lying to her, invoking her supermom powers.

In these three six pack ranges, she became terribly angry, complaining about how useless and horrible Dad was for leaving her with four kids. Her favorite description was that he was not a man because a man did not leave his family. She was the victim with four kids, which made us feel badly for just being alive. Mom became intolerable as she drank more, so we tried to go to the yard or barn, but this required her permission. She would not give it when she wanted an audience for her self-pity rants. We felt trapped. Even when we were able to get permission to go outside, she often called us back in. She complained about something we did or did not do, often hitting us and pulling our hair then making us kneel in the corner.

We became very observant in determining Mom's degree of intoxication. If we were around when she started, we could see the progression with each six pack. If we arrived in the middle of her descension into intoxication, we could determine how much she had drunk with several clues. Her body posture was a primary clue. As she got drunk, she spent more time in her chair while staring at the TV. The beer bottle was beside her on a tray. She often looked down at her feet, admiring how straight her toes were because she did not wear shoes. She made many minor adjustments to her clothes by picking at her dress. It looked like she was picking of hairs or crumbs as she made these minor adjustments. As she progressed, she had trouble holding her head upright and she held her chin closer to her chest. When she was terribly drunk, on her third six pack, she rested her chin on her chest. This was the time to avoid all contact with her as this was her meanest phase.

We learned that she would drink until the beer was gone, then get more, one six pack at a time. She went to different stores so the storekeepers would not know how much she drank. As she got drunker, the worse she drove and the worse she parked the car. She called the welfare check "my check" that she felt she earned by having four kids and being divorced. We learned to expect that she would be drunk by the time we got home from school when her check came. I sought indications into her depth of intoxication as early as possible to avoid becoming entrapped in her hostility. If she were very intoxicated, I could tell by how the car was parked. I would look out the bus window to see if the car were parked too close to the house or at an unusual angle. If I saw any of these, I sought reasons to avoid going into the house. If the car seemed OK, I cautiously entered the house. If we were lucky, the check came late and she had only one six pack and would she be in a good mood. If our luck continued, she would be in a mood to "splurge." These times she celebrated with us by getting a package of Necco wafers. If we were lucky, we could have a root beer, too. We took the fullest advantage of these times since we knew the positive mood would soon wane and we would be pulled into her very dark world of extreme intoxication.

We tried to distance ourselves from Mom's drunken wrath in the yard and barn, but she would yell for one or more of us. She subjected us to unfounded punishment, accusing us of lying or fighting when it was typical rivalry. If we stayed out of voice range, she sent Debra or Gary to get us. Most often it was Debra, who was closest to Mom.

Sometimes, Mom decided we needed to do household chores. Cilla and I often did the laundry. We did five or six loads at a time, dividing the loads of dirty clothes around on the kitchen floor. Because the water supply was limited to what the spring could provide, we did not change the water in the wringer washer nor the rinse tub. We put some Tide powder and a capsule of bluing. Mom said that bluing made the white whiter. I did not understand how a blue substance made things white but I knew better than to question Mom. We washed whites and towels first and colored clothes last. We passed each load from the washer, through the ringer and into the tub of rinse water. After agitating the clothes in the rinse water with our hands, we passed them through the ringer again and into a basket. We hung the clothes on the line in the back yard. We often ran out of space and clothes pins, so we doubled up the clothes. Sometimes they fell on the ground. We shook them off and rehung them. When we finished, we emptied the wash water into a bucket and dumped it in the backyard.

When Mom was drunk, she went to bed early, usually by six thirty. For a while, she sent us to bed early, too. We simply got back up when she was asleep. She finally stopped sending us to bed. When Mom went to bed early, it was a relief for us. We could play without her intervening, irrational demands. Mom snored loudly. She always slept on her side. She said it was because of the bursitis in her shoulders. She said that she could not drink milk because it made her bursitis worse, justifying drinking beer with her meals. We knew she slept on her side so her exceptionally large belly could rest on the mattress. She also always had to have her feet sticking out from under the blankets, have a window open, and the only fan blowing directly on her. The house had to be cold for her. I hated being cold while she was so well insulated with fat. She especially hated the summer humidity, which did not bother me.

Mom conditioned us implicitly and explicitly. She told us directly not to tell Pop and Grandma about her beer drinking. Mom said that it would only upset them unnecessarily. She denied any effects of the alcohol, saying that it had no effect on her. Her consistent denials of any problems associated with her drinking had a cumulative effect on us. We, too, denied any problem to anyone outside the family, though Cilla and I deeply resented our family isolation. Nonetheless, we dutifully protected our alcoholic mother from any outside interference.

Mom could not or would not see and denied the influence alcohol had on her. She often referred to others as being "just a damn drunk." Other times, when the person was acting foolish, she described them as being "drunker than a skunk," "higher than a kite," "feeling no pain," or "three sheets to the wind." She was proud of her reputation of being able to drink any man "under the table." She explained under the table meant that a drunk person would pass out and slide under the table. I was realizing her ability to consume large amounts of alcohol was due to her experience and large size. It took more alcohol for a large person to get drunk. Mom denied ever being drunk, but we knew.

Doing schoolwork at home was impossible. If I tried doing it, I was vulnerable to being found by Mom who would demand that I perform some task for her or I would become her audience to blame me for Dad's leaving. I learned to struggle at school to get my homework done there or on the bus.

Dad surprised us when he came home one day. We were glad to see him, but Mom was less receptive. Within minutes, she was arguing with him for abandoning us. We resorted to our former coping method by going outside or in the barn. One of us would periodically go near the house to monitor the fighting and to help decide when it was safe to go in the house.

Things seemed to be settling into old ways again. Mom and Dad fought still but we were better able to go outside to avoid it. Grandma taught me how to knit yarn using an empty wooden thread spool and four small nails. It made a neat looking ropelike chain. I then braided it like Grandma did to make rugs. I was less ambitious and was making a seat cover. I proudly showed Dad. I felt proud at his interest in what I was doing. He pulled on my braid, stretching it. He commented, "It's strong, too." Unfortunately, he stretched it out of proportion with the remainder of my project. I could not get it to go back to its original form. I abandoned the whole idea with so much work wasted. Yet another time I gave up on a desired activity.

One day, Dad came home and told us that he was going to buy us shoes. We were happy as our sneakers were falling apart. He drove us to Harry's Shoe Barn in the center of Claremont. We got tan colored boots that were much better than our holey sneakers. When we got home, Mom met us at the door. She was furious at Dad. "Where have you been?" she yelled. Dad walked past her and sat in the living room in front of the TV. I did not understand why she was so aggressive as we told her that we got new boots. She ignored us and stomped after him, looking down at him in the chair yelling, "You don't take my kids without telling me." I watched from around the corner in the kitchen.

I did not understand why she was so angry. It was obvious that Dad brought us to get shoes. It was a happy occasion for us, but it now turned into frightful situation. As Dad tried to ignore Mom by watching TV, she got more aggressive. She stepped in front of him. He leaned his head to the side to look at the TV around her. She grabbed him by his shirt, saying "Answer me! Where were you!" She picked him up out of the chair by the front of his shirt and started shaking him. Dad raised his right hand clenched in a fist, then lowered it. I was distracted by Cilla who started screaming and ran out the door. She ran down the driveway, across the road and towards the Simonds Farm. Mom said to me, "Go get her and bring her back." I ran out after her. I called to Cilla several times. She slowed to walking, then stopped, crying beside the road. We walked back. Mom promised that they would stop fighting. The fight continued at a lower level until Dad left.

Mom and Dad's relationship deteriorated. Dad was again gone for days at a time. I came home from school one day to find Dad sitting at the table that I built. He had his head down and was crying. It was the first time that I had seen any man cry. On the table in front of him was his twenty-two-caliber revolver. The one he used to shoot at bats in Springfield. When we walked in the door, Mom said, "Come on kids, we're going for a ride." In the car, Mom explained that Dad was threatening to kill himself. We were of course very scared and concerned, but she said, "Either he will do it or he won't. We'll find out when we get back."

When we returned, Dad was standing in the kitchen. The gun was not around. He seemed OK. A few days later, Dad was gone. Mom said that he was in the mental hospital. He was committed for trying to commit suicide. She expected him to be there for six weeks or longer. When he got out, he returned to living with his mother in Florida. After a few months, when she was drunk, Mom dictated letters for us to write to him. Sometimes Cilla wrote the letter. Sometimes it was me. The last letter she had me write was threatening. She directed me to write that I did not want him to be my dad and would hurt him if he tried to return. I hated writing it but had no choice. She proofread it and mailed it.

We got another dog, Butch. I liked him because he was more fun to play with than Chino. It did not take long before Butch ran off and was gone for days at a time. Sometimes, he came home with a dead woodchuck. Mom made me bring it to the woods and leave it. I had to be sneaky, otherwise Butch would drag it back.

We went on hikes behind the farm. It was the same area that the farmer used to pasture his cows. The cows never let us get close to them, moving away as we approached. The upper pasture was the best place. We had a view of my grandparents' farm across the river. It was a rugged climb, up the hill, through shrubs and over large rocks. Cilla and Gary grew less interested in these hikes, so I began doing them alone. It was a peaceful time for me. Many times, I did not go far, just exploring the woods nearby. I saw rabbits and squirrels a lot. Mom encouraged me to shoot squirrels with the twenty-two-caliber rifle Uncle Bernie gave to me. She had showed me how the gut and skin them. She cooked them with barbeque sauce. She praised me for my hunting skills that provided the family with some good meat.

We liked to play in the old barn across the road. It was smaller, had more small stalls and a loft. What made it most fun was the large pile of loose hay in the middle of the floor. We liked jumping in it from the loft. Gary and I played there most. Cilla joined us sometimes. It was unusual for Debra to come with us because she was only six years old and could not keep up with us much of the time. Perhaps it was the tensions in the home was the reason all four of us were playing in this barn on this day. It was further away and less likely for Mom to call us in.

We were having fun together. There were several ways to climb into the loft, each with different challenges. There were rungs beside one of the stalls that was the most direct route. We could use a stall door to stand on, then climb onto the loft. There was also an old horse drawn hay rake that was more challenging but was how I got to the loft when my siblings were too slow.

We took turns jumping into the pile of hay. We made several jumps when Debra started screaming after one of hers. She laid on top of the pile with her right knee bent but her left leg held straight. Her arms flailed as she screamed obviously in pain but she would not say what was wrong. She just kept screaming and flailing. Cilla was first to notice. Debra had jumped onto a pitchfork that was buried deep in the pile of hay. I went to assist Cilla with Debra. What I saw seemed unbelievable. One tine of the three-tined hay fork went completely through her shoe, the sharp point protruding from the center of her left foot. No wonder she could not move with that hay fork stuck in her foot. I knew about hay forks because my grandfather taught me how to use it to gather and carry loose hay. I was surprised how this could have happened. We had been jumping on that pile of hay for days and many times just today. Why hadn't we found it sooner, before anyone got hurt?

I held Debra's leg while Cilla pulled the hay fork out. Debra's screaming lessened but continued for several more minutes as Cilla and I tried to figure out how we were going to get her home. Debra finally stopped screaming and cried normally. She stood up with Cilla's help. She was able to hobble around. Cilla walked her home. Gary and I followed behind.

Cilla brought Debra in to see Mom. Gary and I watched from the porch. Mom took off Debra's shoe and looked at it. She decided to soak Debra's foot in a solution of Epsom salts. This was common practice for when we stepped on nails. Debra bravely complied as the solution made it hurt even more.

The next morning, Debra's foot was swollen and red. Mom decided to bring her to the doctor. We stayed home with firm instructions to stay inside. Debra returned with a nice bandage and a prescription for an antibiotic. She was incredibly lucky that it went between her bones. I thought lucky would have been not to land on the pitchfork in the first place.

A few weeks later, state highway engineers stopped by to talk with Mom. They were planning to rebuild our road, which was Route 12, the major north-south route on the west side of New Hampshire along the Connecticut River. A man toured our home with a tape recorder. He was noting existing cracks in the walls. As construction progressed, we were told to remain in the house sometimes. I heard three shrieking blasts of a horn, a short silence, then the loud thud sound of blasting. Small rocks fell around our house.

After the blasting, large construction vehicles arrived. They seemed surreal to us. The construction workers called them Ukes, which I learned were Euclid trucks. I was most impressed with the huge Caterpillar scraper. Workers started by tearing down the old barn across the street, where Debra got hurt. The farmland across from our house suddenly turned into a huge pit. They removed large amounts of dirt and built up the area for the new road. It was almost frightening when one of those large scrapers came up our driveway. It was taller and bigger than our house.

Our house shook as it lowered the level of our driveway to meet the new road elevation. I was afraid that our house would fall from the shaking. It shook more with the huge earth mover than with the blasting.

The construction went on all summer. Cilla, sometimes Gary, and I went to work on the farm with Pop and Grandma during this time. Gary often got sent from the fields for making too many mistakes. Mostly, he skipped large areas when we weeded. This made Pop angry because he had to go back over everything to get what he missed. He belittled Gary, calling him stupid and useless. Pop rated a person's value by the quality and quantity of one's work. He believed his criticism of Gary would straighten him out. For Pop, sending Gary out of the field was punishment. For Gary, it was what he wanted most, no work. Cilla and I were angry with Gary because it meant more work for us. Pop told Mom that he did not need Gary, making him even happier. Mom blamed me for letting Gary do so badly.

Pop started some vegetables in a tray in the kitchen under the woodstove at the end of winter. When they started to grow, he brought them to his greenhouse. It was a long narrow building with cinderblock walls and windows in wooden frames as the roof. He heated it with a potbelly stove using mostly coal. He used wood to heat his house but coal for the greenhouse. He explained that coal lasted longer, especially through the night.

I enjoyed being with him in the greenhouse. He had immense pride in his vegetables. He showed me how he watered them with water fortified with sheep manure that he bought in large paper bags. The sheep manure was very dry. He carefully mixed it in the water until he had it evenly dissolved. He used a watering can with a long, narrow spout. The long spout passed easily between his plants in rows and under their developing branches. He had troughs formed in the soil between the rows so that he could control the distribution of the water. As the plants grew larger, he transplanted them to give them more space. Planting the tomatoes a little deeper each time caused them to grow more roots from the stem. By the time they were ready for the field, they had a massive root bundle.

As I watched with fascination, Pop talked about many things. He talked about farming with horses and his transition to modern farming with a tractor. He did a lot those two years of modernization. Pop was a skilled farmer but not a builder. He hired someone to build the greenhouse in 1948. The two-car garage next to it was built the next year. Pop passed on to me what he learned from his many years as a market gardener. With his French language heritage, he referred to everything with a gender. Pop explained about a plant, she likes the sheep manure in the water. She did not like too much heat from his heat lamps at the far end of his greenhouse. Weeds had a masculine gender. Pop explained how to kill him effectively and how to create conditions to prevent his return.

Mom was also proud of her French heritage. French was the dominant language in the house when she was young as Grandma was still learning English. Mom had lost much of her French vocabulary and could only understand it. She could not help me learn the language. However, one of her favorite words to get us to hurry was "Vamboose." She said it was French to hurry. As I later studied French and Spanish in high school, I learned that there was no such French word or phrase. It was closest to the Spanish word "Vamos," meaning "we go" or "vamonos," meaning "let's go."

Pop supplemented the greenhouse space with a temporary cold frame. He did not heat it so it could only protect plants from the frost, not sustained cold weather. Pop built the cold frame with short wooden walls and covered it with windows like those on his greenhouse. When all the vegetables were planted in the fields, he disassembled it and stacked the windows. One time, Gary and I walked around the edge of the stack of windows. Gary was being a little unsteady, so I jumped off and told him to do the same. He continued, growing more unstable. He stepped onto the glass and his foot went through several of the stacked windows. We waited for Pop's wrath, which was more of the same ranting and confirmation of our uselessness. I was unable to defend myself, fearing his anger. Even worse, he left it up to Mom to punish us. She accepted my explanation that Gary did it but held me responsible for letting him. After suffering through Pop's wrath directed at both Gary and me, I alone suffered Mom's wrath. Her demeaning dissertation was longer and more demeaning, calling me stupid and predicting that I would never amount to anything, like my father.

Holding me responsible for Gary's behavior became common. I was punished more than he for what he did. Sometimes, I got punished while he was not held responsible for his own behavior. Mom said that I know better and I should make sure he knew better, too. However, if I tried to intervene in his behavior, he did not respond to any verbal redirection or threats. I got additionally punished for my attempt to physically divert him, which was typically punching him on his shoulder. If I got punished for what he did, I would retaliate against Gary, only to be punished for it again when he complained that I hit him. I soon learned how futile it was to do anything and simply tried to conceal all misbehavior, his and mine. Cilla experienced similar expectations and results with Debra. Certainly, this hurt our relationship with our younger siblings while developing a tenuous but better bond between Cilla and me.

Mom's explanations about from where babies came was limited to a man and a woman could not have a baby unless they were married. I was satisfied with this simple explanation for a while, until she told me that Uncle Bernie was going to get married soon. There was not much notice. Mom said something about why they were getting married so quickly. She said it was because "he had to." I thought that marriage was a choice. It did not make sense but Mom gave her usual deflection, "You'll understand when you are older." I had no choice but to accept this. It was just another assault on my emerging intelligence, which I was getting used to. I deserved an explanation. Mom did not want to explain. When Cousin Victor was born six months later, Cilla and I realized that Aunt Joan had to be pregnant before they got married. Mom seemed anxious when we asked her about it. She said that sometimes women can get pregnant when they are not married. She refused to discuss it further.

I spent a few overnights with Uncle Bernie and Aunt Joan. They lived in a small mobile home on Aunt Joan's father's farm. He was a dairy farmer. Uncle Bernie worked some on this farm and in the Gear Shaper Factory. He talked about fishing out the bathroom window instead of working. He preferred hunting and fishing and barely tolerated working on farms. He was better suited for farm work and not the rigid schedule in a factory.

I was pleasantly surprised when Aunt Joan made pancakes for breakfast. The only time I had pancakes before was when Cilla and I made them. Breakfast was prepared for me only by Grandma on the farm. Grandma usually cooked oatmeal or we had Cheerios. Sitting at the table and having breakfast served to me was surreal. The pancakes tasted great!

There was a frog pond on this farm. I liked trying to catch the big bullfrogs and was sometimes successful. Uncle Bernie showed me how to catch one with a fishpole and a small piece of cloth. He dangled the fishhook baited with cloth in front of the bullfrog. Much to my surprise, the frog jumped at the cloth and got caught on the hook. It was so much easier than sneaking up and pouncing on them.

One day, Uncle Bernie was driving me to Pop and Grandma's farm. He turned into the Howard Johnson's Hotel and Restaurant and stopped by the entrance. He handed me forty-five cents and told me to get him a pack of Camels from the cigarette machine in the lobby. I had not paid much notice to cigarette machines until now. When I stood on front of it to see how to operate it, I read the instructions. It required the money to be placed into the slot and pull a handle under the desired brand. I noticed a prominent sign the said you had to be at least fourteen years old. I was only twelve. I went back to the truck and told Uncle Bernie about the sign. He said that it did not mean anything. I told him that I did not want to get in any trouble. He seemed disgusted with me as he took the change, turned off the truck, and went in to buy his cigarettes. He explained to me several times over the two remaining miles to the farm about how many rules do not mean anything. I felt bad, stuck in yet another dilemma. I liked and respected Uncle Bernie. I wanted so much to please him and follow his guidance but I wanted to follow clear and concise rules. He was making things so much more confusing for me.

My Uncle Bernie's sister-in-law, Alva, came to our house one day. Though there was no relationship to me, we called her Aunt Alva like he did. She said that they were planning on camping in Canada for a week. Her son, Arn, was a year younger than me but wanted me, not Gary, to go with them. She said that she wanted a playmate for Arn but had room for only one person. She did not want Arn to have to choose among his friends, causing any animosity among them. Mom agreed. She gave me five dollars to spend.

It was a long ride. I tried playing the games we played on our California trips but Arn did not want to participate. Alva's mother rode in the front passenger seat. It was implied that I should call her Gram. It felt odd. Alva was not my aunt and her mother was not my grandmother. I did not mind calling her Aunt Alva but Gram was a special title I wanted to reserve for my grandmother. I avoided calling them by name as much as possible.

Alva, her mother, and Arn sang songs a lot, which I did not like doing. We eventually arrived at the campsite. She set up one tent for her and her mother. Arn and I had a smaller tent. I enjoyed swimming in the lake. Arn could not swim and I was not allowed to go beyond waist deep, which was less than ten feet from shore. It was not much fun. I tried to have fun with Arn and called him Arnold once. Alva quickly corrected me, "His name is Arn." I did not realize that Arn was not a nickname and wondered why Alva was so stern with me and why Arn did not correct me sooner.

There was not any opportunity to spend the five dollars my mother had given to me. On our way home, Alva stopped by a department store and pressured me to buy a souvenir. I looked hard. I wanted to make good use of the money. There were no real souvenirs of Canada in this ordinary department store. I spent the money on a garden hose that I knew we could use. I was glad to get back home. With all its turmoil, it was where I felt more comfortable.

Farwell School changed to only grades one through five. I started sixth grade at the Holden School, which was on the top floor. Mr. Morris was my teacher. Cilla started junior high school. Debra and Gary continued to attend Farwell School.

On the first day, Mr. Morris made sixth grade seem exciting. He described what we would be learning. He made it sound like we were going to have an exciting year with him. I distinctly remember he promised to teach us how a crow could recognize up to nine objects without counting. He never did cover that topic.

I developed a friendship with Danny as we rode the bus together. He liked the seat above the bus's rear wheels. He sat slumped next to the window with his knees raised and against the seat in front of him. We were the only sixth graders on this bus. The bus driver told us that we had to hurry because she would not wait for us. This worried me considerably because I had no other way home. Mom would not want to come for me and I did not want her to come if she was drinking. We had no phone to call her. I was most concerned about what Mom would do to me.

Danny and I sat near the back of the room. He got into trouble several times for leaning back in his chair. One day, he fell over backwards and split his scalp. He bled a lot, which concerned me. The nurse brought him to her office. He returned the next day with stitches easily visible in a shaved area on the back of his head. I felt relief. It was like the cut I got on my chin when I fell off my tricycle but he bled a lot more.

The fire escape was scary during fire drills. We had to exit through the second-floor metal fire escape. I could see through the metal rungs to the ground, giving me a sense of being higher and less secure. I was glad to get to the ground. We reentered the building through the front door, for which I was grateful.

I was bored most of the time in sixth grade. I already knew the math from Mrs. Smith's teaching the sixth grade at Farwell School. I hated history and English but did okay. I spent a lot of time daydreaming. One of my favorite pastimes was to imagine that my pencil was a zeppelin. The eraser was the device that extracted helium from the air so I could increase elevation of my airship or let out helium to land. I had imaginary machine guns and rockets to attack targets on my desk. The book was the enemy stronghold. My zeppelin made repeated approaches to the target until it was destroyed in my imagination.

We had a substitute teacher one day. Like kids with a babysitter, the students were noncompliant most of the day. The substitute was getting frustrated with the entire class. As usual, I wanted no part of being identified with misbehavior, so I remained quiet. The worse I ever did was to whisper to Danny. She took the opportunity to avenge her frustration when the final bell rang. She told us to remain seated until she dismissed us. She would not dismiss us until everyone was quiet. My anxiety to catch the bus grew intensely. Most of the students did not care because they walked home. Since we were on the top floor and furthest from the bus, we had to hurry after school so that the bus would not leave without us even on a normal day. It would have been disastrous for me to miss the bus. My stress level increased exponentially as I contemplated the consequences. We had no phone, so I could not call my mother. She would have held me responsible and punished me for missing the bus. She could only come for me if she had gas. Was he awake and sober enough to even come get me? I expected Mom to be upset, blame me for causing her distress, subject me to intense and very demeaning criticism, and dole out punishment such as kneeling while the verbal assault continued. I could no longer tolerate the intense anxiety building within me and walked out. The substitute called for me to return. I refused and told her that I was not talking and had to catch the bus before it left. Once on the bus, I told the driver that Danny would be coming when the teacher let him.

The next day, Mr. Morris called me into his office. It was adjacent to the classroom and directly across from the fire escape. He directed me to sit in the chair beside his desk. He lit a cigarette and started his speech about how terrible I was to defy the substitute. He said, "If you don't want to be here, there are plenty of others who do." This statement confused me. I had to be here by law. Why was he making a point of it? He drew upon his cigarette as the office grew smokier. I tried to explain to him that the bus driver had said that she would not wait for me. He grew angry and told me that was no excuse for my behavior. I knew there was no point in trying to advocate for myself and it would likely worsen my situation. He told me that I would be suspended if I did it again and sent me back to class.

Soon after this, Mr. Morris told us that President Kennedy was shot and was not expected to live. It seemed surreal to me. I did not want to believe it but I knew that Mr. Morris would not lie about anything, especially not an assassination attempt. President Kennedy was well liked and I could not understand why anyone would try to kill him. He also had lots of protection. How could this happen? I remembered that there was an attempt to assassinate Fidel Castro that failed. I also remember the Cuban blockade to prevent the Soviets from placing nuclear missiles in our hemisphere. An intense three days followed with this naval blockade. The possibility of a nuclear war became real. Afterall, we practiced for it. I wondered if Kennedy's assassination was connected to the assignation attempt on Castro and the missile crisis. Though I felt a loss and sadness, it had an insignificant impact on my daily life.

Cilla and I became increasingly aware of the connection between Mom's drinking beer and her moods. We grew keenly aware of the indicators even so subtle as to how the car was parked.

We tried to pick up on the clues as early as possible to avoid engaging with her if she had a lot to drink. We could get some indication about how drunk she was by looking through the bus windows as it came to our stop. If the car was parked awkwardly or too close to the house, we knew that she was drunk and likely in a mood for a fight. We hated these times. We regretted going inside but any delay would make it worse. Mom usually began by complaining about how bad Dad was and how he abandoned us. We were lucky to have her. She worked hard for us every day. Only her extraordinary efforts were keeping us from being in an awful foster home. She seemed to be preying on our natural childhood fear of being abandoned. Like any child, I feared any change to the unknown. I was confident that my grandparents would take at least Cilla and me since we were good farm workers. I wondered why Mom, who praised herself relentless for being such a great mother, would even consider giving us to foster care.

She continued with how terrible her childhood was, how she "went without." She said that she did not have the nice things we have. She had to go barefoot on the farm. This complaint about being barefoot also confused me because she preferred to be barefoot most of the time. She only wore tennis shoes when she left home. I have a lasting image of her saying "you kids will never go without like I did" as she raised her bottle of beer and took a long drink. There are many things we lacked because she spent so much of the limited money on her beer.

I could never determine exactly what she went without that we did not experience. We had old, torn clothes and worn-out shoes. The money my grandfather gave at the end of the summer for our work on the farm bought our school clothes. By the end of the school year, my pants were too small with "high water" legs.

My toes wore holes in sides of my sneakers and the soles started falling off, separating first from the toes.

Sometimes, especially when she was drunk, Mom complained about having to work in a nursing home to buy school clothes. It was in the old Higgins House just up from the farm. We drove by it every time we went to the farm. They raised German shepherds there. She said that she had to walk, regardless of the weather. Walking did not seem too unreasonable to me. I walked at least that far in the fields and woods behind our house. As Mom's self-pity continued, she described how she had to bathe a dead body. She had no choice. She was just told to do it. Each time she repeated this story, she cried. When Mom was drunk and crying, her moods were explosive. She could suddenly explode on any or all of us commanding us to do things, then adding more before we could finish. Sometimes it was the laundry. Other times it was cleaning a room. She interrupted our work to bring her another beer and take away the empty bottle. I tried to get away before her moods exploded but I was seldom successful. She would call me back or send Cilla, Gary, or Debra to get me.

Before the school day ended, my thoughts diverted to what could I expect from Mom when I got home. I had not yet made the connection to the date and her welfare check. I did know that if she got drunk the day before, she was likely to be drunk when I got home. The only way she would be sober is if she ran out of money. I did not want to go into the house but had to or she would come get me and slap, pinch, and pull my hair. If I outran her, she would eventually corner me in the house to wreck her vengeance upon me, charging like an angry bull. Mom was extraordinarily obese, so she was very intimidating when she moved quickly towards us. There were endless reasons for her to complain about me or how I let my brother misbehave. She complained that I was too much like my father. I was going to be just like him. She then went on about how terrible he was, describing him as a terrible father and husband. As she got drunker, she started saying that he was not a man and repeatedly called him a prick. "He can go piss up a rope" and "not worth a piss hole in the snow" were two of her common phrases directed at Dad in his absence. After hours of listening to this, I wondered how she ever lived with him. I also imagined me and Gary pissing up a rope and how messy it would get. The more she belittled him, the more I realized that he was my father and I do share many characteristics with him, such as a drooping eyelid, only mine was worse. Sometimes, Mom would begin crying with rapidly changing emotions. If we agreed or tried to validate her feelings about Dad's poor character, she might suddenly flip her emotion. She would admit to loving Dad. "I had four kids with him!" she shouted and start crying. When she was in this mood, I could quietly slip away and let Cilla and Debra deal with her.

Eventually Mom grew tired and went to bed, bringing relief to our day. When she got an early start on drinking, she was usually in bed by six o'clock. Cilla and I began to collaborate on how to deal with Mom when she was drinking. We noticed a rare time when there was beer left in the refrigerator when Mom went to bed. She usually drank it all before going to bed. When she was the most intoxicated, she had three six packs. Sometimes, she got a fourth one. The only time that there was left over beer was when she had bought four six packs. She liked sixteen-ounce Black Label beer. She bought one six pack with each trip to a different store. She always bought a loaf of bread or a half-gallon of milk. Her intention was to make it appear that she needed the bread or milk and was getting a six pack of beer since she was there.

Cilla showed me the leftover beer in the fridge when Mom went to bed early. We decided to make a sign saying, "Please Stop." We placed it on top of the partial six pack. A few minutes later, we decided that this would make Mom too angry. She would be sober when she found it and would likely start crying. Then she would make our lives miserable with degrading rants about the way we did not appreciate how she suffered. Since this would be an unknown experience for us, we could not predict any punishment. We removed the sign and decided to approach her together sometime.

Weeks later, Cilla decided it was the best time to talk to Mom. She had drunk enough to be happy but not enough to be mean. We summoned our every ounce of courage and approached her in the living room. It was the hardest thing we ever did. We tried to explain to her how hard it was for us when she drank beer. We cried intensely as we explained that she got so mean and scared us. She started crying with us and agreed to stop drinking. It was the happiest day of my life. I went outside to continue with my project.

I was working on building sideboards for my wagon when Mom and Cilla came to me. With Cilla by her side, Mom explained, "You know, when I start drinking, I can't stop." Maybe I knew it but never wanted to admit it. I wanted to think that she could stop anytime she wanted, like she said when she described other people who were just old drunks. Mom continued, "I want to buy this one last six pack. I spoke with Cilla and she agreed. This will be my last one." Mom wanted me to agree, too. I did, but I immediately knew that all our pouring of our hearts and tears were for nothing. I felt a sinking feeling in my chest and overwhelming hopelessness. Mom would never stop drinking beer and our lives would never change.

Chino had six puppies. They looked like Butch, with light brown long hair. Some had black spots like Chino. It was interesting watching the puppies as they nursed and struggled to learn how to walk. Cilla played a major role in naming all the puppies. I was not interested in participating. I hardly cared to remember their names. They were more fun to play with as they grew older. Mom let them into the front yard to chase each other around.

One hot summer day, Mom called us to get in the car for a trip to the store. She had already drunk one six pack and was going to get another. She rushed us more than usual as we climbed into the car. She started it up and backed out of the parking spot when we heard one of the puppies yelping. Mom stopped the car, held her hands over her face and said, "Oh my God, no." She told us to go check the puppy as she sat in the car, covering her face, I can't look." Cilla and I got out of the car. Cilla found the yelping puppy and picked it up. We could not find anything wrong with it. We brought it to Mom who felt its body and focused on a front foot that caused a reaction from the puppy when she touched it. The foot seemed okay. Mom concluded that the tire must have just barely pinched it. We got back in the car and she drove to the store, more carefully than usual. We checked the puppy again when we got home. It seemed fine.

The remainder of the evening was relatively quiet. Mom took her position in front of the TV. She demanded that we serve her as usual. On her demand, we brought potato chips or made a sandwich. She demanded that we put plenty of Miracle Whip and spread it all the way to the edges. As usual, she sent one of us to get another beer for her when she wanted one. Never was there any thank you. The only reward was the servant could have the first swallow from a beer served to her. Cilla sometimes took several swallows. I did not like the taste of beer. She called upon us to change the TV channel or adjust the volume. She expected us to get a pan of water and wash her feet. Afterwards, she wanted baby oil applied to her feet and lower legs. I usually tried to avoid Mom when she was drinking so I rarely was the one to serve her.

I enjoyed the solitude in my walks on the mountain behind us. Only a few times did Cilla and Gary join me. It was exciting exploring nature, the different forest sections and the upper pastures that were returning to forestland. I looked for wildlife. Squirrels and chipmunks were easy to find. I was once startled by a large black snake. When I asked him later, Uncle Bernie told me that it was a milk snake. He explained that it would climb up a cow's leg and get milk from it. I learned later that it was a black racer and no snake milks cows. I never went hiking with my uncle but he did a lot of hunting with his friends.

The house did not have a central heating system. It had the kerosene kitchen stove and a woodstove in the living room. There was a small amount of firewood in the attached shed that connected to the barn. It was my job to bring in the firewood, an arm load at a time, like my grandmother did for her wood-fired kitchen range. In time, I got to operating the woodstove more and eventually was the primary person to keep the fire burning. I had to get up in the cold house to make fire and warm the house before others got up. I did not mind this responsibility because I wanted to warm the house. My siblings could not get a good fire going. I only mildly resented being the first one up that got cold.

The upstairs bedrooms were very cold. Gary and I shared a bed. We had shipping blankets that we got from Pop. They were thick and heavy, more designed for cushioning furniture than heat conservation. It was so cold I hated getting out of bed to go to the bathroom. Once, I tried peeing in the bed between Gary and me so Gary would be blamed. He woke up shouting, "Hey!" I pretended to be asleep and he went back to sleep.

Mom spent most of her time in front of the TV in her chair. Like Pop's chair on the farm, we could sit in it but had to get out when she came into the room. The chair was rarely empty. It was uncomfortable with broken springs. It was also dirty with urine. Once in the chair, Mom resumed demands for us to serve her, "get me another drink" or something to eat or change the channel on the TV. We only got two channels. Channel three was out of Burlington, Vermont. Channel eight was from Poland Springs, Maine. We watched only the shows she wanted. The TV always played loudly and we had to wait for a commercial to talk so not to interrupt Mom's shows. I entertained myself much of the time in my daydreams or with my imaginary spaceship destroying enemies and rescuing victims.

Mom planned little for the future, including firewood for the winter. We were always about to run out. She made Cilla, Gary, and I get more wood from the area around the house. I tried cutting it with an old, wooden bucksaw. I was not strong enough to be efficient and tired quickly. There was a two-man saw that we used for bigger pieces. It was rusty and we were not strong, so it got stuck often.

One day, Mom hurried Cilla and I to get some more firewood. We were trying our hardest but the saw was too rusted and kept getting stuck. Mom came charging out as she did when she wanted to beat us. We stepped back and waited for her onslaught but she grabbed one end of the two-man saw to show us how to do it right. She could not push it and told me to grab the other end. The stuck saw jumped out of the cut when she pulled violently and it came down on her left hand. A tooth made a jagged cut on the back of her hand. It peeled a quarter-size chunk of skin back. Mom tried to act like it was nothing, pushed the chunk of skin back into the wound and continued trying to get the saw working. I tried pulling from the other side. She looked at her hand and tried to cover it with her shirt. It was bleeding more and she realized that she had to take care of it. She said, "Now you know how to do it. Get me some wood." She went back into the house.

Cilla took the other end of the saw and we resumed our struggles. Cilla expressed concern. "Did you see the cut on Mom's hand." I replied that I had. Cilla was fighting back tears when she said, "It looks bad. You could see the fat come out from under the skin and she only pushed it back." I saw what Cilla described but did not share her concern. I was focused on getting some firewood.

I preferred to cut the smaller pieces of wood with an axe. I hit hard on one side, then the other. I repeated this until it broke. Mom showed me how to cut wood with strikes from alternating angles, chipping out pieces of wood. It was easier than using a saw but wasted a lot of wood.

During the winter, we all moved into the living room with the woodstove because it could not heat the whole house. Cilla and Debra shared a full-size bed. Mom had a full-size bed to herself. Gary and I had roll away beds along the walls of the room. It made housekeeping exceedingly difficult with everything so crammed together, so we did little. Mom did less around the house as time went on. Trash and dirt accumulated on the floor, table, and counters so deep that it completely covered the floor with several layers. We ate in the living room using TV trays.

I played with a magnet and string. I imagined flying in my spacecraft and finding magnetic things on the floor. I could also get the magnet to stick to the side of the hot woodstove. When it was hot, I used it to burn my siblings who annoyed me. With no room for furniture, we sat or laid upon our beds. My folding bed had a steel link and the end for storing the bed in the closed position. It was a handle that swiveled down when open. I laid prone on my bed and could turn the handle up in front of my bed. With the linkage as a pilot's flight stick, I pretended to be a pilot steering my spacecraft around the planet and through the solar system. I pretended to have rockets for weapons and shot down invaders.

Whether she had money for beer or not, Mom spent her days watching soap operas. We were not allowed to interrupt her television shows. It was apparent that the television was more important than anything we had to say. We could wait for a commercial. We had to stop talking when the show came back on. The time never seemed to come for us to share what we felt was important.

As the evening drew near, Mom put her hair up. She used a drinking glass half full of water and a comb as she sat in her chair in front of the TV. She dipped the comb into the water and collected a section of her hair. She combed it with repeated dips in the water until it was wetted to her satisfaction. She then twisted the section of hair and pinned it tight to her head with a bobby pin. She continued this process until she had all her hair tightly twisted to her head. She felt around her head to confirm that she had included all her hair. She seemed to be compelled to frequently pat around her head to check the status of her curls. When the beer ran out, she went to bed, leaving the drinking glass with the water and comb next to her chair.

We were expected to shovel the snow from the driveway. It was a long driveway and too much for us. Mom's demand was typical. We had to do the shoveling. Of course, Gary was ineffective and Cilla and I did most of it. Debra always seemed to be the one to stay in and help Mom. Mom eventually conceded and said to just shovel paths for the wheels. Shoveling the plowed snow at the end of the driveway and around the mailbox was a daunting task. Most frustrating was when the highway plow filled it back in. Sometimes, Uncle Bernie came to plow us out.

There were times when I had to get firewood or shovel snow after dark. Going into the barns was challenging with no electricity or working flashlight. The barns were cluttered like our house only the hazards in the barns were just greater. I often tripped and fell over the clutter. I became agile at moving into the dark environment, reducing injuries.

We started noticing that water froze in the kitchen sink on cold mornings until the woodstove heated the house. Ice drops formed on the faucet. Eventually, the water stopped flowing. We had no water. Mom complained to the landlord, Gordon Bemis. He came and eventually gave up. He explained that it was spring feed and the line was too close to the surface. It was hopelessly frozen all winter. Mom said that she would not pay rent unless we had water. Mr. Bemis agreed to this. I am sure that he agreed because forgiving rent was much cheaper than providing reliable water. So, we had no water all winter. Mom said that gave her more money for other bills. What it did was provide more money for beer. Unknowingly, Gordon Bemis contributed to my mother's alcoholism, making our lives worse.

There was an old horse trough by the Farwell School. We got two milk cans from the barn and put them in the trunk. We hauled all our water from there. Since it was a lot of work, we used a lot less water, even for the toilet. Without water, our wastes piled up in the toilet. The pile of dung and paper got so high that I had to hold myself above the seat so as not to touch it. Mom grossly scooped it out with her hand and threw in in the back yard.

There was not enough water, so we just did not take baths. Mom told us to put our dirty clothes in the bathtub. We were expected to wear our clothes for several days. When we desperately needed clean clothes, Mom took us to the laundromat. This was not very often. When we ran out of clean clothes, we had to pull out dirty clothes to wear again. It was gross, digging into dirty and often wet clothes that smelled of urine. This developed a habit that persisted even in times when we had water. We did not realize that we were the stinky kids.

Winters were difficult. We had little firewood. Mom asked Pop for firewood when we visited them on Sundays. We got two bushel baskets and placed them in the car trunk. I continued to be responsible to keep the fire going. When I got up in the morning, it was extremely cold in the house. During the coldest times, ice would form on the water we had stored in the kitchen. I became proficient at starting and building the fire quickly, even though it was unappreciated.

Winter had some good times. In the field behind the house was a valley. The far side of the valley was a place we enjoyed sliding. We had one old runner sled we found in the barn. We had saucer sleds given to us our paternal grandfather. We did not like them because we always spun around and went down the hill backwards, then fell over. We tried laying on them but our legs dragged too much. Pop gave me some old skis he had in his barn. There were no laces, only slots through them. I tried tying them on with bailing string but I kept falling. I decided to build a sled using them. Though it was much heavier and harder to pull than the runner sled, it went much better over the snow. We also realized that we could slide on our backs in the snow, though not very well. The snow formed large, curled drifts at the top of this hill. It was like an ocean wave frozen in place. We built tunnels through it. We tried building snow cabins but it caved in on us.

Once, Gary and I slid together down the hill on my sled. We crashed at the bottom and rolled over each other. It was fun as we rolled around. As we came to a stop, I was on top of Gary as he faced down in the snow. I wiggled to push him deeper in the snow. I was hoping that we would settle into the deep snow. As I wiggled on top of him, I felt his butt cheeks squeeze together. I yelled to be funny, "It hurts." I felt him squeeze hard and laughed, "I'm stuck." I was trying to be funny about my tee-tee getting caught between Gary's butt cheeks. Cilla watched our silliness from the top of the hill. She said, "I'm telling Mom." We did not understand what we did wrong. We were rough but no one was hurt.

Gary and I got home several minutes after Cilla. I propped up my sled against the back wall of the woodshed. Mom came out into the entryway as we walked in. She was noticeably angry, which puzzled us. She started yelling at Gary and I about our private parts. We had no idea what she was talking about. She even said that she knew what our father had taught us. This puzzled us even more because Dad never talked about such things. Mom picked up a piece of firewood and walked over to my sled and said, "If you're going to use your thing that way then place it here" and she pointed at the footrest of my sled. She sacred us. I started to comply with her demand to place my thing on the foot piece. I grabbed my zipper then she slammed the piece on wood on the footrest and said, "I'll cut it off," then threw the piece of wood down and stormed back into the house.

Gary and I were stunned. We had no idea what she was talking about or why she was so upset. We looked at each other and I said, "I almost put my thing out there." We laughed but still did not understand what we had done wrong. We did not know how we would avoid making Mom so angry, again. So angry that she would want to chop off our things.

For Christmas, Mom told me to find a tree in the woods. I was up to the assignment. I liked going in the woods. I searched long and hard to find a perfect Christmas tree. The best I could find was a scraggly looking hemlock. I chopped it with the ax and dragged it home. In the open, it looked even scragglier. I apologized to Mom and said that I would look further up the hill. She said that this was fine. We set it up in the living room and decorated it.

We each received ten dollars from each of my paternal grandparents for Christmas. They were divorced and separately sent a forty-dollar check to Mom. We had a twenty-dollar limit to choose presents. We looked at the Sears catalogue to select something for Mom to buy. I saw a gun that shot large plastic bullets for eight dollars. I saw another one that shot smaller bullets and was much more realistic. It cost seventeen dollars. I told Mom that I wanted the realistic looking gun. She said, "OK." I specifically told her that I did not want the big bullet gun and she assured me that she understood. I explained that if she could not find the gun that I wanted, I would be happy with a car model. She assured me that she understood.

As Christmas came nearer, we watched the presents as they appeared under the tree while we were at school. I got excited as I saw two packages the size that would have the gun I wanted. One was for me and one was for Gary. On Christmas morning, I was so excited and selected that big box. We were required to remove wrapping paper carefully so that it could be used again next year. We had to share scissors to cut the wrapping tape adding to the anxiety of waiting for a less than considerate sibling. I was deeply disappointed to find the very gun that I did not want. I looked at

Mom and said I did not want this one. I expected the usual retort of hurting her feelings but I did not care. I was deeply disappointed after so much anticipation. I added that I wanted a model car if she could not find the gun I wanted. She replied, "I could only find this gun. I did not know that you wanted a model car." By the tone of her voice, I knew that I had to accept what I got. Besides, Gary was thrilled. It was a very disappointing Christmas. The gun performed as I expected, shooting only a few feet. I could throw the bullet farther. She spent only eight of the twenty dollars on Gary and me. I expected that the remainder went to beer.

A few days later, I was awakened by voices in the kitchen. It was not unusual for me to listen for sounds before I got out of bed, whether at home or on the farm. This was unusual because I was usually the first one up to build a fire and it woke me up. Mom was crying and her voice was screeching. I could hear Cilla's voice consoling Mom. Mom was saying, "I know your father taught the boys how to do it." I listened from my bed as the crying and screeching continued. It was obvious now that Mom was very drunk. It was five thirty and still dark outside. I wondered how she could be so drunk, so early. As I listened, I heard her say, "I found him with his pants down and his thing straight up." She oscillated between blaming Dad and what she found mixed with the crying and screeching. I knew my brother did not practice as much discretion as I warned him. From the voices, I figured that Gary fell asleep that way. I wanted to warn him that he was going to get Mom's wrath when he woke up. I quietly got out of bed and went to his side and I woke him up. I quieted his protests and told him to listen. He could hear for himself why I wanted to warn him. Gary was covered by the blanket but his pants were still down. I expect Mom only pulled the covers over him. Gary quickly pulled his pants up. When Mom came into the room, I tried to avoid her attention. She ranted at Gary with Cilla at her side and slightly behind her. When she blamed Dad, I injected that it was not Dad. She did not believe me and stayed with her wrongful conclusion.

Mom's reaction validated my concern from when we were much younger in Springfield. I knew that she would be terribly upset if I had told her about this older boy who showed us his large tee-tee and what he did. I would have explained it to her now but she would not hear it. Her mind was set to believe only what she wanted.

A few weeks later, Mom said that Dad might be coming home again. This both puzzled and worried me. I had listened to her say so many terrible things about him. Every time she drank, she descended into her troubles, being left with four kids to take care of, and how it was all Dad's fault. She frequently detailed all his shortcomings and how she was glad to be free of him.

Everyone tried to normalize Dad's return. The odds were very much against Dad. Mom had poisoned our thoughts of him for many months. We were all crowded into the living room and kitchen for the winter. Mom and Dad slept in the downstairs bedroom, which was very cold, the way Mom liked it. We ate in the living room as usual, using trays or just a plate on our lap.

I remained responsible for maintaining the firewood and stove. Dad helped a lot with cutting and splitting it. I used an ax intended for cutting, not so much for splitting, like my grandfather. I had a wedge and sledgehammer for bigger pieces. It was challenging to place the one wedge so that the piece would split. If it did not split, the wedge was stuck. I tried to get it to split using the ax. If this did not work, I had to pry the wedge out and try again. I was most appreciative of Dad's help cutting wood with the bucksaw. He was strong so that it did not get stuck so much for him.

During a particularly heavy snowstorm, Dad decided that he, Gary, and I should start shoveling before it got too deep and hard to move. Dad directed me to the center of the driveway. He warned me to never leave a shovel lying down as it would soon be covered with snow and hard to find. He and Gary started up by the barn, where he parked the car. His working with Gary was fine with me. I accepted that he showed favoritism and glad that he kept Gary away from me.

I created a path and imagined it to be a road. It was much like playing with my toys under barn on the farm, building roads with them. As the snow fell, it recollected in my roadway, so I had to go back over it. I imagined that I was pushing a snowplow on the front of a truck as the snow rolled up in front of it. I could angle the shovel to recreate the highway snowplow effect. Now and then, I looked up to see Dad and Gary shoveling intently from the car and working their way towards me. Gary seemed to be in Dad's way, like he did with me whenever we had to shovel snow. I was glad that Dad was keeping him away from me.

Suddenly, without warning, Gary entered my cleared area. He came from behind me so that I was startled with his sudden appearance. He immediately started knocking down the banks that I had built. I told him to leave. He said, "Dad told me to." I was furious. All the hate Mom spewed about Dad boiled within me. I yelled that I hated him and Gary. I threw down the shovel purposefully making it lay flat and submerged in the deep snow. Dad told me to stand it up. I refused and told him to stand it up himself and stomped into the house.

Mom was in the kitchen. I cried hard and could barely speak as I told her that Dad told Gary to ruin what I had shoveled. Dad came in as I tried to stop my hysterical crying. He tried to explain his good intentions to have Gary help me. He did not realize how much Gary interfered with my efforts. In retrospect, if Dad had sent Gary to another spot, it would not have bothered me. However, when Gary was left alone to work on a project, he was completely ineffective. Mom sent me to the living room and Dad and Gary went back to shoveling snow. I did my part alone a while later.

As spring approached, we could return to our bedrooms upstairs. We slept in double beds. Once sent to bed, we were not allowed to talk. If we did, we would be verbally reprimanded from Mom. Mom expected Dad to do the physical discipline that she used to do in his absence. If we talked after being told to be quiet, we would "get the belt." One night I was awakened with the belt striking the blankets over my butt. Dad left our room, telling us to be quiet, now. I started to protest, "It was not us." Then I realized that my sisters might get the belt, so I remained quiet. It did not hurt through the blankets, anyway.

We were not allowed downstairs after being sent to bed. This was like when we lived in Springfield. Once we were in bed, our parents sat quietly by the television. If we had to use the bathroom, Mom told us to "hold it 'til morning." The window in our room opened onto the porch roof. We would get into a lot of trouble if we climbed onto the roof. We realized that we could pee out this window instead of trying to hold it until morning. In the dark, we could hear our pee as it rolled off the roof and splattered on the ground, like rain. We tried to make it flow slowly so that it did not make enough noise that Mom could hear, since it fell directly outside the living room window.

Mom also expected Dad to be the disciplinarian when we rode in the car, whether he was driving or not. He would reach over the front seat and swat us with his hand. He would only reach our knees and it did not hurt. We did not like the feeling of being punished. Once, Mom warned us to be quiet and we continued to whisper, Dad placed his hand over the seat, leaving it behind his seat and directly in front of us. We felt that it was a signal that he would hit us if we misbehaved. After a short while, Cilla and I started being silly and decided to take a new risk. Since we were not making that much noise to begin with, we felt more courageous than usual. We tickled Dad's hand. Dad wiggled his fingers. We repeated this a few times. It seemed to be a game to communicate that Mom was being unreasonable and he did not really want to punish us. All this interaction with Dad was without Mom realizing what was happening right behind her back. After a while, he brought his hand back into the front. I felt a strange connection with Dad. Something Mom did not know; an unspoken shared feeling that she was often unreasonable.

We came home from school one day when Mom told us that Dad left and would not ever return. He went back to living with his mother in Florida. We were only surprised that we did not see it coming. Mom and Dad argued, but no more than usual. Regardless of how it happened for him to decide to leave, things seemed more normal without him.

When Mom was drunk, she ranted about Dad living with another woman in Windsor, Vermont. She seemed to develop greater hatred of him and belittled the other woman, calling her his whore. One afternoon, she told us to get in the car. She sped towards Windsor, saying Dad was getting out of work soon. She had to drive quickly so that we could meet him at his workplace when he came out. I did not understand why this was suddenly so urgent. She drove recklessly, passing into on-coming traffic and swerving on and off the road. It was a scary ride like the rides when she and Dad were together and fighting.

She parked outside the Cone-Blanchard Shop and pointed to a door, saying Dad would be coming out there. She sent Cilla, Gary, and I to catch his attention. Dad seemed surprised to see us but was truly kind in greeting us. He asked, "Where's your mother?" We pointed towards the car. He walked over to talk with Mom as we got back into the car. He explained that he had a new family with obligations. He promised to find some time to spend with us, but he never did. I did not expect he would. If he ever came, he would have to deal with Mom's wrath. Mom never accepted that she was the one who drove him away. Certainly, we felt that Dad abandoned us to his new life. It was Mom's excuse for our descension into poverty. We could accept poverty. The physical and verbal abuse with its unpredictability was the most difficult. There was no assistance or relief for these feelings. People did not deal with alcoholism or understand the effects on the children. Though we liked having Dad around, we had gotten very used to life without him. The weather was better, so we spent more time outside.

We depended solely on welfare again. Mrs. Rene was our social worker. Mostly we saw her in her office on Broad Street in Claremont. We waited outside while Mom met with her. A few times, Mrs. Rene came to our house. Even at home, we waited outside while she met with Mom.

Mom unexpectedly got a young goat. It was most logical to keep it in the old horse stall in the barn. I happily took on the responsibility for its care. I found some old leather strapping in the barn and made a collar for him. I used a chain and cement blocks to tie him in the yard. When he ate most of the vegetation, I moved him to a new location. There were plenty of places for him. As he got stronger, he dragged the blocks. I found a pipe that I could drive through one of the openings in the blocks to hold him in place. Though he was undoubtedly my pet, Mom and Cilla came up with his name, Herbie, after Herbie the Love Bug character.

Herbie was playful. I often walked him around on the chain. He liked to run fast but changed directions unpredictable, sometimes taking me off my feet. We played a lot with a red wagon. I tried to get Herbie to pull the wagon but he wanted nothing of it. However, he liked riding in the wagon. Mom rarely took pictures with her Brownie camera but decided to take a picture of the goat in the wagon. She told Cilla to take the wagon from me and took her picture with Herbie in the wagon. I was hurt by this because Herbie would only ride the wagon when I pulled it. He was my pet. I alone took care of him. He was my playmate. I wanted a picture of me pulling the goat. Mom only wanted a picture of Cilla.

The nuns from church stopped by one Sunday afternoon and asked for Mom. They saw us in the yard and were concerned about why we stopped going to church and catechism. They were most concerned that we were approaching the age when we need to confirm our religion, one of the seven sacraments. Mom explained that we were on welfare and that we did not have money for gas. The nuns explained that they attend the service in Claremont, then travel to the service in Charlestown. They offered to pick us up as they drove by. Though they invited Mom to join us, she declined. We rode to church with the nuns through the summer, until we completed Confirmation, then stopped. Mom resumed taking us for a short while afterwards. Mom stayed in the car, doing crossword puzzles, or reading the romance novels Cousin Annette La Frank gave to her while we attended services. She said that she did not have clothes good enough for church. Mom only had housecoats that fit her. She had jean shorts that she wore when we went to the store or farm. She wore dirty white tennis shoes, which she hated. She complained that they were too narrow for her broad feet. Mom seemed more concerned about how people judged her.

Zippers, the cat, came home after several days of being gone. The right side of his face was badly swollen. Mom decided that he "had to be put out of his misery." The way we euthanized cats was to tie them in a burlap sack with a rock and throw them into the river. The next Sunday afternoon, Mom told me to catch the cat and prepare him so that we can put him out of his misery on the way to visit Pop and Gram. We all climbed into the car. I carried Zippers in the sack with a rock from beside the barn. Mom stopped beside the road on Lovers Lane, just before the toll bridge. I climbed down the steep bank with the cat. I found a place with good footing on the edge of the water and swung the bag with the cat and the rock as hard as I could to assure it landed in deep water. I spun like a discus hurler. I heard the bag tear as I released it. I hoped that the tear was small and would still hold the cat. The bag splashed about eight feet from shore and sank immediately. I was relieved that it sank with the cat. Suddenly, Zipper's head popped out of the water and he swam to shore. I tried to catch him but he was too fast and got by me. He ran up the bank much too agile for me to catch him. I went back to the car and told Mom. She told me not to worry about it and the cat would die on his own. Three days later, Zippers returned home. His infection had cleared. Mom said the river water must have helped him. So, life returned to normal for the cat that escaped from death row.

We found a new way to break up the boredom of our long summer. There were many spare teat cups in the barn that were once used to milk cows. They caught our interest because they were oddly shaped, strong, flexible rubber. We tried many ways to have fun with them. We threw them at targets, used them as swords to fight each other, and tried to stack them. Nothing seemed to work very well with them but they were too interesting to give up. We often sat on the edge of the bank and watched traffic. We placed one of these teat cups in the road to see if cars would hit it. Mostly, they just steered around it.

Cilla had an idea to stand near the road and pretended to be looking at something in the sky. One of us would watch the people in the car and see if we were able to fool them. Most of the time we did. For some unknown reason, we decided to add the teat cups to our game. One of us would place one in the road and quickly run up the bank. When we distracted the drivers by pretending to be looking at something in the sky, they would often hit the teat cup. No harm was ever done because the cups just bounced about and eventually bounced out of the road.

Cars would only cause the teat cups to roll a short distance. They bounced into the air when trucks hit them, so we preferred to sucker truck drivers into hitting them. Once a tractor trailer truck hit one, causing it to bounce between the cab and trailer and onto the top of the trailer. We rejoiced at seeing the rubber teat cup rolling around on the top of the trailer as it drove away. Though it seemed disappointing to lose one, we had plenty more. As much as we tried, we could never duplicate this event. We eventually got bored with this game or Mom yelled for us to get away from the road.

Mickey was a boy my age that lived in the house to our north. He came by occasionally. He played at some of our activities but grew bored with them. He asked if we had ever smoked a cigarette. He asked if we could get one from our mother. Mom was smoking cigarettes during this time. At his request, we took one of Mom's and met him at the back window in the barn loft. He had matches. Cilla, Gary, and I tried the cigarette. I coughed violently and did not want to try it again. Cilla and Gary listened to Mickey's advice on how to hold your cough. He encouraged them to continue because it would make them become grown up. I left them to finish the cigarette with Mickey.

On one of our hikes through the pasture behind our house, we saw Mickey with another, much older boy. They were on top of the hill where we slide in the winter. They had a wagon much like ours. We climbed up the hill to meet them. Mickey introduced us to Bruce who was much taller than me and very skinny. Mickey got in the wagon and prepared to go down the hill. We tried to convince him not to, but he did anyway. He got going extremely fast, bounced out of control, and crashed about three quarters of the way down the hill. He and the wagon continued tumbling to the bottom. Mickey started screaming, writhing, and rolling around much like the dog George in Southview when it got hit by the car. We ran to Mickey to try to help him. Bruce got to him first. He was leaning over Mickey as we got to him. Bruce looked up at us with one hand near Mickey but not touching him. In his other hand, he raised a folding knife much larger than my grandfather's jackknife. He opened the knife with one hand and pointed it at each of us and said, "If you tell anyone about this, I will kill you." We were shocked and immediately backed away and ran home. Though we worried about Mickey, we trusted that he would get help eventually. Later, we learned that Mickey broke his hip and that he healed fine. We never saw Bruce again. We did not see a lot of Mickey either.

Collateral damage during the later grade school years

There were many times that my parents promised that things would be better after an event, such as moving to a new home.

If that event or time was achieved, life was better at first, then we returned to the steady decline. Each expected improvement ultimately resulted in a worsening of our condition. It was the move to the Bemis Farm that had so much promise for happiness with the greatest set back. Mom felt ties to her farming roots. This move was with the greatest excitement and hope, but it marked the greatest decline for our family. It propelled our descent into deep poverty, neglect, unsanitary conditions, food poisoning, social decline, and the isolation that comes with protecting the family's terrible secret. We were socially isolated. We never had friends to our house nor did we go to theirs. Peer relationships were limited to school. Frequent moves made it difficult for us to develop any meaningful connections to friends our sense of connection to any community. All our relationships at home, school, and community were under strict limitations imposed by our mother. We carefully followed rules to avoid unwanted attention and never talked about anything in our home.

Cilla and I grew increasingly super parentified. Simple parentification involves just taking care of a younger sibling; dressing, feeding, etc. Ours was quite distorted. We not only took care of our younger siblings; we were expected to control their behavior far beyond sibling mentoring. We were punished most severely for our younger siblings' misbehavior while they received little or no punishment, eroding our relationships. As Mom progressed into deep self-pity and intoxication, she was unconcerned about our emotional well-being. The children took care of the parent's physical and emotional needs and most of the household. We were dutiful servants as we tried to meet her demands to show that we appreciated what she does and gave up for us. I very much resented delivering more beer to her. I did not want to feed the monster it created. Since my siblings liked the reward of the "first swig," I let them do it. I did not notice that I was doing highly responsible chores that my peers did not do. Few grade school students were responsible for wood fires, cutting and splitting firewood, doing mounds of laundry, mowing the lawn, caring for younger siblings, caring for an intoxicated parent, and euthanizing pets without supervision.

Mom would not recognize that we were separate individuals and not extensions of herself. It was partly why she refused to do anything different for any of us, no matter how minor. Another part was to keep her life simple and easy as possible. She refused to even hold out my food and mixed it into the Shepard's pie or separated out mine before she added huge gobs of butter that I disliked. She even took food off my plate when she wanted it. She thought nothing of wiping our faces with her snot-filled tissue. The children did almost all the house and yard work, even serving her food, drink and changing the television channel when she was closer. She shared the characteristic of many alcoholics. Her needs came first regardless of how much she said her kids came first.

Like many children of alcoholics, I avoided conflict or anything too difficult. I gave up easily. There was already more conflict than I could endure. I dropped boy scouts, baseball, and even key collecting. Mom did many things that eroded my self-esteem. Her kids were less important than the television show. We were not allowed to interrupt her shows. She discounted our truth for what she wanted to believe. She accused Dad of teaching masturbation. When I told her that it was not him and wanted to tell her who, she refused to allow even my attempt to explain. Hours of kneeling and verbal badgering had an accumulative effect on me. A hatred for my mother was growing inside me. My emotions were conflicted. I loved my mother but hated what she did when she drank. I tried to avoid the monster that came out with alcohol.

I struggled to make sense of my crazy world. Mom called some people "damn drunks." She was not a drunk because she could "handle her liquor." She said that she could drink any man under the table. I did not understand what she meant for a while then I figured out that the man would get so drunk that he would slide under the table. It did not surprise me that Mom could win such a contest. I had at least a rudimentary understanding of the effects of alcohol and the size of the body. Little people got drunker, faster. Mom had a huge body mass to absorb lots of alcohol. She also mentioned that she always ate something when she drank to offset the alcohol's effects.

I tried so hard to make sense of her nonsense. I tried to understand but Mom often refused to answer my questions with her most common put off, "You'll understand when you are older," like knowledge comes magically with a certain age. As a result, we got none of the sex education or social skills other children commonly get from their parents. Cilla and I began to realize that things were not right but were powerless to change anything. We still lacked the courage to approach out maternal grandparents, who we thought were the only ones with the power to help us. We had no friends or unrelated supportive adults. Mom had successfully isolated us in her alcoholic dungeon. No adults intervened, not even the social worker.

It is a normal human quest to understand and control the environment around us. Humans like order and symmetry. Classifying objects increases understanding. Finding similarities and differences within these categories increased my understanding. Learning from an alcoholic frequently disrupts this knowledge building. What made sense once, made no sense later. I was just beginning to learn that my mother's explanations sometimes contradicted other sources. I dutifully accepted her views but I was learning that other sources better supported the order and symmetry I sought. I began to realize the inconsistencies in Pop's expectations in how to do things. I was led to believe that it was my fault that I was unable to make sense of the nonsense. I was learning to reject the nonsense and quietly form my own understanding. I found sanctuary in my daydreams.

Cilla and I suffered traumatic stress. There was physical abuse but the emotional abuse was unrelenting. We suffered Mom's wrath for everything that did not meet her expectations, regardless of whether we had any responsibility or control. We were responsible for our younger siblings care and behavior. We were punished more than they were punished for their infractions, even in when we were in no position to do anything about it. We felt her anger as her volatile moods swinged as she blamed our father. We looked for indicators for predictability in Mom's behavior, hoping to avoid her or attempt to intervene in her tortuous dominance. It was extremely stressful because we had no control, yet all the responsibility. Constantly seeking mitigation, avoidance, and self-defense caused unrelenting stress.

As difficult as it was, it was the home we knew and felt most comfortable. Mom's warnings that she was keeping us out of foster care was effective on my siblings. I was confident that Cilla and I could live with my grandparents. Nonetheless, we preferred to stay home. We were trapped but felt comfortable in tumultuous security.

Many people say that they remember little about their childhood. This is good. It shows that there was nothing remarkable. Their childhood was safe with loving relationships. I remember minute details throughout my childhood. Most were harmful things. Making sense of them was critical for my survival. There were few good times that I remember as well.

Again, these were the times I sought to feel valued and safe. Cilla remembered these times when I discussed them with her. She had suppressed them, which was her way of coping in her adult life. I often felt guilty for having mentioned childhood experiences that upset her.

THE JUNIOR HIGH
SCHOOL YEARS

I started seventh grade. The junior high was in the same building as the Charlestown High School. It was the third time changing schools without moving. I was used to changing schools with all our moves, so it did not bother me to be an outsider again. This time, I was not entirely alone in the move. I maintained a connection with Danny and we developed a few more friends. Older boys started teasing us that soon all the seventh-grade boys will be called to the girls' locker room and told to take our clothes off. I did not believe it at first. How could anyone require such a thing? The rumor continued and grew in validity when a teacher gave me a form for my mother to sign. It was permission for a physical exam. Now, the rumor grew more valid when the teacher explained that the girls' locker room was used because it was bigger. The prospect of taking my clothes off in front of anyone frightened me. Doing it where girls were free to enter made it much worse.

The day came when all the seventh-grade boys were called to the girls' locker room. I kept hoping that the rumor was not true but now realized that it was. I walked through the halls with the others and cautiously entered the girls' locker. It seemed extraordinarily weird to pass through a door marked "Girls." Inside, there was a large room with benches around the outside walls. There was an office space to the left. A large open room with showers was next to it. To the right was a smaller room filled with lockers. It was much like the boys' locker room except that the open room was larger. I now understood that the rumors were true and why they used this room. I still wondered about taking our clothes off and if girls would walk in at any time.

There was a doctor, a nurse, and another woman with a clipboard. The doctor told us to line up alphabetically by last name around the benches and the woman with the clipboard verified our names. The doctor set up in front of the showers with a chair and a small table beside him. He told us to take off our shirts. He did not say anything about removing our pants so I felt relieved that the part about everyone having to strip naked was not true. We cycled through as the medical team checked our vision, hearing, listened to our breathing and heart, took our temperature, pulse, and blood pressure. The doctor also felt our necks and under our jaws.

After completing this part of the exam, the doctor told us to strip down to our underwear. Now, I was getting nervous. The line advanced towards the doctor again. This time, each boy was told to face the doctor and lower his underpants. So, the rumor was true, almost. It seemed that I was not alone in being reluctant to expose my private parts. Several times the doctor told a boy to lower his pants more, raising his voice as if he was annoyed. Since I was near the end of the line, it took a while for me to get to the doctor. I saw the backside of each boy and the doctor was placing his hands in the boy's groin for a few seconds, then telling him to turn his head and cough, then cough again. Sometimes he had the boy repeat the cough a third or fourth time. I did not know what was going on and grew increasingly anxious as the line continued. After the doctor finished what he was doing, the nurse weighed and measured the boy's height. The woman with the chart was making notes as the doctor told her and recording the weight and height. The doctor spent extra time on my friend Richard. He seemed frustrated and told Richard to sit aside for further examination, then continued with the line.

My turn finally came. I felt so nervous and so weak that I could barely stand. I very much dreaded the aspect of exposing myself. It did not matter to me that he was a doctor or that there were two women. I was used to my mother barging in on me when I was naked so the presence of women did not bother. I just hated lowering my pants in front of anyone. Knowing that the doctor would not be patient, I took a deep breath, dropped my pants, making sure that I dropped them to the level so that he required of others so that he would not yell at me. I did not want any delay, wanting it to be done as soon as possible. I stood up straight as he commanded of the others. I took a deep breath and held it.

I did not know what to expect. I knew by his motions with the other boys that he was touching them somehow. I did not expect it when he immediately touched my scrotum and felt for my testicles. He grabbed each one and made it slide back and forth between his fingers a couple of times. I gasped and stood slightly onto my toes in reflex. I feared that it would seriously hurt if he squeezed, but he did not. Still, his fingers on my most intimate and sensitive parts were extremely unsettling to me. He then slid a finger up one side of my scrotum past my penis and under my skin. It surprised me that he could go so deep up and into my groin with his finger. It hurt. I could not resist standing on my

toes as I tried to minimize the pain. He commanded, "Cough."
I was still stunned by these unexpected and those humiliating
touches that I did not respond right away. He repeated, "Cough!"
Somewhat in shock, I responded with a slight cough to which
he told me to cough harder. I felt like an animal being treated
in this way, so vulnerable, helpless, exposed, naked with painful
fingers sticking into me. I coughed with much greater force as I
wanted this to end. Suddenly, I felt the relief when he removed
his finger but it suddenly went up the other side and deep into
my groin again. He said cough to which I responded right away.
I was thinking, "Please let this end." I tried unsuccessfully to let
my mind drift away into one of my daydreams. The pain in my
groin and the humiliation of being so exposed was overwhelming.
He pulled my underwear part way up and told me to see the nurse
doing the weight and height. I adjusted my underwear to cover
myself better and moved to the nurse, my groin still aching. It
was worse than the rumor. We were not just exposed naked; we
were being examined and touched in a way that I could not have
imagined. I hoped that this was almost over.

After the doctor examined all our groins, he had us face him
as we stood around the room in just our underwear. He walked
by, looking from our head to our toes and back again. I was glad
and a bit surprised that we could keep our underwear on, thinking
this might be the time that we would all become naked described
in the rumor. The doctor stopped at my friend Danny and asked
him about his toes. Danny replied that he was born with only four
toes on one foot. I had never noticed. The doctor did not seem
surprised and directed the nurse to note it. He then had us face the
wall and did the same visual examination. The doctor examined
a couple of boys' backs. He dictated what to write in their charts,
describing how their backs curved differently. He told us to get
dressed, except Richard. I was relieved and dressed quickly. I was

ready to get out of there. As we filed out, the doctor told Richard to lie on the bench on his back. Later, Richard admitted that he had only one nut and that he would have to have surgery if the other one did not come down on its own. I did not know what this meant but hoped the best for my friend. I was extremely glad that it was not me.

I did not mention anything about the physical to my mother when I got home. I feared that she would make me show her how the doctor examined me if I told her about it. I was beginning to realize that I had no one with whom I could talk about such things. There was no one to reliably warn and advise me of what to expect in the future. Without realizing it, I was a stinky, naïve kid. I could and did warn my brother on what to expect when his time arrived.

We rode the bus that picked us up at the bottom of our driveway. Waiting for the bus was brutal during cold winter mornings. We had winter jackets but no sweaters. Mom did not let us put on our jackets until we were ready to go outside. She said that if we put our coats on too soon, we would start to sweat. If we sweat in our coats inside the house, we would freeze outside. Since our house was cold, it would have been good to warm up the inside of the jacket before going outside. Instead, we went from being cold to being colder.

One cold morning, the bus stalled after we got on. The driver said that we would have to wait for help that would come when they realized we were not at school. The bus got cold and people bundled their jackets tightly against the increasingly penetrating cold. I was cold but satisfied because we were out of the wind. Eventually, someone arrived in a pickup. He looked under the hood then connected to the battery. The bus started. I told Mom about it when I got home from school. She did not even realize the bus was broken down right in front of our house. I told her how cold it was and she said that I should have invited everyone to come into our home. I did not think that I had permission to do such a mass invite. Most importantly, I did not want everyone on that bus to see how we lived. I was becoming more aware of how other people's homes looked and did not want them to see how I lived.

Mr. Jones, my math teacher, seemed nice but too old to be teaching. He seemed competent and was very patient in his instruction. I already knew all the math he was teaching, so it did not affect me. I withdrew into my imagination. He had a strange cough and often took some cough syrup he had in his desk drawer. This was his last year of teaching. I learned later that he was an alcoholic and the cough syrup was brandy. I did not understand why this was a problem. I never saw any mood swings, lies, or inconsistent rules like with my mother.

One day in Mr. Jones' class, Donnie started bullying me again. He called me names and threatened to beat me up. He did not tell me why. He often did the same in the sixth grade, so I just avoided him. However, he sat next to me in math class and the threats resumed with greater intensity.

On the other side of me was Wayne. Wayne was huge, well over six feet tall and more than two hundred pounds. He had stayed back several times and was almost sixteen. He saw Donnie picking on me and called him on it. Wayne said, "He's my friend. Leave him alone." This surprised me because I did not know Wayne. I thought that he would more likely bully me than defend me. Donnie immediately stopped and turned away. Donnie completely stopped bothering even in classes without Wayne. A short while later, Wayne dropped out of school so I expected Donnie to resume his bullying but he never did. Wayne must have really scared him.

We moved between classes. I hated the slow pace. We were required to stay on the right up the stairs and to take one at a time. I got scolded many times for skipping stairs. Once, when I passed by the gymnasium, I heard loud sounds of older boys playing with a basketball. Pudgy Fisk was throwing full court and making some baskets. His sister, June, was in my class. Despite his basketball skills, his later fame was as a catcher for the Red Sox.

Our English teacher had great difficulty maintaining order in the classroom. One day was worse than the others. When he could not gain compliance, he threatened to keep the whole class after school. He followed through on his threat when the students did not become quiet. He told us all to report after school for detention. If we did not, we would get three days of detention. Remembering my sixth-grade experience with Mr. Morris, I decided that I needed to comply. He kept us only long enough to take attendance, then dismissed us. I had no way of notifying Mom because we had no phone. Danny called his parents and his father was going to bring him home. Since they went right by my house, I asked if I could ride with him. He was happy to help me. Unfortunately, his father arrived on a motorcycle. I had no choice but to walk home. I made it about a mile when I saw Mom driving down the hill at a high rate of speed. She saw me and barely stopped in time to pick me up. She continued to the school, explaining that she had no idea why I was not on the bus. I tried to explain that I was quiet but the teacher kept the whole class. She was angry and I was glad that it she did not seem to be angry with me.

Mom stormed into the principal's office. Mr. Gould was at his desk. She expressed her anger and exaggerated our situation. She said that I was in great danger walking along the road by myself. My father had threatened us and she was afraid that he might kidnap and kill me. At first, I thought that Mom was disclosing something I did not know about my father. As I thought more, I realized that it was not at all true. The principal admitted that the English teacher was wrong to keep us after school without the required twenty-four-hour notice. Mr. Gould added that teachers should not be keeping a whole class after school and assured her that it would never happen again.

I did not like how Mom lied but I was pleased that she stood up for me. I wish that Mom presented the truth about our situation. Unexpected trips were a hardship for our family. Mom had to receive kids from different schools at different times. She also did not have the resources for extra trips. The truth was compelling without having to exaggerate. She did not have to demonize my father when it was not true. I was far more concerned about whether she was sober enough to drive safely.

It was practically impossible to do homework at home. We did not have a space for a flat surface upon which to write. The open book on my lap served as my desk. There was too much fighting with Mom and my siblings to focus on schoolwork. Mom did not hesitate to interrupt me to do something for her. If I could not get my work done on the bus, it did not get done. Fortunately, I could do my math quickly and always managed to get it done. Reading assignments were impossible to do at home or on the bus. I tried to study for tests on the way to school as best I could.

With the water frozen in the winter, Mom stopped paying rent so she had more money for beer. Unknowingly, the landlord enabled Mom's alcoholism freeing more money for beer. With more beer, there was more days of intoxication and horror. Cilla and I discussed the idea of pleading with Mom about her drinking and realized how futile it was. We learned how Mom was keeping her drinking from Pop and Grandma by the way she spoke with them. We started to consider asking Pop and Grandma for help. Pop rarely stopped by our house. If he did when Mom was drinking, she went into the bathroom and spoke through the door. Pop was always busy, so he dropped off his vegetables, "day old" bread, overripe bananas, or whatever groceries he found with a good deal. We also realized that Mom went to a different store each time she bought beer so that the storekeeper would not know how much she drank. We felt that we could get help from Pop and Grandma. We also knew that it would upset Mom. We struggled with this decision.

Thanksgiving, Christmas, and Easter were always celebrated on the farm. Grandma made lots of pies, cakes, and cookies. There was turkey for thanksgiving and ham for Christmas and Easter. Aunt Alice and Uncle Beau moved back from California. Grandma was so happy to have her whole family at her home for the holidays. Uncle Beau watched Gary and I playing chess. As I beat Gary, he came to me and said that he wanted me to teach him. It made me feel important to be able to teach an adult a skill. When I indicated that I was ready, Uncle Beau said, "No, not now, I'm too drunk to remember." I was puzzled and disappointed. I also could not understand how anyone could be too drunk to remember this game. Even though Mom did poorly when she was drunk, she would be willing to try something. She broke the promises when she sobered. I was beginning to realize why Pop and Grandma never spoke well about Uncle Beau and switched to French in my presence. I also began to understand how his driving seemed clumsy. His reputation was to spin his tires unintentionally in my grandparents' driveway every time he left. Mom said that he always did jackrabbit starts. I remember riding with him a few times and my head being jerked back with every start. People would say that Uncle Beau could cause your head to go into the back seat. Aunt Alice and Uncle Beau divorced shortly after this.

Pop often offered a shot of brandy to the adults. Grandma never drank brandy but once in a great while had a small glass of sherry. I watched Mom's behavior when Pop offered the brandy. She always refused at first but later accepted. We knew that she would want beer afterwards. I could see her escalating struggle after the one shot of brandy. She patiently waited for an opportunity to complain about pressing bills. She complained that the car needed a tire. Pop gave her money to buy one. When she spent it on beer on the way home, she explained that she would get money from her "check," which was the welfare money. We needed milk and bread and she only got a six pack while she was there. She drank one six pack and went for another. She had enough money to continue with a third, bringing us into another evening of horror. We never had the courage tell Pop to please do not give her money. He was still the family patriarch subverting family members to his power. He felt his generosity was helpful. Instead, it kept us dependent on him.

The days went by. We delayed for quite a while, until we felt life was nearly unbearable. When we finally had the opportunity and the courage, we told Pop and Grandma. They were silent when we told them, as though the information shocked them. Finally, Pop looked at Grandma and said, "Lilly told us that she was not drinking anymore." When Pop first made this comment, I felt that he was not going to believe us. The tone of his voice and his body language with his head held low indicated that he saddened and believed what we said. I then realized that they did, at one time, realize Mom had a drinking problem. I knew Pop had some understanding of alcoholism those times he talked about his father's drinking. He said that his father could tip up a pint of whiskey and down the whole thing without swallowing. Pop then said, "I told the store not to sell her any more beer." He seemed disappointed that they did not respect his wishes. We knew better. Pop may have century old expectations that the patriarch still commands even the adult members of the family. I remembered now how Mom came out of a store one time terribly angry about what Pop had told them. The storekeeper knew that Pop had no power over him. It soon looked like Pop and Grandma would not be able to help. The only people we thought might help us were just as powerless as we were. It was obvious that we would remain on our own. I regretted needlessly causing concern for my grandparents. I worried that they did not believe us. They did not want to believe Mom lied to them about her drinking. We got no relief and only made things worse for Pop and Gram. We regretted trying to involve them. It was entirely our problem, now.

We found more ways to stay out of Mom's way when she was drinking. I liked trying to build things. Our long driveway was exceedingly difficult to shovel, so I decided to build a snowplow. There were several things around the barn but I was most limited by having only a hand saw, hammer, and bent nails. I had a screwdriver but no screws. The nails are what I was able to scrounge from unused wooden things. There were the remains of old cart with large steel wheels. I decided to convert it into a snowplow. With the large wheels, the wooden plank plow was easy to lift for moving through the snow, pushing up snowbanks, and back and forth movement. The problem was that the means I had to attach the plow to the frame kept breaking on me. I finally gave up because I was spending more energy fixing my plow than just shoveling the snow.

We were awakened early one morning when the barn roof collapsed from the weight of the snow. Mom and I immediately worried about Herbie. Mom told me to go get him. She remained in the house while I went to the barn. The roof had fallen in and around the stalls where Herbie was. I peeked in and saw a lot of debris blocking the way. I worked my way through the small openings of the broken beams to gain access to Herbie's stall. I struggled with some heavy debris and managed to get the bottom half of the door open enough for Herbie to get out. I carried him through the demolition and into the house. I thought later how dangerous it was for me to enter the collapsed, unstable barn. It was one more subtle message to me about Mom's priority to care for "dumb animals who cannot care for themselves" even more than her own children. She was willing to risk my life for the goat.

Mom's concern for animal life over human life did not come from her father. Pop laughed when he spoke about a teenage prank he did. He and his friend tied two cats' tails together and threw them over the clothesline. They screamed and howled as they tore each other apart. He also spoke about how a friend could not get a cow out of the barn so he tied the tail of another cow to it. The cow pulled the other's tail off. He also spoke about a neighbor's dog that often bothered him when he cut ice from the river. He rubbed turpentine under the dog's tail. It yelped while dragging its ass all the way home. The only pet my grandfather liked was a cat that hunted mice in his barns and garden.

Our social worker, Mrs. Rene, rarely made visits to our home. We followed Mom's rules about the limits on what to tell her and she would do all the talking. She especially did not need to know that Mom drank beer. Mom said that Mrs. Rene would take us away to awful foster homes if we told her anything. Mom threatened us, saying that she was the only one keeping us from such an awful fate. We went outside every time Mrs. Rene arrived. After one of her visits, Mom complained that she had to take us to a dentist even though we had healthy teeth. Somehow, she found Dr. McIntyre. He worked out of the same mobile home in which he lived. His dental chair was in his living room, next to the kitchen. Mom liked him because he offered her a beer while she waited. He found and repaired fourteen cavities in my teeth. She did not mind taking us to this dentist for the free beer. His bills were paid by our Medicaid. Besides hating dentists, we hated that each visit kicked off a drinking binge by Mom. Her worst binges were when she described a reason to celebrate and "splurge." Reasons could be the car passing inspection or a store clerk's error giving her extra money in change. At these times, we might get a bottle of root beer to share and a roll of NECCO wafers.

We had no toothpaste to brush our teeth. When we had a toothbrush, I avoided using it because others used it, too. The only time we brushed our teeth is when we were staying on the farm. We had our own toothbrushes there. Grandma always brushed her teeth using Pepsodent powder and went to the dentist twice a year. If she ran out of Pepsodent, she used baking soda or salt. Grandma's teeth sharply contrasted Pop's teeth that were completely covered with plaque for lack of dental care. It was like a solid band in his mouth, yet he had "healthy teeth."

Our birthdays were mostly in the middle of the month when money had run out. There were no presents and rarely a birthday cake. My divorced paternal grandparents each sent us a card with two dollars in it. Mom convinced us that we should give this money to her to support the family because she was low on money. Eventually, she just took it.

Cilla and I spent our entire summers on the farm. Gary came sometimes and did a lot less work than Cilla and I did. We all did the weeding. As crops ripened, Cilla was mostly responsible for the farm stand meeting customers. Pop and I kept her and his commercial markets supplied. Pop and I got up early and picked a load of corn for his Claremont markets. Each trailer load was three thousand ears of corn. Pop wore a rain suit because there was so much dew on the corn, he would get soaked. He gave me one of his old rain pants. It helped to keep me reasonably dry but made movement much more difficult. I struggled to meet Pop's expectations to keep up with him.

He taught me to drive the tractor so I could go pick corn for his Springfield markets while he delivered to his Claremont Markets. I was so proud to drive it all by myself. He used to back into the field over two rows, picking them first. Backing over these made picking and loading the trailer much more productive. Backing the tractor and trailer was incredibly challenging at first. I eventually got exceptionally good at backing the wagon. Making the right angle turn into the field from the roadway on the first try was my only remaining challenge. If I worked hard, I had enough time to pick a wagon load by myself. Because Pop saw no reason to go faster than thirty-five miles an hour, I had almost two hours before his return. I remembered the stories Pop told. He started farming with horses and drove a Ford Model T to town. Around the time I was born, Pop bought his first Ford tractor and an International Harvester truck.

Pop always battled the wildlife to protect his vegetables. Grandma even called it waging war against them or we would have nothing to sell. Dad gave to Pop his double-barreled shotgun to scare away the black birds he called grackles. He did not have to hit any. Just scare them off, which worked for short periods of time. If he did manage to kill one, he placed the carcass in the corn tassel to scare off others. This did not seem to work very well, either.

Racoons were another foe. He set leg hold traps in key locations around the farm. One particularly good location was where the culvert passed under Route Five. He checked the traps every morning. He carried a pickax handle to beat them to death. There was no need to waste a bullet.

When I was ten years old, Uncle Bernie gave me a brand new twenty-two-caliber, single shot rifle. Pop gave me bullets to scare away the birds while he went to town. The twenty-two did not make enough noise. The birds only flew a short distance and settled into the corn again. I was like a gambler hoping for that one big score. I felt that I needed to produce a dead bird to please Pop when he returned. Instead, I used the whole box of bullets with no results, compelled like the gambler. I suffered Pop's verbal wrath for using a whole box for the remainder of the day. I wished Pop would have realized that a twenty-two is less effective than a twelve-gauge shotgun at scaring away birds.

Pop did not like the pigeons because they made a mess in his barn. I was much more effective at killing these. I seldom missed. He also hated chipmunks because they would nibble on his produce stored in the barn. Rat shot worked well on chipmunks. Rat shot had a lot of little pellets like a twenty-two-caliber shotgun.

Pop also sent me to check the traps. It was easy to shoot the trapped racoons between the eyes. They stared at me and growled. I pulled the trigger and the hole suddenly appeared between their eyes. Their growl faded as they fell over. I dragged them back to bury in the field so their bodies could help fertilize the garden.

Uncle Bernie joined the National Guard. Mom said it was so he would not get drafted into the army, which would require going to war. He did not speak much about it other than he did not care much for the National Guard. The National Guard remained in this country. Uncle Bernie also did not like working on the farm. He thought Pop should pay him an hourly wage. We all knew that this was not possible. The farm did not make enough money. He got a job at Fellows Gear Shaper where Dad used to work. He joked about going into the bathroom and fishing out the window. The Black River flowed next to the plant and had a dam to provide hydropower. The bathroom window was next the dam where fish hung out in the still waters.

Summers on the farm were hard, lonely work but an escape from Mom's wrath. Cilla and I benefitted greatly by learning Pop and Grandma's old-fashioned values. Grandma had an overly broad definition of a sin, far beyond the ten commandments and in much greater detail. Grandma also baked pies for the Paddock Restaurant. She often worked in their kitchen Friday and Saturday evenings, cooking, cleaning, and baking. Pop drove her there and picked her up. Grandma did not drive. She used to drive on the road until drivers' licenses were required in nineteen hundred twenty-eight.

Early and midsummers were dominated with the constant weeding of the garden. Pop referred to crop sections as fields: corn, potato, tomato, squash, etc. He closely monitored their condition and planned a schedule according to the weeds. We worked each field to completion at which time, Pop told us where to go next. With each change in field, Pop gave us specific directions and demonstrations on how to do it. Tomatoes required special care around and under the growing vines. He showed us how to watch for the tomato worm. If there seemed to be fewer leaves on a vine, look on the ground underneath it. If there was a tomato worm, he would leave small, dark clumps or manure droppings. The worms were perfectly camouflaged and difficult to find. Their droppings gave away their position.

Pop put a lot of care into his tomatoes. He once confided in me that tomatoes made more money per acre than any other crop. When it was very dry, tomatoes were the crop he watered. We had to put water in pails and wheelbarrow them out to the plants. Pop's instructions required a half a pail to each plant. He had two hundred fifty plants. He assigned gender and emotions to his plants describing how she liked the water and it made her happy. I worked with Pop most of the time. He could control the heavy wheelbarrow. Sometimes, I was left alone to do it. The wheelbarrow was heavy and difficult to balance. I had to stop and set it down many times to regain balance to avoid spilling the water as my arms tired. The soils were soft, making it impossible to push the wheelbarrow. I had to turn it around and pull it. This made balancing it more challenging. Sometimes I cheated on the amounts. I watered three tomato plants per pail instead of two.

The corn fields were the longest and most boring with their eight-hundred-foot-long rows. We were each assigned a row and struggled to keep up with Pop while not missing any weeds. Pop inspected our work and scolded us mercilessly if we missed too many weeds. He told us how stupid we were and how he did not have enough time to go back over what we did. His language attacked our self-esteem. Good people did good work. If you did not do a good job, you had less value as a person. There were times that we worked alone in the fields. We argued with each other about doing a fair share of the work. Gary often fell far behind. When Cilla and I complained, he would skip long sections, deliberately walking past weeds. This infuriated Cilla and I as we knew that we would bare Pop's wrath more than he. Our redemption came from the skipped portions were deep in the field. Pop inspected the edges. He did not see the weeds until harvest time. By then, the weeds were quite tall but his wrath was less.

Sometimes the boredom was briefly interrupted with the excitement of finding a toad. Pop valued toads for the insects they ate, so he wanted us to be careful of them. Toads defended themselves by peeing on you. I learned the best way to catch them was by the head and let their butt hang free. This way, when they peed, it went harmlessly into the air and on the ground. Pop allowed us to briefly move them but did not want us to waste time playing with them. The hoeing had to get done.

The perpetual, high pitched sound of sand pipers grew annoying. They lived at the far edge of the farm where water ponded during heavy rains. They built their nests on the ground in the tall grass. They had long legs. It was interesting watching them. They moved slowly, raised their legs high, then slowly placed them down as they seemed to carefully select a place. When necessary, they ran very quickly. They seemed reluctant to fly. I could never get close to any.

During these quiet times in the fields, I could wander in my daydreams inspired by what I saw on television. I imagined living with Indians like being captured from a show like Wagon Train. Perhaps I could live with extraterrestrial aliens like I saw on the Twilight Zone. I did not like the part when they examined my internal organs. I imagined living in the present but with superpowers of invisibility, like the *Invisible Man*, a book I read. I also imagined being able to stop time, like I saw on a *Wild, Wild West* show. I found greater peace in the life I imagined in my daydreams or some mischievous way of dealing with my present conditions. Being able to disappear during the unpleasant times was most appealing to me. The next best thing was to numb out, turning down the volume on the criticism and thinking about what I did well.

It was peaceful in the fields. We could hear the crowing of the chickens back at the barn. Much of it seemed without purpose and became a bit annoying. When there was an obvious change in tone and energy from one chicken, Grandma explained that she had just laid an egg. When we finished hoeing, I checked for the eggs. It was one of my favorite things. It was like a scavenger hunt. Sometimes they laid eggs in the nests, sometimes on the floor. Chickens had a pecking order. If the dominant hens were in the nests, lower hens had to stay on the floor. I liked the challenge of checking under a sitting hen. Some let me slide my hand gently under them. They did not like my intrusion and shifted around. Some jumped out of the nest. Sometimes, I got an angry chicken that pecked me. I met her challenge by distracting her with one hand as I slid the other one under her.

Grandma butchered the chickens when they stopped laying eggs. She brought a tub of boiling hot water to a post under the barn. She placed the bird in a tapered peck-sized basket with an enlarged hole in the bottom. She pulled the bird's head through the hole and held it while she cut its throat. As the bird thrashed around, she explained that the basket keeps it from running away even with its throat cut. The basket also kept it from splashing blood everywhere. When it stopped thrashing, she placed it in her tub of hot water. She held it by its feet as she rolled it around, soaking all the feathers. The hot water made it possible to pull the feathers out. She then hung the bird by its feet on the post. She cut through its butt and pulled out the internal organs, letting them fall on the ground. She kept the heart, gizzard, and liver.

She cut open the gizzard and removed its contents. The cat came and started eating what fell on the ground and Grandma left it for him. I had dreams about being butchered with someone pulling my organs from between my legs as I spread them apart like the chicken's legs. It was not a nightmare nor did I feel any fear. I marveled at my organs as best I understood them as they were pulled out. I enjoyed these dreams, perhaps because I got some odd special attention that I craved.

We could hear the mechanic in the neighborhood as he revved engines he serviced. Pop felt it was unnecessary to make so much noise. Pop also complained when someone left his garage while revving his engine and squealing his tires. Soon after going to bed most nights, someone left squealing tires with each shifting of the gears.

Pop and Grandma talked about the neighbors, most of whom I did not know. They especially complained about the neighbors across the road. Pop used to own the land where he had his sugar house when I was younger. He sold it because the riverbanks were falling into the river. He thought all the land would eventually fall in. The people bought it for its river frontage. They liked to party, building bonfires, and drinking beer. I was quite familiar with how people change as they get drunk. These neighbors liked to party at night and grew very loud. It was hard to sleep as they shouted and argued. There was a woman with a young child who ran up to her and nursed on her breast in their yard for all to see. Grandma complained that the child was much too old to be nursing and the woman's lack of discretion to allow it to continue. Pop did not seem to regret selling the property. He just complained.

As the crops ripened, Pop opened the stand. Within a few days, there was enough for Pop to begin delivering to markets.

Whenever he left, he assigned us work to do before he returned. It was good to be free from his constant supervision, but worrisome that he would inspect our work on returned. Even though only Gary's work was poor quality, we all received Pop's criticism. There were times we all grew tired and bored and skipped a few feet in the middle of a row of corn.

When we came out of the field for dinner and supper, Grandma sent us to the sink in the cellar to wash our hands. Picking red tomatoes oddly stained our hands green. It was exceedingly difficult to get it off. We could use Comet powder sparingly. Once, when Grandma finished picking tomatoes with us, she used Lestoil. It seemed to effortlessly melt the green off our hands.

Picking fall crops was fun. I especially liked picking squash. I stood by the wagon and Pop tossed the squash to me. I caught them and placed them in the crates on the trailer. I had to be careful not to damage the stem or blossom end. Pop was good at tossing them and I got good at catching them. Once all the crates were full, I drove the tractor to the barn. We unloaded the heavy, full crates and got more empty crates. The process continued. I liked this because catching the squashes was both challenging and fun. It was a quite different routine. Perhaps nicest part of all was when Pop praised me many times for the good catches.

Digging potatoes was also fun, hard work. It began with walking beside the potato digger. Pop drove the tractor while Cilla walked on one side and I walked on the other. Our jobs were to prevent the potato vines from catching and plugging the front of the digger. We pushed vines that overhung the edge of the digger into the conveyor belt with a broom handle. Potatoes and vines fell out the back. After digging the rows Pop wanted for the day, we gathered the potatoes in bushel baskets. After the potatoes were all in the baskets, we went with the tractor and trailer to pick them up. Pop rinsed them off and we stored them in the garage for later grading and bagging. Pop and Grandma usually did this, weighing each bag on hanging scales. I often helped by bringing a new basket and taking away the filled bags in banana boxes. They always made certain to give extra, more than what people paid. Anything sold by the pound was significantly over the quantity the customer wanted. Corn was sold by the dozen but always with thirteen ears, more if they were small.

Pop liked to watch boxing matches, the news, and *The Lawrence Welk Show*. I hated *The Lawrence Welk* Show. It was nothing but boring music. The news in the sixties was often about the riots. I could hear Pop's solution to the race riots, "Just put them on a boat and send them back to Africa." Grandma sometimes tried to calm Pop. Pop's seemingly racist comments were out of character for me. He was looking for an easy, safe solution. He also often complained about the "damn Jews" when they haggled over prices. Grandma tried to quell these rants, "They are your best customers." My bedtime was before the boxing matches came on television but I could listen from my bed, upstairs. Pop said that he boxed when he was younger. I could hear him criticize boxers and get excited when his favorite boxer scored.

I listened to the news reports about the riots. The closest demonstrations were at Dartmouth College where they took over buildings. Pop and Uncle Bernie complained and feared that negroes and hippies were trying to take over the country. I tried to relate to the people Pop said should go back to Africa. They were no more from Africa than he was from France. Grandma and he were French-Canadian descendants. What if someone suggested that we get on a boat and go back to France. We would have no place to stay. At least they were bilingual and would be able to speak French. Grandma did not learn English until she was thirteen years old, when she came with her family from Canada. Most of the African descendants no longer spoke the language.

There was also an intense fear of communism that I did not understand. I could understand the invasion of a communist country but the greatest concern was that our democracy would become communistic by some sort of take over. I understood that no one could own anything in a communist country. It all belonged to the government. I felt confident that would never happen in this country. I believed that the people in communist countries only accepted it because they had no choice. I saw no difference between communism and a dictatorship. Both had a single person in charge.

Dad started visiting us again. He was committed to his new family in Windsor but wanted to maintain a connection with his children. He brought Cilla to get a dress for her eighth-grade graduation. Cilla was so proud and cherished the dress. Mom immediate blew her temper. She refused to allow Dad to spend money on Cilla unless he spent the same amount on the others. We were all fine with Cilla getting special treatment for her special occasion but Mom refused to allow Cilla to wear the dress. We were willing to wait for our special time. Mom was continuing her past practice of making it impossible for Dad. Cilla defiantly wore the dress to her graduation. Dad stopped visiting us. Mom drove him away, again.

In the eighth grade now, I was becoming more aware of my surroundings and my friends. I started taking algebra, which was the most interesting thing in school. I struggled to understand what the English and history teachers wanted. I had gotten some bad advice from my mother on a science assignment and got a D.

I stopped asking for her help. I did not need her help with algebra. She could not do it anyway because she never studied it. It seemed odd to me that I was only in the eighth grade and ahead of what my mother learned in high school. She continued to boast that she was the first one in the family to graduate high school. She also reminded me that I would not do so well in high school.

Daisy Hronek was my algebra teacher. Mom said that she went to school with her. I already liked math but Mrs. Hronek made it so much more interesting. Her love of math and teaching it was compelling. I quickly understood everything she taught us. Mrs. Hronek gave periodic, chapter tests. Every Friday she gave a fifty-question, ten-minute quiz to sharpen our skills. It was an exercise to increase our speed and accuracy. I usually got perfect scores. As the year progressed, the tests got harder as there was less arithmetic and more algebra. After one new concept, I got one wrong, scoring ninety-eight percent. The next highest score was seventy-six, then sixty-four. I was so proud but a little disappointed by my single, simple mistake. Nonetheless, I was immensely proud that I did so much better than everyone else and anxious to tell my mother.

I ran into the house when I got home. Mom was sitting in front of the TV, watching her soap operas as usual. She was sober so it was a good time to tell her how well I did. When I told her that I got a ninety-eight, she immediately responded, "What did you get wrong?" I started to explain how I made the simple mistake even though I wanted her to understand how much better I did than everyone else. As I explained my mistake to her, I noticed that she was still focused on her soap opera. I suspected that she was not listening to me. As I continued to describe my mistake, I realized that she would not understand as she had never studied algebra. I stopped mid-sentence. She did not respond to my unusual breaking point, staring at the television. I looked at her a few more seconds as she remained focused on the television and had no interest in what I was saying. I had learned that her TV shows were more important than anything we had to say. I walked away and never told her of my successes again. It hurt that my mother was more interested in a dumb soap opera than my achievements. It taught me to be self-motivated, now knowing that I would never get any encouragement from her.

Some mischievous boys threw spit balls during science class. They waited until the teacher was writing on the board. They grew braver and made paper airplanes and flew them out the open windows. Donny boasted about setting one on fire before throwing it out the window. They got caught when the teacher downstairs returned a plane that flew into her window.

I learned about nutrients and calories in food. There was no easy reference to look these up nor were there any food labels. The instruction validated my grandparents' value of eating good vegetables. We learned that sweets like cake and candy should be taken in moderation. Too many calories would make you gain weight.

This teaching about regulating calories conflicted with my mother's assurances that people are heavy because they were meant to be that way. She referred to her being big boned as the reason she was heavier than most but also stronger. She felt that we should all be big boned. I was beginning to realize the huge amounts of food Mom ate when she drank beer contributed to her increasing obesity. I suspected that the beer also had a great deal of calories.

My peers' language had many sexual inuendoes. I tried to assemble them into an understanding of sex and sexual relationships. There was a lot of pressure aligning one's personal value with one's sexual prowess. Some popular phrases included "get bent," "eat it," "suck it," "don't let your meat loaf," "keep it in your sneaker," "corn hole," "first base," "rubbers," hickeys," "Bang her," and "knocked up." I wondered what the difference was between making out and making it, if any. I wondered what the four bases were that people were achieving in their sexual relationships. I was confident that humping was sex but did it mean doggy style sex? I knew a male dog's back formed a round hump when it mounted a female. "Colder than a witch's tit" was a common phrase. Similarly, a popular mocking phrase was, "Tough titty said the kitty because the milk's no good." Neither made much sense to me.

I tried to combine these with Mom's aggressive vigilance to prevent us from playing with ourselves and a James Bond seduction scene she seemed to like. When drunk, Mom often boasted she knew everything about sex. She also repeated what I heard Pop joke about, "The stool goes beside the cow, not behind it." I thought that anyone trying to milk the cow from behind would certainly be kicked and risked being showered in cow urine or manure. I did not get the warning that the stool behind the cow facilitated having sex with the cow. She described being surprised by finding a farm hand sitting on a fence "playing with himself" when she was a young girl. Depending on Mom's mood and level of intoxication, she sometimes laughed when she told the story. Other times she cried, describing herself as a victim, traumatized by the sight. It would have been nice to have a dad that could explain some of these terms.

We played roughly during recess. Titty twisters were common. Mostly, they were sneak attacks. They hurt. Keeping one arm across one's chest was the best defense. Wayne liked to wrestle like he did with his two older brothers. He was strong, fast, and rough.

Wayne instilled a culture of violence among us. We competed to establish a hierarchy of fighting skills. Wayne encouraged me to fight Richard because he spoke badly of Danny. I tried to get him to fight but he would not. I unintentionally caused his nose to bleed as I pushed him around. He wiped the blood and said, "Are you happy now?" I felt badly. I never wanted to hurt anyone.

As mean as he was during recess, Wayne tried to coach me on how to dress better. I realized that he only wanted his friends to look good so that he looked good, but I appreciated the advice. I did not have much choice for clothes. One day, I wore a black turtleneck sweater and a red plain shirt Grandma had given to me. He thought it looked nice, so I wore it again the next day. I was disappointed when Wayne explained that I should not wear the same thing two consecutive days. He said that it should be washed before I wore it again. His advice conflicted with how we always wore our clothes until they were obviously dirty.

Wayne complained that I smelled one day. I told him that it must be my coat. It was a wool coat, again given to me by Grandma. I spilled kerosene on it when I collected it for the kitchen stove. We never washed our jackets. He explained that I did not smell like kerosene, more like puppy. I knew then that it was me and not the jacket. We had no water to take baths. I was powerless to prevent it.

During our third winter at the Bemis farm, Mrs. Rene came for an unexpected visit. Afterwards, Mom said that we had to move. She added that Mrs. Rene did not like that we had to get our water from the horse trough. Mrs. Rene would have seen the milk cans for water in the kitchen. I sensed some animosity against Debra. Mom said that she told her teacher something she should not have. I suspected that the teacher complained how Debra smelled. If someone told Debra that she should bathe more frequently, Debra would have used the excuse that we had no water to take baths. Mom did not coach Debra on what to say to people like she did Cilla and me. She relied on Cilla to do it. The teacher's complaint most likely prompted a referral to the Welfare Department, resulting in Mrs. Rene's surprise visit.

We moved to an apartment on the Old Claremont Road near the top of Lovers Lane. It was right around the corner from where she threw beer bottles at Dad while he tried to change the flat tire after the races. Mom said that it was a better apartment but it cost fifty-five dollars a month, five more than she was paying BEMIS, and she would have to pay all winter. The greater problem was that we could not have a goat and had too many pets.

Mom found someone who was interest in buying Herbie. They drove into the yard and talked to Mom. I brought Herbie to them then stood back and watched. The man held Herbie by his collar and occasionally rubbed him. They took the goat and left. I asked Mom about their conversation. She said that he paid eight dollars. I asked if they were going to take good care of him. She replied, "They're probably going to eat him." I thought this was a cold response from my mother. If they were planning on eating him and she knew it, she could have at least lied to me. She lied about so many things but protecting my feelings did not seem to matter to her.

The time for us to move came closer. Mom decided the dogs had to be put out of their misery because they would have to be tied at the new place. Both had been allowed to roam freely and would return to this house since it was only a couple miles away. She got Dad's twenty-two caliber pistol and brought Chino out behind the barn. We waited a long time but did not hear any shots. We became very worried because Mom was drinking, she might accidentally shoot herself. Mom came back around with the dog running near her. She said that she could not do it. Then she said that if she got drunk enough, she probably could. I was surprised when she admitted to purposefully getting drunk. She always denied that she ever got drunk. So, Mom set out to get drunk, which she did well. Several hours later, she staggered out behind the barn with the gun and dog. Several minutes passed and still no gun shot. Again, she returned, saying she could not do it.

The day for moving came. Something had to be done with the dogs. She was sober as she pushed them into separate burlap bags, added a cement block to each, and tied them shut. I helped her carry them to the well near the barn. She lowered them into the well using a rope. She waited a few minutes, then pulled them back out. She had me dig the hole to bury them while she went back to packing. I was surprised about how she did this without emotion when she was sober but could not kill them when she was drinking.

The new apartment had a long, narrow, dark kitchen, an average size living room, a long, narrow bathroom downstairs. Upstairs, Gary and I shared an extremely small bedroom. Mom, Cilla, and Debra had a large bedroom upstairs. Gary and I had our two rollaway beds and a shared bureau in our room, leaving little floor space. We moved only what we could fit into the new apartment. We left the rest behind. We also left the house in a terrible mess with deep trash scattered about.

After were got partially settled in the new apartment, Mom felt the need to reward herself. She went to the neighborhood store, Ray's Store. She drank that six pack and went for another. When she returned, she announced that she got a job for me. I would help Ray and Aggie stock the shelves after school and Saturday mornings. Aggie especially wanted me to carry up the beer from the basement to help her keep the coolers full. They were going to pay me one dollar per hour. This was generous when the minimum wage was ninety-five cents for adults. Children could work at any wage. I was twelve years old.

Ray asked me to keep track of my hours and present him a bill at the end of the week. Most days, I hurried and got everything done within fifteen minutes, which Ray insisted as my minimum time. I was extremely nervous when I presented him with my first bill for one dollar and twenty-five cents. He pressed the button to open the cash register and paid me, saying "Thank you."

I was so proud to earn money on my own. I ran home to show Mom. She shared my joy, then said, "I know you want to contribute that to the family. You are such a good boy." Sadly, I was happy to do it and put it in the money dish she kept in the cupboard.

For weeks I hustled to Ray's Store after school and Saturday mornings only to put the money in the dish. I watched Mom buy beer with the money from the state and use mine for essentials such as bread and milk when money was low. I had some relief from the sense that my money did not go directly to beer, but I knew it helped her use more welfare money to spend on beer. I was only deceiving myself.

As I grew older, my new friends started asking me to spend time with them outside of school. I was hampered because I did not have a bike or telephone like they had. I got up the courage and with tears welling in my eyes, I asked Mom if I could save my money to buy a bike. She was upset with my selfish request, "I thought that you wanted to contribute to the family!" I continued with my request and she finally consented, "It's your money anyway." I saved up ten dollars and bought an old bike from a friend. It was in terrible condition. One pedal was missing. The threads were destroyed, so a new pedal could not screw into it.

This made the bike extremely hard to pedal using the post and one pedal. My friends all had three-speed bikes. I struggled to keep up with them.

After buying the ten-dollar bike, I returned to placing my earnings in Mom's money dish. After a few weeks of falling behind my friends, I again tearfully approached Mom to keep the money I earned. I got a similar response then consent to keep my money. I saved up forty dollars and bought a new, three-speed bike.

The next problem to arise when trying to coordinate with my friends was not having a telephone. All the school forms that had asked for a telephone number accepted "no phone" in the space because it was not unusual for families to have no phone. We never had a phone. Mom sent me to use Ray and Aggie's phone to call Grandma a few times. It was a toll call even though it was just across the river. It was in a different state. Mom gave me twenty cents to pay Ray and Aggie. She always sent me in to store at such times when she did not want to do it. Ray and Aggie's phone was in their kitchen. They started to complain about the intrusions that were becoming more frequent. So, having our own phone would be a relief in many ways. Cilla and I checked out the cost and I decided that I could pay for it. It had to be in Mom's name because it required an adult. We got a two-party phone. It was a huge social leap for Cilla and me to have more contact with our friends.

Toll calls had to go through the operator. A new system began when we could dial direct but an operator would interrupt the call, asking for our number. The telephone company sent instructions and numbers so we could practice free of charge. I told Mom that I wanted to try. She said, "Just don't give them your number." I called the free number. An operator came on and asked for my number. I told her that I thought these calls were free. She explained that she still needed my number and it would show as no charge on our bill. I told her the number. From behind me, Mom said, "You fool." The call went through with its congratulations. I hung up and left the room. I did not bother to offer the explanation to Mom. She had called me a fool. It hurt. Many times, I have been told how stupid I was by her and my grandfather. This one hurt most because she had never called me that before and it was my phone for which I was paying and my decision to make.

Even though we had water, we had fallen into the routine of putting dirty clothes in the tub. We had to wear them more than one day before Mom even let us put them in the dirty laundry. So, when the ones in the tub were cleaner than the ones we were wearing, we pulled them out to reuse them. They were quite dirty and smelly. Pulling dirty clothes from that huge pile was gross. Adding to it, I knew Mom put her urine-soaked menstruation rags in it. It was equally gross to take all the dirty laundry out of the tub then put it back into the tub after a bath. Cilla and I did the wash, but not very often. It was so hard to dress to the standards that my peers expected.

I began spending more time with my friends now that we had a phone to coordinate with them. Mom embarrassed me in front of my friends whether she was drunk or sober. She was especially silly when she was drunk. Even when she was sober, she still acted very immature. Much of what she said and did made no sense. She tried to involve herself in what we were doing. When she was three six packs drunk, she was very hostile to me, trying to argue all the time. I avoided bringing my friends to my home. When Mom was hostile drunk, I just left. She was in bed when I returned.

Wayne had a pool table in his basement and we spent a lot of time there. We also swam in the Connecticut River across from his house. Sometimes we went to the town pool, but it was cold and the lifeguards were strict. We had much more fun in the river, where it was less safe. We also liked to skip stones on the water. We challenged each other who could get the most splashes. We sought flat, round rocks. The technique involved getting low to the surface of the water, throwing hard and spinning the rock. On the best throws, the rock skimmed across the surface at the end. Though it was a superior throw and should have won, our competition criteria required distinct splashes, but skimming stone still earned special recognition among us.

With my success at driving tractors, I became interested in driving the car. We had a nineteen forty-eight Studebaker that my father had when he returned the last time. It was three-speed on the column with a lever for overdrive. Mom promised that she would teach me how to drive it. She would not even explain how the three-speed on the column shifted. I was familiar with the gearbox of the tractor but could not figure out her shifting pattern. She shifted with extraordinary movements of her hand and arm, flailing her elbow outwardly. Had she simply described the correlation of the floor shift is like the column shift, I would have known. Her wild arm movements disguised it.

Uncle Bernie told us about a rock quarry made during the construction of Interstate Ninety-One along the Vermont border with New Hampshire. It had filled in with water, which made a good place to swim. As we searched for the place, Mother noticed that the access road was rough and steep. She built up speed to make it up the hill. This speed made it hard for her to control the car and made us nervous. With her obesity, her large belly rubbed against the steering wheel and limited her ability to steer with the bouncing car. Over the top of the hill, the road circled the huge quarry as it slowly descended. It was beautiful. The water was clear, greenish-blue color. We could see large boulders in the deepest end.

We enjoyed swimming in the quarry several times. Mother came into the water sometimes. She had no swimsuit so she just came in with the shirt and shorts she normally wore. She could not swim but enjoyed wading in the shallow area. Cilla and I liked to swim out to the large boulders that projected out of the water where it was over our heads. While we were out there one day, Mom lost her footing. She was falling face forward and got my attention when she said, "Uh Oh! I can't get my feet under me." I jumped off the rock and swam as hard as I could, not even taking a breath. Many thoughts raced through my mind. Would I be able to lift her large body in the chest deep water? If I had to drive the car, I still did not know how to shift it. She managed to right herself just as I got there.

Uncle Beau, Aunt Alice, and my cousins came to the quarry once. I rode with Uncle Beau to help him find the place. When I showed him the steep hill, he stopped to study it. I told him that he needed to get a head start. He said that he would be fine. He put the car in low gear and drove up it slowly. It was a much better ascent than my mother's. I began to realize that Mom was not always right about the best way to drive.

One summer evening, our neighboring friends came over to play. Their mother did not like them associating with us. Their father was a successful contractor and we were on welfare. They sometimes sneaked over. Robert was Gary's age and in Gary's class. Paul was ten, two years younger than Robert, three years younger than me. We went outside but Paul remained inside. He was trying to get Mom to teach him how to drive. I felt confident that he was wasting his time because Mom would teach me first. I did not count on how drunk Mom was. A few minutes later, Mom came out with her keys in her hand, staggering down the two stairs off the porch. Paul was behind her. As they walked to the car, I asked what she was doing. She said that she was going to show Paul a couple of things. I protested, reminding her that she promised me. She told me that she was going to show him a couple of things, then I could have a turn.

Paul got in the driver's seat and Mom sat beside him on the passenger side. The engine roared and they backed awkwardly out of the parking space. The engine roared again and they drove around the house down the bank behind the house. The car stopped and they seemed to be taking a long time. I walked around the house and watched them, pacing back and forth, anxious for my turn. It was starting to get dark. Suddenly, the headlights came on and the engine roared much more than I ever heard it roar. The car came extremely fast up the hill towards me. The front of the car raised higher as it crested the hill coming directly at me. I jumped out of the way. The car roared past me and slammed into the tree in front of the house. The engine continued to roar as the rear wheels came off the ground, spinning fast, crashed back to the ground. The wheels spun on the grass briefly, then the engine stopped.

It all seemed so impossible to be real. I yelled "No!" as loud as I could, as if I had some power to undo what happened. Paul got out of the driver's side and ran home. I saw Mom's head much lower than normal. She was wiggling on the front seat. I went to the door driver's door that Paul left open. Mom was trying to get up off the floor and onto the seat. I ran around the back of the car to the passenger side. I saw better that the front end of the car was caved in, the hood buckled up and the bumper wrapped around the tree. I was amazed about the amount damage. Mom's door would not open. I pulled with all my might and it screeched and groaned as it opened part way and stopped. I pushed with all my might to get it open wider. Mom was sideways, facing the driver's side with her back to me. She had her left arm on the seat and her right arm on the dashboard. Her right leg was over the top of her left leg. She was not moving her right leg and trying to push herself up with her left leg. Her right leg was twisted and obviously badly broken.

By now, I was crying uncontrollably and still trying to think how to help my mother. She told me to grab her right arm and pull her up. I did this. Even though I was strong for a twelve-year-old, she was grossly overweight. I pulled as hard as I could. We managed to wiggle her onto the seat. Her right leg remained motionless on top of her left leg. She explained that she tried to apply the brake but reached across with her right leg out of habit.

In my hysteria, I tried to decide what to do next. Cilla was staying on the farm that day, so I did not have her to help me. The lady in the adjoining apartment came to Gary, Debra, and me. We were all crying and hysterical. She said that she had already called the ambulance and they would be here soon. She offered us an aspirin to help us calm down. I thought how strange that was. Aspirin was for headaches. It did not calm people. I told her that I did not want an aspirin. Gary and Debra took one. Mom asked her to call Pop and Grandma.

Mom called for me to come closer to her. She had taken a mint from her pocket and was chewing on it. She often did this to cover her drinking when she went to the store. She told me to go into the house and get all the beer bottles out. She said, "Don't forget the ones in the fridge." I dutifully complied. I ran into the house, got a paper bag, took all the empty bottles from the trash and the four remaining in the refrigerator. I moved quickly and quietly so not be noticed. Everyone was focused on the wrecked car, my screaming siblings, and my mother. I ran to the back of the house and on the edge of the wooded area. I carefully set the bag down so as not to make a sound that would alert anyone. I returned to Mom. She asked if I did as she said. I assured her that I did. She asked again about the ones in the fridge and I assured her that I got those, too.

The ambulance arrived. They drove the oversized Cadillac station wagon along beside the wrecked car. It was very dark now and the flashing lights made the scene feel worse. Two men assessed Mom. They removed the stretcher from the back of the ambulance and placed it alongside the car nearest to Mom. They tried unsuccessfully to lift her. She was far too heavy for them. They helped her move her legs to the outside of the car. I could see the pain in my mother's face. She stopped frequently. Other men arrived in their own cars. The men did their best to help her with the broken leg. They helped her stand and pivot on her left leg. They helped her lower herself onto the stretcher. One man held her broken leg, which hurt Mom a lot. With two on each side of the stretcher, they lifted Mom into the back of the ambulance. They drove away as I watched helplessly.

We were still sobbing with our attention turning towards our own care. The neighbor offered to look after us overnight. I thanked her and told her that I expected my grandfather. Pop arrived a short while later and told us to get some clothes. We went to the farm with him. He restrained himself from asking about what happened and gave us some assurance. It was the most nurturing that I had ever seen him. It must be that he sensed how scared and upset that we were. Grandma helped us settle down and wash up for bed. I finally fell asleep.

The next morning, Uncle Bernie asked me about the condition of the car. I described how the front end was damaged with the bumper around the tree. He told me to come with him and we drove to my house. Uncle Bernie examined the car closely. He tried to open the hood but it was too badly crumpled. As it crushed rearward, the hood buckled up, leaving openings on each side. Uncle Bernie looked through these holes and examined the engine. He took out his jackknife and reached through one of these openings. He hooked onto something and pulled hard until it broke free. He explained that he had to cut the fan belt so he could start the car. He got in the driver's seat and started the car. The doors would not close so he left them open. He backed the car up, drove around the tree and parked it in its usual location. I thought that we would get back into his pickup and drive back to the farm but he went into our apartment. He did not say anything as he looked around the kitchen. He looked in the fridge, then more around the kitchen. He noticed the open cardboard milk carton beside the kitchen sink where Mom put her beer caps. He picked it up, investigated it as he shook it around. I did not think he would care about the beer caps. I thought that he was like Pop and Grandma who did not want to talk about it. He put the carton back and then we left.

After we drove a short distance, Uncle Bernie said, "Was your mom drinking?" I quickly replied, "No." He paused, seemingly searching for words and said, "There were eight beer caps in the milk carton." Uncle Bernie was telling me that he knew that I was lying. I suddenly felt that I had let my mother down. I never thought about the beer caps or their significance. He did not need to say anything more and did not expect me to say anything, either. He did not need to call me a liar as I compromised my personal integrity to honor my mother's wishes. Words were not necessary to validate our mutual understanding that Mom had been drinking. I felt some relief that he saw only eight caps. Mom had been drinking a lot more than eight, so I still partially protected her wishes. I did not know why she kept some beer caps in the carton near instead of directly into the trash inches away. She had another carton beside her on floor beside the couch. Sometimes she had a full beer next to her while she finished one. It made more sense to have a carton there for the beer caps. Fortunately, Uncle Bernie did not check there.

Pop and Grandma brought us to visit Mom in the hospital. She was in bed with her leg in traction. She was going to surgery the next day. I knew people with broken legs got casts but she said that she was too big for a cast. The doctor was going to pin a rod to her upper leg bone.

After her surgery, Dr. Shoemaker showed me her X-ray. He pointed to the screws into her bone that held the long metal rod against her thigh bone. He said that he put extra screws to make sure it held against her weight when she was able to walk on it. For the next few weeks, she would have to use crutches. Mom was always happy to see the doctor. She called him Papa Shoe-Shoe. I thought it was disrespectful but he did not complain. He was a skilled orthopedic surgeon and deserved more respect. She was lucky that he was available for her. If it were not for his skills, she would have been in traction for weeks.

Everyone agreed that we would all stay on the farm until Mom was well enough to return home. Pop, Grandma, Cilla, and I went to get clothes. Most of them were in the bathtub and had to be washed, which Grandma did. Grandma dug through the huge pile in the bathtub. She did not complain or judge in any way. Uncle Bernie helped set up a bed for Mom downstairs, in the front room of the farmhouse.

Cilla and I were quite comfortable with life on the farm. We did our usual early summer chores of weeding. When Mom came, she struggled to get up the stairs into the house. Once inside, her bed was close to the kitchen and the bathroom, so it was a good place for her to recover. I was more relaxed during this time than any other time during my childhood. We were safe on the farm and Mom was sober.

Working with Pop was unusually pleasant. He seemed to enjoy having us on the farm. With the extra help, we finished our morning's work early and headed back to wait for lunch. It was a nice, sunny day and I was feeling safe and relaxed. As I approached the house, I saw Mom sitting on the porch. She looked good and seemed to be doing much better now that she was not drinking beer. I greeted her as I walked up the stairs. When I got closer, she pulled something out from under her dress and said, "Here, take this." She handed me something with such timing and speed that I did not see what it was until it was in my hand. It was a heavy, wet rag. She said, "Put it in the hamper from Grandma to wash." I was stunned by the weight, wetness, and warmth of the rag. I did not want to touch it but did not have a chance to reject it. It was already in my hand. Mom added, "You should wash your hands because it has pee in it."

All my pleasant feelings disappeared. I felt betrayed and treated like her lowly servant with no individual value. If I knew what she was handing to me, I would have refused. Mom was literally on the rag during her period. She used rags, washed them, and reused them. Apparently, Grandma did, too, only very discretely. Grandma had some humility while Mom was just disgusting. Today, she obviously did not want to struggle to the bathroom on crutches. When she saw me coming, she decided to pee into the rag and make me take care of it. It ruined all the good feeling I had about Mom being sober. She proved to me that she saw me as being at her disposal for the grossest of tasks, even when she was sober. I was deeply hurt by this incident. I avoided contact with her just as when she was drinking at home. My love-hate relationship with my mother became more complicated than simply a drunk and sober duality relationship.

After a while, our honeymoon ended. Mom decided that she could be at home. Gram said that we could stay for as long as Mom needed but respected her wishes to go home. I was happy on the farm and expected to stay there until school started. I even thought that we might start school in Springfield.

We set up the couch so Mom could sleep downstairs. She tried but could not sleep on the couch. She managed to go upstairs to sleep each night. She used the crutches as she was taught at the hospital. She used only one on the opposite side of the rail. With the crutch and the rail, she managed to get up the stairs ever so slowly and with great effort. I stood behind her to make certain that she did not fall backwards. Since the bathroom was downstairs, she used a pee pot during the night. We all took turns dumping it in the morning.

We settled at home. Oddly, I felt uncomfortable at home. I was accustomed to being uneasy on the farm with the strict rules. Now, at home, I felt unsupported. One very scary incident was when I saw Mom fall. She tried to step over the dog and suddenly fell face first over the dog, striking the couch and floor. The dog squirmed out from under her and ran into the kitchen. I ran to her and expected her to have done serious harm to her broken leg. She was OK. She explained that she did not want to disturb the dog and her toe got caught inside her pajama pants. I thought how foolish it is that she has such concern for animals. I was accustomed to Mom respecting the animal more than me, but

I never saw Mom place herself in such jeopardy for an animal. I was very capable of stepping over the dog but would have made him move if I were trying to go where Mom was going.

When her check came, Mom called Ray's Store. They were happy to have me back to help Aggie with stocking. She asked them to sell beer to her and I would pick it up. They refused because they would lose their vender's license. This is when I learned how addicted my mother had become. She had me walk with her to the store. She struggled on crutches even for short distances in the house. Now, she was walking almost a quarter mile to the store to get her beer. She stopped every few feet to rest. Mom paid for her beer. She took it off the counter and handed it to me to carry home, which was acceptable to Ray and Aggie. The best part was she did not go for a second six pack, so she did not get as drunk as before. She did go a second time once and nearly fell several times. I struggled to keep her upright as her weight was several times more than mine. Then she decided to just buy two six packs. Even with the two six packs, she was drinking less with her broken leg. Also, being handicapped, she could not easily beat us. With no car, there were no scary drunken rides. Though life at home was less peaceful than on the farm, it was still better than before the accident.

With Mom's broken leg, she had trouble reaching her feet. Debra washed her feet using a wash pan. This practice continued even when Mom healed enough to wash her own feet. When she was drunk, she would tell Debra to wash her feet. Debra always complied. I did not mind too much bringing a pan of water for her but I refused to wah her feet. Mom would tell the Biblical story of the man who washed Jesus' feet went to heaven. It bothered me a lot because it seemed like she was comparing herself to Jesus. As Debra washed Mom's feet and trimmed her toenails, Mom would say to Debra that she was such a good daughter. "I know you will always be around to take care of me. The others won't, but you will." From an early age, Mom groomed Debra to take care of her at a higher priority than Debra's own life.

As Mom's leg healed, Dr. Shoemaker told her to start bearing more weight on it. Soon, she was walking without crutches. Pop found an old Plymouth Fury for two hundred dollars. Our lives started to return to normal. We could go to a regular grocery store and visit Pop and Grandma every Sunday. Unfortunately, Mom had easier access to her beer and was back to her three six-pack a day binge when she had money. Her anger against my dad returned along with her desire to argue with us. Just as before, there was no escape. If we stayed outside, she called us in. Any attempts to avoid her only intensified her anger and verbal assaults. Similarly, if we talked back, she intensified the verbal assault and a physical attack was imminent. When we were younger, the spanking was the end of it. Now, hitting did not end the onslaught. Arguments could continue even in public. Mom was only more discrete about it in public. Instead of hitting us, she pinched our necks and arms or pulled our hair.

Even though Mom could negotiate the stairs, she still used the pee pot upstairs. Now, she filled it near the brim during nights when she had been drinking. It was challenging to carry it downstairs and dump it in the toilet without spilling any. We all took turns. Mom allowed us to use it rather than go downstairs. I realized this was mostly to justify making it a chore for all of us. I never used it. I would not want to go into the girls' room and expose myself especially when it was just as easy to go downstairs and use the toilet. I finally revolted against the pee pot chore. I stood with great courage against my mother and refused. I said that I did not use it and I was not going to dump it. I was surprised when she agreed so easily.

The tub filled with dirty clothes just like the days when we had no water. Mom still barged in when I cleared it to take a bath. She walked past me to the toilet. I found a door hook and installed it on the door. Finally, I could have certain privacy. Mom still pushed against the door opening it just enough to look in. She demanded that I open it right away. I wrapped myself in a towel and left the room, regardless of the state of my bath. When she left, I returned to get dressed.

I still hated handling the dirty clothes after my bath. I felt the disgusting wet ones unsuccessfully trying to move them with the dry clothes. I treated them as though they were wet with Mom's urine. I usually put off taking a bath until after Cilla and I did the laundry, which was not very often. I was getting bullied at school again.

Mom drove us into town to her friend's house for a visit. She commanded us to stay in the car as usual. It was hot in the car so we had the windows down. Stanley was nearby. I did not know him well but he struck up a conversation. As we spoke, he came closer. He was being sarcastic as he criticized us for staying in the car. He confirmed that our mother would punish us if we got out. Mom had been in the house for an exceptionally long time, now, and I wondered when she would be coming out. In the meantime, Stanley started challenging me to fight. When he was confident that I would not leave the car, he spit in my hair. It was gross, yet I was still more afraid of my mother than Stanley's humiliation. Finally, Mom came out and we left. I tried to wash my hair in the bathroom sink when we got home.

I am not sure what Mom was doing in that house. I know that she often spoke about real men that would love to treat her well. She hinted at her large breasts. She said women in her family all had large breasts. I noticed that this seemed to be true with Grandma and Aunt Alice. Mom's huge breast were only partly due to the genetics. I knew that their immense size was due mostly to her obesity. I did not see how anyone would find these attractive. I thought that she was gross.

We stopped a few times at a farm in North Charlestown. Again, we waited in the car while Mom went inside. Mom was cheerful when she came out. Though the farmer was older, she thought that he liked her. She said that he was looking for a housekeeper but she thought it would develop into much more. She fantasized about how happy we could be on his farm and that he was rich. Mom stopped there only one other time. It was brief and she spoke no more about him. The farm was sold. They demolished the farm buildings and built a Tampax factory on it.

Mom cut our hair with clippers. I was teased about my haircut. The crew cuts we had been deemed immature, only little kids had them. I asked Mom if I could let the top grow like other kids. She resisted at first. Mom saw nothing wrong with what she was doing and I should be thankful that she does a good job. After asking for weeks, she eventually agreed. My friends soon pointed out that my hair was parted on the wrong side. Mom parted it from her perspective as she cut my hair. She parted it form her left to right, not mine. My friends noted the poor quality of my haircut. After repeatedly pleading, Mom finally agreed to bring me to Martel's Barber Shop. He was slow and Mom was impatient. She dropped me off, with strict instructions that I was to leave upon her return. She did not want to wait for me. I was still waiting my turn when Mom drove in. Mr. Martel tried to assure me that I was next. I tried to explain that I had no choice but to leave with my mother. I did not know how it explain it without giving away any family relationship secrets. I knew that it was unusual for a mother to be so dominant that I could not wait like everyone else waits. Eventually, Danny told me about Don Ferland's Barber Shop in North Charlestown. He was fast and had early Saturday morning hours. Finally, I got professional haircuts. It helped my self-esteem considerably.

Mom was first one in the family to graduate high school. Grandma told me about when she and Pop went to school. Pop completed the sixth grade and she finished the eighth grade. Pop went to school where he lived in Salem, Massachusetts. She attended school in Canada before her family moved to Claremont. This was considered enough education at those times. She suggested that even though Pop completed sixth grade, he did not learn very much. He was one of the troublemakers. Grandma also showed to me her bathing suit. I asked her about Pop's. She explained that boys did not wear bathing suits. This puzzled me. Did he swim with his clothes on? Grandma said that he took his clothes off. I thought nudity was not allowed in our family. I also wondered why a boy would want to swim naked.

I admired Coach Silva in gym class. He taught us sports and was complimentary of things we did. I liked playing defense in soccer the best. I could block the ball and kick it hard to an offense player on my team. Couch Silva showed us how to do things properly. Even when we did it wrong, he found a portion that we did correctly, complimented us and kindly showed how we could improve. He could tell us how to improve without shame. I especially liked soccer and baseball, perhaps because I did best at these. Joining the school teams was entirely out of the question. Mom said that she did not have the gas money to transport me. I also realized that she would not always be sober enough to bring me.

One day, while playing volleyball in the gym, my glasses kept slipping off. I decided to place them on the bleachers far away from the court. Someone hit the ball high, nearly hitting the ceiling. I watched as it crested and descended towards my glasses. It seemed to fly with surreal slow motion and directly upon my glasses. My glasses bounced from the impact of the ball and went in two different directions. The nose bridge was broken. I brought them home to Mom. She repaired them with white adhesive tape. They looked awful and felt too loose. Kids picked on me. They called me "four eyes" much more than before. Mom said that we did not have enough money to get them fixed. I had always had trouble keeping them clean. I could only wipe smudges with my shirt so a film built up on the lens. The lenses always had a foggy film on them. Glasses were just too much trouble for the little benefit so I stopped wearing them.

Antagonists liked to call me "born in the sand." I hated it then. It was said in such a manner that it compared me to dirt. I was as worthless as dirt in the yard that no one wanted on their shoes. Making it worse, Pop always derogatorily referred to my father as "Sanborn" when he spoke poorly of him. My mother also referred to him that way, especially when she was drunk and, in her mood, to blame him for all her troubles. I tried to defend myself by explaining that Sanborn was English and I identify with my grandparent's French heritage. It never worked, so I tried ignoring them, which also did not work. After many years of this, I researched the name and learned that the family indeed had roots on a sandy bank in England. It also had a family crest. I became proud of knowing this part of my heritage and responded with agreement and a genuine curiosity about the heritage of anyone who called me "born in the sand." Most had no clue of their heritage.

Kids also picked on me about my lunch. Mom always made peanut sandwiches with margarine. Every school day morning, she placed eight slices of bread for our four sandwiches on the countertop. She then put peanut margarine on one slice and margarine on the other. She did it quickly and sloppily. There was just enough peanut butter to coat the bread. The margarine had big chinks. I hated the taste of margarine and I especially hated the lumps. I started to complain and got the usual dissertation about starving people in the world and I should be thankful that she keeps us out of awful foster homes. I asked if she would eliminate the margarine in my sandwich. She said, "No, I make them all the same." I asked if I could make my own. Again, she said "No." I struggled to eat around these large clumps of margarine.

Boys carried their books on their hips and girls carried theirs in front with their arms across them. The students who carried their lunch used brown paper bags and plastic sandwich bags. Mom placed our sandwich and two cookies in a plastic bread wrapper. She refused to waste money on paper bags. Plastic sandwich bags were not necessary with the plastic bread bag. Wonder Bread had a noticeable, colorful checkered design that was very predominant. Carrying my lunch in this colorful Wonder Bread bag was a loud signal to everyone that we were too poor to even buy brown bags. Even worse, because Mom did not use four loaves every day, we had to carry the empty bag back home. So, we carried this lower-class social identifier to and from school.

Jeff was a new kid in the eighth grade. Like many boys, he tried to establish himself in the hierarchy of dominance. Pat was in the undisputed lead. We all liked and respected him. No one challenged him. Pat matured earlier than most of us and was strong and athletic. For a reason that I could not understand,

Jeff challenged my friend Wayne to a fight after school. Wayne and I often wrestled. He was good, fast, and strong and always got the better of me. Wayne learned from his two older brothers. Looking at Jeff, I did not think he could beat me, but I sensed a lot of anxiety in my friend. When talking with Wayne, I knew it was not that he was afraid to fight. He did not understand why Jeff wanted to fight and especially why he picked a fight with him. Maybe he picked Wayne because Wayne was now shorter than most of us. Jeff's challenge began during shop class, with only boys. We worked on our wood projects. The girls went to a home economics class for cooking and sewing. When Mr. Cain, the shop teacher, was helping someone, we could move about and talk with others. Several people went to Jeff to try to convince him that he had picked on the wrong person. We all expected that Wayne would win decisively. Pat was the one to finally convince him. By the end of class, Jeff went to Wayne and apologized. They shook hands. Jeff was accepted by most of us and never was there another time he needed to prove himself. Jeff was popular with the girls, making me a little jealous of him. I easily beat him in math, so I was happy.

I had perfect attendance through junior high school. I did not like school any more than anyone else. I hated being home alone with Mom more. School was a safe place with unchanging rules and predictable outcomes. I excelled algebra and enjoyed the praise from Mrs. Hronek. She was the best and nicest teacher I had known. I was doing fine in the other classes. I hated history. I saw no value in learning what happened so long ago. Mr. Purington managed to make class interesting. I mostly liked how he presented things and not the topics. He liked to enforce discipline in his class with the threat of "beating with the raw end of a wet noodle."

During Mr. Purington's class is when bullies wrecked their havoc when he turned his back to the class. Mickey sat next to me. He liked to snap me with rubber bands. I asked him to stop many times but he liked getting away with doing it behind Mr. Purington's back. One day I had a rubber band. Just snapping him back was not enough. I wanted to do something decisive. I got a staple from the stapler. I straightened one side and bent the other enough to form an angle to hold onto the rubber band. When Mr. Purington turned his back, I launched the staple at Mickey's thigh like a slingshot. In its flight, it turned like an arrow. It stuck into Mickey's leg, through his pants and into his skin enough to show blood. I was satisfied and Mickey stopped snapping me with rubber bands.

I was proud to show Mom my report card with all the good grades. As she signed each quarter's report, she reminded me that junior high school was easy. I would have a lot harder time in high school and would not get such good grades. I was already beginning to doubt her warning. She never took algebra. Taking this high school class in the eighth grade validated that I could do high school math well.

I had great anticipation for the eighth-grade graduation ceremony. I was hoping that Dad would attend. Unfortunately, I developed a reaction to poison ivy. I reacted so severely that my arms, face, and legs swelled. I could barely open my eyes. I knew the poison ivy plant well and avoided it. Since Gary had developed it before me, we blamed him for passing it to me through the common bathroom towel. Since then, I realized that many germs can be transmitted through this towel. Ever since, I have avoided using a common towel to dry my hands. I either let them remain wet or wipe my hands on my clothes.

Collateral damages during the junior high school years.

Cilla and I had become increasingly aware that our lives were profoundly affected by our mother's drinking. Still, we were reluctant to consider her an alcoholic. Mom's denial was so powerful that it distorted our view of our family condition. Mom controlled our minds and body with violence, intimidation, humiliation, and shame. She blamed us for her being a victim, burdened with four children. We were more her servants than children learning to become competent and independent. Both my mother and grandfather continually reminded me that I was not good enough to do well in school. Mom's motive seemed to be to keep us around to take care of her. Pop similarly wanted us to work on his farm.

Mom often told us that we came first but she practiced the opposite. Most notably was the lack of money to buy basic needs. Growing up on welfare is poverty in ordinary circumstances. When she diverted a significant amount of the money to alcohol, the family struggled well below the poverty level. Feeding her addiction monster came first, not her kids. We were secondary to even the poor, dumb animals.

Mom treated us more as extensions of herself than as independent persons worthy of respect. We cared for her needs more than she met ours. The meager welfare income was because she had us as dependents. As time progressed and we grew older, we took care of everything including heating with firewood, cooking meals, doing laundry, and what little housework got done. She refused to compromise even for simple things such as reducing or even eliminating butter in my peanut butter sandwich or letting me make my own sandwich.

Mom also groomed us for our life roles. She wanted me to be a truck driver and remain near home to help her financially because Dad had abandoned her. I willingly gave her the money

I earned. Even stone cold sober, she tricked me into taking care of her urine-soaked rag in my bare hands. Mom groomed Gary to fail with subtle comments such as always falling on his head. She groomed Debra to take care of her physical needs such as washing her feet and emptying the urine pail. Mom harassed Cilla about her relationships with boys, accusing her of sexual activity that was unfounded.

Mom labeled herself as super mom. Being a mother gave women special abilities and honor. The title "Mom" was a term of endearment that I felt less and less. Cilla and I started calling her "Mother." It was an undeniable fact that she was my mother. I did not feel she deserved my acceptance of endearment to be "Mom."

My mother was saving us from a horrible foster placement. She frequently reminded us that we had it much better than she had as a child. We could see some of Pop's strict control of the family in the way she controlled us. There was a remarkable difference. Though Pop methods were similar with intimidation, there was no real violence to validate what Mother described as "getting the belt." Pop spoke of the whole family as having higher level morality and identifying and defending against harmful people and beliefs. Pop was always at his mental and physical best, never letting his guard down. Mother allowed her alcoholism to bring her to incapacitation, mentally at first and eventually physically. Each time Mother drank, she transgressed through happy, demanding, mean, self-pity then outright hostility. Our relief came when she went to bed.

Cilla and I grew more aware of our social status and resented it. We had little power over the social signals we displayed such as our clothes, hygiene, the Wonder Bread lunch bag, and isolation from social groups and events.

We were isolated from any authority that might help us and there was little oversight from the Welfare Department. We were kept from talking with the welfare lady, Mrs. Rene. Had she taken some initiative and learned more about our demise, Mrs. Rene would have had to do more and likely had few resources at her disposal. It was better to just not notice. When we went to Pop and Gram for assistance, we learned their lack of power over Mother's addiction. All we did was sadden them, then regretted telling them. Most of all, we lived in a society that did not respond to the clues and realize we were a family that needed intense assistance. Even when a teacher reported Debra's poor hygiene, there was little follow up.

We recognized that we did not fit with the rest of society. It is not racism when everyone is the same race. It is classism. We felt the prejudice of being in a social class that burdened a society that would rather ignore our existence. My mother accepted the limitations of our social class by telling me other people could do things that we could not. I resented these constraints.

I was learning that Mother was not always right. I was already far beyond her education in math. I could escape her domineering control in several ways. Her drunken early bedtimes gave me my first opportunities to develop some autonomy. Spending time out of the house with my friends gave me access to real world experiences independent of Mother's interpretations and control. I could develop my own identity and values with my peers. I was beginning mild defiance by avoiding her to be with these friends.

We all tend to perform a little differently in our various activities such as work, school, extended family, and community. We may even play different psychological roles in these places. These differences are more extreme with children in alcoholic homes. My mother's extreme dominance necessitated separation of my activities. In every place, no one knew the extent of what was going on in my home. I was hypervigilant and super responsible in all areas. I strived to foresee and head off anything that might interfere with my responsibility to perform above expectations in all areas. My stress levels were always high.

Adults with the responsibility failed or chose not to notice our family condition. Most notable was the welfare worker. Her interventions were minimal but at least there was some benefit. We got some dental care and moved out of a house with no water during the winter.

I was beginning to benefit from adults outside the family. They were teachers. Mrs. Hronek's praise and encouragement in algebra boosted my confidence. Coach Silva was a strong, competent role model who recognized and encouraged my efforts. I benefitted when a teacher who reported my little sister's account for why she could not take a bath because we had no water.

HIGH SCHOOL YEARS

Adding to the many things going on in my life, five communities pooled resources to build Fall Mountain Regional High School. It made many more courses available, including calculus, which was not offered in Charlestown. At this time, I only knew calculus was a higher-level math course, so I was in favor of it. Mother told me that I would never make it into such a high-level course. She was wrong.

There were a lot of surveys about what the students wanted for such things as school colors and a mascot. I had little interest in it but some girls were highly motivated and campaign intensely to win their choices. Their campaigns became intense.

School officials informed us of the rules for the new high school. The dress code was strict. Jeans were not allowed. Boys had to wear dress pants. Shirts had to have a collar and hair had to be cut to stay off the collar and ears. Leather shoes, not sneakers, were required. Sneakers and a school issue gym uniform were required for gym class. We had to buy the gym uniform for two dollars and fifty cents. Mother was angry about it even though I used my own money to buy it, the sneakers and all my school clothes. Girls had to wear dresses. The length of girls' dresses was tightly regulated. When there was a question about the length of the dress, girls knelt on a chair. The dress had to be no more than two inches off the chair. I remember seeing girls being measured in the office went I passed by as we passed through the halls. They were sent home when their dress was too short. I remember one girl crying intensely.

All students would ride the bus. The school was in the geographic center of the five towns, in the most rural area. The driveway alone was longer than the previous students walked to school. No student could drive to school. Later, there was an exception for those who had a job that required them to start very soon after school. These requests were verified and exceedingly rare.

We were assigned lockers. They were in section of two. Two narrow upright sections to hold our jackets and a compartment above for books. The combination lock had a pass key in the handle. There was little time between classes or at the end of lunch to exchange books. Many of us set the lock halfway through the combination. This way, we only had to turn the combination to the final number to open the locker. It made it much easier when everyone was trying to get into these lockers at the same time. Occasionally, an angry student walked down the hall spinning each locker combination, thereby defeating anyone's attempt for quick access.

I was five feet, nine inches tall and weighed one hundred sixty-five pounds, exactly my father's size, when I started high school. I was younger than most of my fellow students, starting high school at thirteen years old. I was rapidly growing bigger than the ones who had bullied me. I was also in higher level classes than they were. I only saw them in gym class, study hall and lunch. I outgrew them intellectually more than physically.

It took a while for me to get acclimated to the much bigger school and students from the other towns. There was some intense rivalry between people from Walpole and Charlestown. We were previously sports competitors, now we were supposed to be on the same team. Academically, we were competing for the higher grades. One of these Walpole students was Glen. He took up the bullying the Charlestown bullies stopped. He was always sarcastic and condescending to me. I could beat him both physically and academically, but this did not stop him. One day, an opportunity presented itself and I took the opportunity. We were both entering the English class at the same time. I was on the outside of the corner. It was clear that he intended to humiliate me by crowding me out, making me wait to let him in the classroom. On an impulse, I turned prematurely, quickly, and strongly crashing into him, which caused him to crash into the lockers lining the hallway. Since he carried his books on his hip like the rest of us, his books and papers scattered as he stumbled and fell to the floor. It made him late to class. When the teacher complained, he said it was my fault. I apologized to the teacher, saying it was an accident. Nothing came of it. I had made it clear to Glen that I was willing to do this and perhaps other things if he continued to bully me. Not only would I fight back, but I was also clever enough to get away with it. He backed off to a much more tolerable level. I could ignore his occasional sarcasm. Spaz, queer, moron, and dip shit were common insults projected upon inferiors.

A common mischief during lunch time was to pop an empty milk cartoon by stomping on it. Most of the time, teachers supervising lunch would punish such activity with a detention. Some mischief makers managed to pop it without the teacher being able to identify the culprit. Other teachers did not bother to try. The greatest prank was when someone managed to coax another into stomping on a full cartoon believing that it was empty. Milk sprayed, making a terrible mess. The culprit was easy to identify with milk running down his leg. Penance was to clean it up. A mop and pail were available in the utility at the rear of the kitchen.

Even though I could demonstrate my intellectual and physical abilities, there are subtle actions to keep me in my place, the lower social class. They would not let me join their social groups. Each group had its own subculture. There were the jocks. Even the jocks had divisions according to the sport they played. There were the socialites, delinquents, and geeks. I came closest to the geek class but remained mostly in the class with other low-income students. One example of how I was kept in my place was when we were playing basketball in gym class. We played a lot more basketball than I liked because I was not good at it. During a game, Matt thought it was funny to sneak up behind Jon and pull his pants down as he shot a basket. Jon was humiliated with his pants around his knees and underwear exposed. Matt laughed, pointing at him to intensify the humiliation. Matt backed away from Jon, towards me, and still laughing. I grabbed his pant legs but only pulled them down a couple of inches. Matt immediately stopped laughing, turned towards me saying, "What's wrong with you?" as he readjusted his pants. That comment hurt. I did less than what he had done to Jon but I am someone with something wrong. Matt remained a class clown through high school. He enjoyed attention I sought to avoid.

Cilla, more than I, felt the social pressures at school. I was physically bullied less. Many of them were no longer coming to school, whether they were truant or drop out. I was also growing bigger while some bullies stopped growing. I was beginning to understand that it was easier for bullies to demean and bring others down to their level than it was to build themselves up. They attacked weak people, such as me, who was doing better academically than they were doing. I could not escape the ridicule related to my low-income social class, the poor kids. I did not have the financial means to buy the nicer things, to do proper hygiene, or experience the social activities that help young people develop. There was also much resistance from my family, "other people do those things," followed by excuses explaining we could not. Of course, there was never enough money. I was growing more resentful of the money lost to my mother's beer drinking.

I was especially ridiculed for such things as carrying my lunch in a Wonder Bread bag. When I wore a jacket, I could stuff it in a pocket but it still bulged noticeably. One day, our social worker Mrs. Rene, came to visit. She told us about the free lunch program. We filled out some forms and were automatically qualified because we were on welfare. It required me to go to the nurse, Mrs. MacIver, every Monday morning and sign a form. She then gave me a meal ticket. The same meal ticket that other students bought each week. Everyone knew why I went to the nurse on Mondays. With this small exception, I was like a normal kid. I ate normal hot lunch, using a regular lunch ticket. Every kid just wants to be normal. This was one small way to help my self-esteem in a big way.

The free hot lunch program was going well. One day, the nurse asked if we were able to contribute any money to the program. I asked Mother when I got home. She said for me to tell the nurse that Mrs. Rene said that we did not have to pay anything. I dutifully told the nurse, "Mrs. Rene said that we don't have to pay," the next time I signed for the meal ticket. The nurse responded, "Mrs. Rene does not run the program." She then seemed to regret her response and told me not to worry. This was all still much less than any humiliation I endured from my fellow students when I carried the Wonder Bread bag.

We were required to read *"The Catcher in the Rye"* by JD Salinger. It seemed like a formidable task at first but as I read the book, I felt a connection to Holden. He was unhappy with his life. He had several people criticizing him but maintained his dignity despite these assaults on his self-esteem. He was also a daydreamer, which I did a lot. Like me, his only confidant was his sister with whom he had a tenuous relationship. With all these negative influences in his life, he maintained his personal integrity. Holden and I had a lot in common. I also liked the *"The Grapes of Wrath."* I could identify with the family struggles, the poverty, and the fear of the vehicle breaking down. *"The Voyage to the Center of the Earth"* and *"The Voyage to the Moon"* gave to me the science fiction I needed to fuel my daydreams.

There was a lot of discussion at school about naming the yearbook, deciding on *"The Lamplighter."* I asked Mother about what a yearbook was. She said that I did not need one until my graduation year. She shamed me to continue contributing my earnings to the household again. When the yearbooks came, I realized how important they were in connecting with classmates and school spirit. Years later, I strongly resented my mother's selfishness or at the very least a disregard for her kids' needs and feelings. I missed buying the very first yearbook published at this new school when I could have paid for it with my own earnings. It was only three and a half dollars. Something I could have easily bought with my own earnings.

Cilla started babysitting at the neighbors. Alec was my friend Wayne's older brother. He had three young sons. Sometimes

Wayne and I visited Cilla and played cards while she babysat. With my success in science classes, Wayne asked if I knew how to make alcohol. I set up some fermentation: yeast, sugar, and water in two sealed jars. After three weeks, one exploded. We tried the other one. It tasted horrible. They fermented yeast dominated the flavor. I did not have the ability to distill it.

Cilla refused to give her babysitting money to Mother like I did, even though Mother pressured her as she did me. Cilla felt strongly that she earned her money and wanted to spend it on clothes and music. She was very much into the Beatles. She tried to get me interested but music was not that important to me, then. Years later, Cilla told me about the intense fights she was having with Mother. Mother was even accusing her of having sex with my friends when we stopped by during her baby sitting. Her accusations were baseless but that did not matter to super Mother. She could tell by using her motherhood superpowers. I suspected that Mother's motive was to sabotage Cilla's growing independence by making it intolerable.

Cilla and Gary developed a regular smoking habit. We did not fully understand the health effects. I was not interested mostly because I did not like it but I felt it was just a waste of hard-earned money. One day, while playing with my friends, we were setting off firecrackers. Wayne liked putting one under a soup can and launching it in the air. It went surprisingly high. I thought about how funny it would be to put one in a cigarette, like the exploding cigars on TV. I also hoped that it might discourage Gary from smoking. I brought one home and waited for Gary to leave his cigarettes unattended. I pulled one from the back and carefully rolled it between my fingers to get the tobacco to fall out. I removed most of the tobacco from the firecracker. I cut the fuse to about one-quarter inch long and inserted the firecracker into the empty cigarette. Since firecracker's diameter was less than the cigarette, I carefully packed the tobacco beside the firecracker using tweezers. Finally, with great effort, I packed the tobacco on the end. Getting the density to look normal without crushing the paper was the hardest part.

I waited for hours for Gary to smoke a cigarette. I was disappointed that I was not home when he finally lit the trap I had set. He described it to me when I got home. He said that he lit the cigarette and took a draw on it. Within a few seconds, he heard the strange hiss of the fuse. It puzzled him and he lifted the cigarette to look closely at it. Just then it exploded. He said it blew the cigarette completely out of his hand and scattered flaming pieces all over the room. He struggled to extinguish the embers in several places. Though I was pleased with my success, I felt a bit guilty about the danger I presented to my little brother. It was in vain as he continued smoking.

Coach Silva was one of the Charlestown teachers that came to Fall Mountain Regional High School to be the physical education teacher. I was additionally pleased when he taught my biology course. Even though he taught basically from the book, I admired his knowledge and explanations. He was very capable of helping students understand complex structures and relationships. His tests were fair and I did well.

Coach Silva conducted gym class with equal skill and fairness. He was required to test our physical abilities, even gymnastics. We were tested on pull ups, sit ups, standing on our heads, climbing a rope, etc. I climbed the rope well, all the way to the ceiling, thanks to my farm boy strength. However, the height scared me. The trampoline was fun. Jimmy Gardner was fantastic on it and the high bar. He looked like an Olympian.

Outside, we played our usual soccer, baseball, and tag football. I did well, most of the time. I still liked playing a defensive position in soccer the best. I was doing better at baseball, both batting and fielding. I did not like football. Even though it was tag football, blocking was violent. I got hit hard once. Hard enough that I felt hurt deep inside my abdomen. Later, I developed a hernia. I am not sure if it was this injury or my grandfather's pressing me to work beyond my strength.

Coach Silva seemed be unhappily fulfilling the requirement when he made showering after gym class mandatory. He made sure everyone was in the shower room before we could come out. So many of us crowded naked in the showers. I was uncomfortable being naked but accepted that there was no choice.

My classmate, Joanne Dunham, lived in the trailer park near my house. We rode the bus together. Her family moved to the trailer park nearer Claremont early in our freshman year but still rode the same bus. She was a nice, quiet girl who was liked by all her classmates. She did not come to school on the third day, which was unusual for her. No one noticed anything wrong until she did not come home. Her parents thought that she was in school all day. We later learned that she was abducted from the bus stop. There was an intensive search for her and there were many rumors. Three days later, my friend Danny's father found her body using his dog. Joanne's new home was not far from his farm. I understood Danny's father's dedication to persist in searching for her. He was a kind, considerate and devoted church member. We learned that she was found not far from the bus stop. Later, the rumors were that she was raped. There were many suspects and lots of finger pointing and worrying about the safety of others who waited for the bus or walked to school. Her killer was never found. We have never forgotten her. Our senior yearbook was dedicated in her memory.

Mother continued bringing inconsistency in my life. I later learned that she was trying to establish a relationship with Herb Blake, a mechanic in North Charlestown. She first went to him looking for discounted services due to our plight. From there she tried to develop an intimate relationship. It surprised me because he was already married. He apparently rebuffed her, making her angry. She ranted about it for a while then decided to call the police. When Chief Joe Gibson arrived, she came out on the porch to meet him. Cilla stood behind her. Chief Gibson stood outside his car with the door open, one foot inside the car. I listened from across the driveway, on the opposite side of his car. Mother said that Herb tried to pick up Cilla along the road. I knew this was a lie and was surprised to hear my mother make such an accusation. She went on to explain that the police should consider him as a suspect in the Joanne Dunham murder. Chief Gibson tried to appease her while seemingly giving no credibility to what she was saying. I expected that Mother's statement made no sense with what the police must have already known about Joanne's murder. Chief Gibson appeared uncomfortable with the conversation and struggled to end it as he slowly got back in his car. Afterwards, Mother was satisfied that the police would now make Herb's life exceedingly difficult. This blatantly false seriously damaged my trust in my mother. Lying was wrong. Purposely trying to severely hurt someone with a lie was incomprehensible to me.

One Saturday morning, I was doing dishes in the kitchen. Cilla had babysat late the night before and was sleeping upstairs. Mother was sitting in her usual place near the television. We heard Cilla yelling at Gary. Normally, such yelling was brief when Gary retreated. This time, the yelling grew more intense followed by some loud banging. I thought Mother would go intervene but she could not climb stairs very well. We suspected that Gary was getting bigger and would no longer retreat from Cilla and he was hurting her. I ran up the stairs to protect my sister. When I got to her bedroom, I saw what I never expected. Cilla was straddling Gary who was on the floor on his back. She had his ears in her hands and she was slamming his head repeatedly on the floor. I was greatly relieved that Cilla was alright. I was not so worried about Gary, knowing that he was likely getting what he deserved. I laughed as I watched Gary so helpless against Cilla's volatile temper. Nonetheless, Mother sent me to settle the ruckus. I approached Cilla and started to take her left arm. She rose off Gary with my gentle pull but gave one last hard punch to his chest with her right hand. Gary was crying and slowly crawled away. Cilla in all her fury yelled, "He would not leave my room and let me sleep when I told him to get out." We left Cilla alone.

School continued with all the other things in our lives. There were seven periods at school. Everyone was expected to take a full course load of five classes. Lab science classes were paired with a study hall so that once weekly there was a double period for the lab. Gym class was twice weekly with the other three days as study hall. Drivers education was also twice weekly during one of these study halls. Since there were so many students taking study halls, the primary place was the cafeteria. During the staggered lunch times, it was in the large room that opened from three classrooms with movable walls.

Two teachers were assigned to study hall duty. Seats were assigned so that the teacher could quickly go about the cafeteria to complete the attendance in a timely manner. They took attendance first, then students with passes from their classroom teacher could be signed out. If there was not already too many with passes to the library, others could go to a certain limit. One day, my neighbor Mickey sat on the table with his feet on the seat during attendance. Mr. Kerylow taught math, including calculus. His wife was a gym teacher. He was tall and strong with a deep voice. He politely told Mickey to sit in the seat. Mickey refused. Mr. Kerylow told him that he must sit in the seat or go to the office. Mickey said, "F*** you!" Mr. Kerylow grabbed Mickey by the front of his shirt using his left hand. He continued to hold the pen and clip board in his right hand in the same position as when he took attendance. He picked Mickey off the table with one hand, carried him to the wall and held him up against the wall, Mickey's toes barely touching the floor. He held Mickey at his eye level, I could not hear what he was saying to him. Mr. Kerylow then carried Mickey out of the cafeteria and across the hall to the office. He placed Mickey in a chair in the office and spoke briefly to the secretary. Mr. Kerylow then returned to taking attendance as though nothing happened. I never saw Mickey again. I was impressed with Mr. Kerylow's strength and calm demeanor when others would show intense anger.

As a freshman, I took geometry with Mrs. Hicks. She was a good teacher but extremely strict. I did not like geometry. It seemed like a lot of memorization for no particular benefit. We were expected to memorize theorem proofs and write them perfectly for the quiz. My home was far too chaotic to study. Fortunately, geometry was first period. I could memorize the theorem on the bus ride to school and regurgitate the proof for the quiz, then promptly forget it. It was two years later that geometry made any sense to me. It was during my junior year, while studying trigonometry in advanced math.

As a sophomore, I took algebra two. I was so happy to have Mrs. Hronek again. While waiting in the hall with her before class began one day, she asked me what I was going to study in college. I told her what my family had always told me. I would not be going to college. We could not afford it. My mother was encouraging me to be a truck driver because they made a lot of money. Mrs. Hronek said that money from a family was not necessary to attend college. This puzzled me. I shared the reasons repeated so many times from my mother that I would not be able to go to college. Others accepted my explanation but Mrs. Hronek would not accept it. After class, she said, "Come with me." She brought me to the guidance counselor, Mr. Livengood. After Mrs. Hronek briefly explained my abilities and lack of money, she asked him to explain how I could attend college. I had never heard about scholarships. He assured me that he could find the money for me to attend college if I kept my grades up. We should start the process in September of my senior year. He suggested Saint Michael's College. He said that it was a good school and he had just completed a master's program there. By doing this simple act of encouragement, Mrs. Hronek became the most influential person in directing my life away from poverty and alcoholism. Mrs. Hronek's influence went beyond this brief encounter. She had demonstrated to me many traits, including intelligence, caring, dedication, trustworthiness, and so much more. It was because she had earned my trust that I would even consider what she was suggesting so contrary to the messages I got from my family.

I discussed this with Mother when I got home. She tried to convince me that college was not necessary. All I needed was a good high school education and I could make plenty of money as a truck driver. I countered with my passion for math and science. I wanted to either teach math or become a doctor. She conceded, "Alright. You should mention this to your grandfather because he is the only one with any money to help me."

Cilla, Gary, and I continued working on the farm every summer. Cilla mostly worked the vegetable stand while Grandma tended to her household chores. Gary and I worked with Pop in the field. Gary kept making mistakes. Pop's anger increased to the point that he sent Gary back to the house. For Pop, this was a great punishment, to tell someone that their work is unacceptable. For Gary, it was a reward. It was like some students who like to get suspended from school. Gary's reward made more work for me. Making matters worse, I had to listen to Pop complain about Gary and how it was my father's fault. Compounding my agony was when Pop told Mom and she nagged me about how I failed to control my brother. This contributed to my deteriorating relationship with my brother.

Grandma was a true matriarch, working, caring, and praying for her family. She was teaching us more of her home remedies. She explained the importance of having regular bowel movements. She treated cuts with iodine or mercurochrome. These were dark, reddish brown solutions in a small glass bottle with a glass applicator attached to the inside of the bottle cap. It had a burning sensation as it killed the germs. Band aides were limited so we just did our best to keep it clean. She dug out slivers with a needle. Sometimes she pulled the bigger ones out with tweezers. She treated nausea with a combination of vinegar and baking soda. We had to swallow it while it was still fizzing. It would either make us feel better or cause us to vomit. Either way, we got better. Grandma taught us the importance of a healthy diet. She described a mistake a neighbor's son made by eating too many green apples. He developed intense stomach pains. He had to jump back and forth over a chair until his bowels finally move.

I waited to find the courage and an opportunity to tell Pop that I wanted to go to college like Mother told me to do. Finally, one day while hoeing cucumbers, I took a deep breath and told him, "I want to go to college." My grandfather immediately responded with a loud, degrading "What!?" I defended myself by explaining what Mrs. Hronek told me that I should go. He said that she was wrong. He added that I was too stupid to even hoe cucumbers properly. I would never be able to attend college. For the remainder of the day, he barraged me with similar degrading criticism. He told me that I was too stupid, like my father. He went to college and failed as soon as he started it. I withdrew emotionally and tried hard to tune out his words but they burned deep inside me. As my anger grew, I remembered how Mrs. Hronek and the guidance counselor assured me that there would be a way to go to college with scholarships and loans. I decided that I would do it without his help. I was doubly motivated to prove him wrong by succeeding at college and without his help. Negatively comparing me to my father was taking a toll on me, too. Yes, half of me came from my father but my father was never so cruel as my mother. No matter how much he criticized my father, he could not undo the connection. I never mentioned college to him again.

Mother decided it was time to have "the talk" with me. She called me from my room and told me to sit beside her. She took a long drink from her beer then started by explaining. A little boy's privates were sometimes called peanuts because they were about the size of peanuts. She explained that a woman got pregnant when "a man stuck his thing in her." She asked if I understood what she meant. I said I did because she obviously did not want to say any more and I did not care to listen to her vague descriptions. She said "Good, then you can explain this to your brother." I agreed. She added, "Because his thing is the first thing around the corner when he came downstairs in the morning." He wore only his underwear so it was obvious. She then explained that we can relax an unwanted erection by rubbing our inner thighs and demonstrated rubbing her hands with thumbs pressing hard on the inner thighs while bending forward. We could do this until we got married, then it would be different. I realized that Mother had no idea what she was talking about because it did not work. I did speak to Gary and told him that he should put his pants on if he was going downstairs with a hard on. He was embarrassed that it was noticed and corrected the problem.

Gary told Mother that he wanted to start shaving. I had been wanting to for a long time for her approval. My sideburns and mustache were looking quite scruffy. I was surprised and disappointed when Mother readily agreed that Gary could start shaving. I expected her to tell him that I had to be the first one. We were both disappointed when Mother would not buy razors for us. She gave us her tube of Nair, the cream she used to remove hair on her legs and upper lip. It burned our skin, making it obvious to our peers that we used women's hair cream on our face. It was another source of ridicule by our peers. I decided to stop applying it to my sideburns, which made large, reddened areas. It was bad enough having a red upper lip for several days. I later took an advantage porkchop sideburns popularized by Elvis Presley. Growing these sideburns covered the acne with which I struggled. Mother did not provide proper hygiene materials to treat it.

Mother cut costs in other areas. We did not have toothbrushes, toothpaste, or fingernail clippers. We shared a common comb, which I hated using. The nail clippers were unnecessary because we bit our nails. Oddly, Mother yelled at us for biting our nails even though she bit hers. Additionally, nail biters were ridiculed at school. I decided that I would stop biting mine, which I did abruptly with strong will power. The problem now was that my fingernails grew long. With no clippers, I peeled them off, often tearing too close, causing painful fingertips that sometimes bled.

To get away from Mother and to have some fun, we played hide and seek in the wooded area across the street. It was perfectly set up with natural boundaries, stone wall on the north, power lines on the east, a brook on the south, and an open field on the west. Those days, we drank from the brook with no concern. Mom assured us that if the water was flowing, it was safe to drink. My school buddies made it more exciting. Sometimes, we used BB guns and played war. I climbed to the top of a small pine tree and watched Chester walk by, directly below me. However, I leaned a little too much and the top bent over and broke. I fell backwards, still holding the broken treetop. I hit the ground hard on my back with the treetop on top of me. I had heard the phase, "getting the wind knocked out," but this was the first time that I had felt it. I could not breathe for a few seconds, then got up like nothing had happened.

The next-door neighbors had a large, clear area in front of their house. It would be a nice place to play soccer. I discussed asking for permission with my friends. Robert warned me that they would not let us. I decided to try. When I knocked on the front door, the woman called from an adjacent window, "Yes." I explained that we would like to play soccer in her field. She said no, adding that we had plenty of other places to play. She added that they operated a pottery business and did not want us interfering with her business. I did not understand how we would impact her business but accepted her decision. I felt that she was being cruel and selfish.

Her field was covered with tall grass most of the time. There were some dead mullein stems sticking up. These woody stems made good swords and spears. I sneaked over now and then to grab one, nervously listening for the neighbor's voice yelling at me. They either did not notice or care.

Our religion became important, again. We were the age when we are supposed to receive the Catholic sacrament of Confirmation. The first sacrament was baptism soon after birth. The second was the First Holy Communion at six years old. Confirmation is a practice during early adolescence when good Catholics confirm their faith. Cilla, Gary, and I were within the accepted age for Confirmation. Mother brought is to church again, but she did not come inside. She did not like the way church members stared at her. I expect that she felt judged for our condition, especially our clothes. Due to her large size, Mother had only one dress. It hung over her like a tent. She had only tennis shoes, which she hated because they restricted her broad feet. So, Mother remained in the car while we attended Mass followed by Catechism. She read the paper and romance novels or worked on her crossword puzzles. She also did these things at home when she had no beer. The Catechism classes prepared us specifically for Confirmation. We did it all in a great religious ceremony with many of our friends from school. With this done, we stopped going to church.

Every Sunday afternoon, we went to the farm to visit Pop and Grandma. One day, we had the rare occasion when Uncle Pat came. Uncle Pat was Pop's brother. His name was really Philip but everyone called him Pat. This was common in our family, beginning with Pop. His name was Vital but everyone called him Vic. My name is George but my maternal family called me Michael, my middle name.

Uncle Pat asked us about our plans for when we grew up. I proudly told him that I wanted to be a priest. I expected Uncle Pat to praise me because he was active in our church and played the organ during services. I did not expect his response, "Well, that's an easy enough life." It puzzled me because I often heard from priests at how hard they were working. I began seriously reconsidering my choice of profession.

We rarely had friends to our house. Primarily, we worried that Mom would be drinking and very irrational. Drunk or sober, Mom's behavior was quite different when one of us had a friend in our house. She seemed more like a silly schoolgirl trying to impress the friend. Her silliness was intensified when she was drinking.

It was exceedingly rare that Danny and I connected outside of school. After school communications were hampered because he lived in North Charlestown and had a Claremont telephone exchange. Calling him by telephone was a toll call. We managed to go to each other's house only a couple of times. His first time at mine, we went across the street into the woods. I brought my twenty-two-caliber rifle, hoping to get a woodchuck or squirrel. We did not find anything to shoot but enjoyed walking through the woods. As we came out, Danny wanted to see a spent bullet. I shot into a sand bank and he dug it out. As we continued towards my house, we saw a game warden talking to our neighbor. They were looking at the beaver dam. He looked at us and continued talking with the neighbor. I thought nothing of it and put my gun away when I got home. As he drove away, he noticed us in the yard and drove in. He confirmed that it was us that shot the bullet. He said that we were too close to houses and asked if I had a hunting license. I produced it and he took the information. I disagreed with him that we were less than the three hundred feet required. I added that we even had the bullet, so no danger was presented to anyone. He persisted in lecturing me about being wrong so I expressed my desire to go measure it. It only angered him. He said that his normal area was Keene and he was in this area only to cover the warden who was on vacation. He did not like that I was being a wise guy to him and said that he would leave it up to the area warden whether to take my license from me. He affirmed that if I were wise to any other game warden that I would lose my license. This really soured my respect of him and other law enforcement. He seemed like a bigger bully than any school bully. I was developing a stereotyped understanding of bullies as lacking reason and intelligence. He confirmed this idea.

When I was in junior high school, one of the daring challenges was to jump the entire set of stairs beside the school. Hesitant at first, I worked my way into it. I ran at half speed, landed on a stair halfway down, then jumped to the bottom. I did not make it all the way the first attempt to jump the entire set of stairs. I fell on the bottom two stairs. I confronted my fears and went all in. I ran at full speed and vaulted the entire set of stairs. The landing was hard, but it was thrilling. I gained admiration among my reckless peers. I landed harder than usual once and bruised my heel. I hobbled around for days. I stopped jumping the stairs.

I started high school and Gary attended the junior high school now. One day, Mother was waiting for me to get off the bus at home. She told me to get in the car and that Gary was at the doctor's office. We drove to the doctor's office in Charlestown. The receptionist escorted us into one of the examination rooms. The doctor was swabbing blood out of Gary's ear as he laid on the examination table. My brother did not look well. He was pale and unusually quiet. The doctor explained that the ambulance was on the way and Gary would be transported to Dartmouth-Hitchcock Medical Center. Springfield Hospital is the hospital where we would normally go. Dartmouth-Hitchcock was for the most serious cases. He explained that blood was coming from

Gary's ear because he had a fractured skull. They found him at the bottom of the stairs I used to jump. I knew right away that Gary had jumped the stairs and crashed, hitting his head on the ground. No one verified that happened but I knew. I was not going to tell them. Gary knew that I used to jump these stairs. Mother would blame me for Gary's injury if she knew.

The ambulance arrived and they transferred Gary onto the stretcher. As they loaded him into the back of the ambulance, they invited me to ride in the front seat with the driver. Mother told me to go with Gary and she would follow in the car. I got in the front seat. It felt strange in the front of the large Cadillac ambulance. The driver got in and told me to put on my seatbelt. I struggled a little with the lap belt. This was the first time that I had ever worn one. Our cars did not even have seatbelts.

The driver fastened his seatbelt. The car was already running with its lights flashing. He shifted it into drive and drove out of the parking lot and onto the highway. He accelerated quickly while turning on the siren. The seriousness of Gary's condition started to impact me. It felt like a heavy weight just appeared on my chest. The driver drove past cars that were pulling over for him. The seriousness felt even heavier. He drove past the tollbooth at the Cheshire Bridge. The attendant was out of the booth and had traffic stopped. I had only seen him do this for the trains that crossed this bridge owned by the railroad company. We drove onto the new interstate highway. He turned off the siren with the lesser traffic. I tried to look at the speedometer but could not see it very well. As we traveled at this high rate, the driver glanced at me a couple of times. He said, "It's OK, you can cry." I realized then that he was also worried about me. Though I understood that my brother's condition was serious, I did not feel like crying. I thought the driver expected me to cry and, if

I did not, there must be something wrong with me. He might think that I did not care about my brother. I forced myself to cry because I thought he expected it.

We drove off the interstate highway, through the Town of Hanover and around the hospital to the emergency entrance. Traffic got out of our way. We did not need the siren. I suspected that the people of Hanover were used to ambulances going to this large hospital. The driver quickly and skillfully backed up to the entrance. I got out and watched as they unloaded Gary. He was quiet as he looked towards me. He still looked pale. I followed into the hallway and was directed to sit in a chair as they brought Gary into an examination room. It seemed like a long time until Mother arrived. The nurse updated her on their progress. Gary was in the Xray Department. As we waited for an awfully long time, the doctor came and explained that Gary was doing fine at this time. He was worried that his brain might swell, so he would have to stay in the hospital at least overnight so they could monitor him. We went in to see Gary. We could not stay long. We said our goodbyes and went home.

I went to school the next day and Mother went to the hospital. Gary was home when I got off the bus after school. He was supposed to stay in bed for three days and take it easy for a week. He recovered fine.

I was doing well in school, despite Mother's prediction that I would struggle. She asked me one day, "Are you still saying your prayers at night?" I assured her that I was. She replied, "No wonder you are so lucky." Given Uncle Pat's comment about easy life and knowing my scholastic success was related to my hard work, I began to seriously question the influence of faith upon my life. I especially wondered. If I was so lucky and life so easy, why was it so hard with Mother's drinking?

I spent more time with my friends to escape the madness at home when Mother drank. I did not spend much time with them over the summer because I was required to help my grandfather on the farm. Friends were a welcomed means to escape for me during school times. At school was the best time for me to coordinate activities with them. We often road our bikes around the area. Sometimes we met at Wayne's house to play pool. Other times we went swimming in the Connecticut River. Other times we explored the Fort at Number Four that was being constructed. They had the main meeting building with a tower and a few attached buildings. We could wiggle between the upright logs barricading the complex. Once inside the perimeter, one of us climbed up the overlapping log corners and into the window on the main building. Once inside, we could unlatch the door and let the others in.

It was remarkably interesting being inside this large, quiet, and historically significant place. We looked at some of the artifacts that were being collected and displayed. There were cabinets of arrowheads. Some old-fashioned tools that I knew how to use from my grandfather. I could operate a hand scythe. There were two-man saws, two-handled planners, drills, and odd-looking axes. There was a canoe made with birch bark. The view of the river from the tower was fascinating. I could imagine watching for aggressive natives sneaking up on the fortress.

Chester's younger brother Donny tagged along with us one hot summer day. We sneaked into the fort as usual but Donny wanted to go into the gift shop. I paid little attention to him as I looked at the exhibits in the cool meeting hall. I heard him bust the shutter boards over one of the windows. He started tossing merchandise out to us, saying "Here, take this." Maple sugar, maple butter, wooden tomahawks, and wooden guns dropped to the ground. We told him to stop and tried to put it back in the window but he just tossed it out again. We then heard a distance siren. Donny said, "Hurry up, the alarm went off." We wanted no part of this and abandoned Donny. We sped away on our bikes as we listened to the siren getting closer. When the siren got close, we rode off the road into the hayfield where we laid down in the tall grass. The police car went by us. We got back up and rode as hard as we could and stopped in a shady spot on the dump road. Donny rode up to us a few minutes later. He had some of the maple products and wanted to share it with us. I tried some maple cream, which seemed strange. I worked with my grandfather to make maple sugar. This maple cream was white, making it look odd, unlike any maple product I knew. I scooped it out with my finger. It was too sweet for me. I did not eat any more and wondered how someone might use it.

In school, I struggled with writing English and History assignments. Science made sense to me. I measured things and wrote in a prescribed format from hypothesis to conclusion. The English and History formats were different and did not make sense to me. If someone could have shown to me the similarities in these formats, it would have helped me greatly. I wrote an exceedingly long history report on the history of Charlestown. I spent a lot of time in the town library. My report had a lot of detail about the people and places in town. I got a C. Mr. Andreoli tried to explain to me that I had no discussion. Though I liked him personally, I grew very frustrated because I had no idea what he wanted, yet I wanted to please him. I wrote a factual and accurate report. He seemed to want something intangible to me. My independent thoughts and opinions have been discouraged especially by my family but also often in school.

Mrs. Gude, my English teacher assigned a position paper as homework. Working at home was impossible for me. There was no place other than sitting in a chair with a book. Even the floor was too covered with trash to provide a workspace. The greatest obstacle to working at home was the chaos and my mother's disregard for our needs. I struggled to write on the moving bus. I wrote about the days of my grandfather's youth and how he never had homework. I wrote how modern schools would not recognize how he had chores when he got home. Mrs. Gude wrote an angry response that my "nostalgia" was "irrational." I got a D. At least I passed.

History and English did not have the detailed structure like Science and Math. Without this structure, I floundered and guessed at what the teacher wanted. Perhaps it was presented in class. Because it was so hard for me to follow the boring instruction, I often fell into daydreaming during class. If the writing structure was presented, I missed it.

I had a toothache. Mother did her usual and told me that it would go away. As the days passed, it got worse. She told me to treat it with an aspirin tablet beside it. It provided little relief. She finally agreed to take me to a dentist. Dr. McIntyre had retired so she took me to Dr. Dexter in Claremont. He said that I needed two root canal treatments. These lasted over a period of several appointments and would take several weeks. I hated the feeling of the rasping tool he shoved down the root canal. He applied a temporary cap in between these appointments.

Mother developed a boil on the surgical site on her broken leg. It was a large and reddened swelling. She went to the doctor who immediately admitted her to the hospital. She had surgery to lance it and a draining tube placed in it. She was on intravenous antibiotics and had to stay in the hospital a few days.

The family decided that we were old enough to stay at home and take care of ourselves. There was enough food that we had been preparing ourselves and could continue without Mother. We were quite capable of getting up and getting on the school bus ourselves, which we had been doing anyways. Uncle Bernie checked in a few times to make sure we were OK.

I realized that I had my final dental appointment during this time Mother was in the hospital. I had no way of getting to it so I called the office and told them. They were not happy with the short notice. On the day of the appointment, while I was in class, the office called my school. I did not know why I was summoned to the office. It frightened me because I had never been called to the office. Only troublemakers got called to the office. When I walked in, the secretary handed me a note with a phone number. She said that it was Dr. Dexter's office and I had to call the immediately. I was not allowed to use the office phone and she directed me to the pay phone in the lobby. I did not have any change so I called the operator. I asked to make a call and have it charged to my home phone. The operator asked me if there was anyone at home to accept my request. I told her, "No." She then warned, "We charge extra for these calls." I did not care at this point. My stress level was at its maximum. I was already fighting back tears. Dr. Dexter's secretary answered. She said that they were waiting for me to finalize the root canal. I told her that I called to cancel the appointment. She replied abruptly that I called too late. I tried to explain to her that my only ride was in the hospital but she seemed uncaring, adding "The State is not going to be happy about paying for an appointment for nothing." As tears started escaping down my cheeks, I told her that it was impossible for me to get there. She said something about their patients must be responsible enough to attend their appointments. She explained how important it was to finish the root canal because the cap would wear out quickly. I never went back and the root canal was never finished.

My friends were all older than me. They were working on getting their driver's license. We all had jobs but no cars. Sometimes, someone was able to borrow a family car for an evening, but it was rare. We usually went to Claremont and rode around and listened to music. It got to be boring after a while and we sought more interesting things to do.

Wayne asked Chester and me if we were interested in working with Peter and him for a farmer, Bob Frizzell. Bob had a partner, his brother-in-law, Harry Fuchslocher. They had a lot of bailed hay to get in and wanted two more workers. We agreed. It was hard work picking up the heavy bails and stacking them on the truck. Harry drove the truck while Bob was still bailing. We rode the truck back to the barn. There was an elevator to transfer the hay into the bar. The elevator was a conveyor from outside and through a window in the barn. Chester and I worked hard. We were used to it. I noticed that Wayne and Peter goofed off a lot. At the end of the day, Bob brought us into his office and paid us one dollar, twenty-five cents per hour. Ten cents more than minimum wage. We expected to be paid less than minimum wage due to our age and farm exception. Bob took our phone numbers for the next time. We were thrilled.

A few days later, Bob called. Harry picked me up on the way to the hayfields around Tampax in North Charlestown. With him was Chester but not Wayne and Peter. As we worked, Chester speculated that Bob's technique was to ask workers with whom he was unhappy to find more helpers. When he got good workers, he stopped calling the poorer workers. Bob was hard-driving perfectionist and had trouble finding workers that met his standards. Sometimes, Mr. Bryce, our music teacher, helped with the truck driving. It seemed weird working with a teacher and seeing him in a different setting. I hated music classes, so seeing an ordinary and even fun side of him gave me a different impression. I learned how he rehabilitated pipe organs in many area churches. He sought large popular trees to make the pipes.

When Bob drove the truck, he set the dashboard throttle and jumped out to throw bails onto the truck, then jump back in to keep the truck on course. Bob taught me how to stack with interlacing bails to build a stable load. It is the toughest job in that I handled every bail and had to place it solidly and accurately into other bails. Sometimes bails came to me simultaneously from both sides. I did this while trying to remain standing on a moving truck in a rough field.

Bob liked our work and often had us doing other things on the farm. We cleaned the cattle stalls, helped build a barn, and help tear down an old one. Sometimes we worked in the section with the huge bull. He sneaked up on me once. I escaped by jumping into the next stall but he pursued me. I finally gained enough of a lead to jump to the other side of the barn. Another time, I noticed he was sneaking up behind Chester. I alert Chester who was heavy and not nearly as agile as me. Chester just turned and faced the bull then hit him on the head with his shovel. The bull stopped, shook his head, then walked away. I thought Chester was courageous but a bit reckless. As the months passed, Bob paid us more. When minimum wage reached one dollar, forty-five cents per hour, he paid us one dollar, sixty cents per hour.

Like my grandfather, Bob did not like the pigeons because they made messes in his barn, defecating on the hay. Chester and I were happy to shoot them for him. Though I was a good shot and seldom missed, Chester was much better. He took much longer shots and still hit the target. Later, Bob complained about there were too many feral cats on his farm. He liked having a few to keep the rats in check but he felt that there were too many. We were happy to help him reduce the population.

My younger sister Debra had amassed numerous animals at home and it was getting to be a problem. She was upset one day when her cat clawed her hamster through the bars of its cage. Mother said that she had to find homes for most of them. We took the big white rabbit on our ride one evening in Richard's car. We got the idea to leave it in Dunkin' Donuts. I put it in a large paper bag and sat at the counter, placing the bag and rabbit on the floor. We bought a donut and waited for the rabbit to emerge. The rabbit stayed in the bag. As time passed and we finished our donuts, I opened the bag slightly to encourage the rabbit to come out. There was no response from the rabbit. I looked in the bag and the rabbit seemed content just resting in the bag. Finally, we had to leave. I grabbed the bag near the bottom, causing the rabbit to slide out on the floor. It still just sat there, under the counter. We went across the street and watched. Finally, the rabbit took a step forward just as the waitress was delivering a cup of coffee and donut. She stopped, screamed, and the coffee and donut flew in opposite directions. We hid behind Richard's car, fearing that we would be identified and connected to the rabbit. Eventually, a small boy came out with the rabbit in his arms. I told him that it was my rabbit and thanked him for finding it. He proudly returned it to me, thinking he did a great service.

We went to Burger Village with the rabbit in the bag. Inside, they had phone booths with folding doors. I brought the rabbit into one of the booths and pretended to make a call. When I left, I slid the rabbit out of the bag just as I did at Dunkin' Donuts. We waited outside for a reaction but none came. We eventually gave up and joked that they probably made burgers out of it.

Debra also had three bantam chickens and a rooster that needed new homes. We took them the next weekend. We decided to try JC Penny's. These were much noisier than the rabbit in the paper bag. People in the store noticed us as we looked around the display shelves and tables. I placed the bag under one of the displays and started to walk away. The poultry started jumping out of the bag and fluttering around the displays. A store employee watched me and yelled "Hey, you can't leave that" as I tried to walk away. He started to approach me and we ran out of the store. We wasted no time in getting in the car and driving away. We decided that this was enough fun and Debra needed to find the homes for any other animals.

Uncle Bernie with George and Dorothy Goodwin opened the B & G Sporting Goods Store in the old Curve-In Restaurant in Springfield, Vermont. It was located directly across from the popular boat landing on the Connecticut River, next to the Cheshire Toll Bridge. It also had a grill. I worked there without pay to help my uncle start his new business. I usually worked the grill on weekends. George showed me about all the hunting and fishing equipment. I spent my savings on a bow and arrow and eventually bought a twelve-gauge shotgun. I was too young so I bought it in my grandfather's name.

George took me hunting and taught me how to stalk game. He hunted pheasants and ducks using his black Labrador retrievers. They were amazing animals. The dogs were great at finding hiding birds, scaring them up to be shot, and retrieving the birds when he killed them. The dogs also responded to George's hand signals on where to search for hiding or fallen birds. I never killed anything but enjoyed spending time with him and learning about life in the forests. He once mentioned that he wished his son had spent more time with him. He was grown up now. He used to run away. George's health was failing and he said that he would never chase his son when he ran off. I did not understand why he would not try to control him. George explained, "There was no point in chasing him. He would always eventually have to come back." I thought how Mother would never be able to catch me. Like George explained about his son, I had no other place to go so I would have to return to Mother.

Mother accepted Ollie, a female black Labrador retriever, that the owner could not handle. I was fascinated because she seemed smart like George's dogs. She loved going on walks in the woods with me and especially swimming in the brook. She would dive in deep water and pull on a root. I worried that she was going to drown, then she popped up with a broken root in her mouth.

When I got home from school one day. Mother showed me a bite mark on her hand. She said that Ollie jumped in the car and would not get out. When she reached to pull her out, Ollie bit her. I believed my mother but she was also drunk. I decided to recreate the event and Ollie responded the same way with me. She rolled her lips back, exposing her teeth and growled viciously. I was quicker than my mother so I could grab her and pull her out of the car. Ollie stayed a distance from me, growling and showing her teeth. I went in the house, got my gun, then a shovel from the garage. I called to Ollie and started in the direction of our usual walk. She happily came along. I let her play in the brook while I dug the hole. When I was ready, I called for her and commanded her to sit. I shot her between her eyes. She fell backwards into her death throws. I felt emotionally numb and confused and turned away as I waited for the death throws to stop. I had lots of fun with this dog but did not want anyone to be hurt by her. I buried her and walked slowly home.

As I got closer to being sixteen years old, Dorothy suggested that I get a job as an orderly in the hospital. I got the job on weekends during the winter. I helped with skiers who broke their legs. The education nurse taught me how to handle people with injured limbs. I got patients from the car, helped them through examinations, X-ray, casting and back into the car. I also helped on the medical-surgical floor, especially moving patients in and out of bed or to other areas of the hospital. I also carried the heavy emergency defibrillator to any cardiac codes.

I was hurrying down the hallway one time to go help put a patient back into bed. I heard someone breathing hard as I went by his room. He called to me as I went by. He was insistent, so I went into his room to see if there was something quick that I could do for him. He was sitting on the edge of the bed with his arms elevated on the bed table to relieve pressure on his chest. He had oxygen nasal canula but breathing through his mouth like he just completed a one-hundred-yard dash. His skin was blue. He repeatedly stretched his arm towards me then waved it towards himself. He said, "Come 'ere." I approached him and asked, "What can I do for you?" He replied, "Give me a cigarette." I explained that not only did I not have any, but he would also not be allowed to have it with the oxygen. He said, "I don't care, get me a cigarette." I said, "Sorry, I cannot" and left his room to go help the nurse put the other patient in bed. He called for me to return but I kept going. I told the nurse about it. She assured me that what I did was fine.

He died later that night. It had a profound impact on me. I could accept but not understand my mother's addiction to alcohol. This patient taught me about cigarette addiction. His lungs were so bad that his skin was blue from the deoxygenated blood throughout his entire body. I had seen blue lips and even blue fingertips from swimming in very cold water. Never had I seen someone whose entire body was blue. He breathed like I might after a one-hundred-yard sprint. I hated that feeling but it only lasted for a few seconds. I could not imagine how it must be to live weeks, maybe months, not being able to catch your breath. Even in this terminal condition, he still had to have a cigarette. The effects on a smoker would never get better, only worse until death.

Earning more money, now, my plans for college were coming more into focus. I opened a savings account at Connecticut River Bank in Charlestown. Because I was a minor, I had to have my mother's name on the account, too. She went to the bank to help me open the account. It required the use of a bank book when making deposits and withdrawals.

It was major news when Dr. Martin Luther King was assassinated. I was aware of the riots around the country. I understood little about why this was happening. I remember the comments, especially from my grandfather and uncle. They were worried that the protestors were going to take over the country and take over our land and homes. My grandfather supported the back to Africa movement. When Dr. King was assassinated, my grandfather and uncle expected things would improve but the protests increase. This topic was not discussed at school. I saw no immediate threat to me.

I completed chemistry with Mr. Lammela. There was a lot of memorization but he helped it make sense and connections for better understanding. I especially remember one day when he said that he could boil water with a walnut. We all thought he was crazy but played along. He put about five milliliters of water in a test tube. He stuck a half walnut on the end of a metal probe. He lit the walnut with a match. I was surprised that the walnut burned. Mr. Lammela held the test tube of water in a clamp over the burning walnut. We all watched in awe but now realized that he could boil water with a walnut. The nut burned out just before the water came to a full boil but we could see the bubbles forming on the side of the glass. This exciting demonstration was Mr. Lamella's introduction to heat and calories. I learned that some foods had so many calories that they could burn like this walnut.

I studied second year algebra with my favorite teacher, Mrs. Hronek, while studying chemistry. I enjoyed statistical relationships and probabilities. We learned a lot about graphing and interpreting them. I made the correlation between balancing chemical equations (stoichiometry) and algebraic equations. Neither teacher showed this connection, which was typical across the education disciplines. Students were left to make their own connections. I wondered about the validity of my observation, but never asked.

Next, I studied Advanced Biology with Mr. Hall, who was also my driver's education teacher. Mr. Hall taught us much of the details in anatomy and physiology. He would work one-on-one with us during the labs. We learned to identify the anatomy and developed skilled to dissect and exam it. We used microscopes to see the difference in the cells. He left teaching to enter medical school.

Mr. Winslow taught advance math, which was mostly trigonometry, while I studied advance biology. He helped me make more sense of geometry, but it was never exciting as my other math courses.

The Apollo Space Program was proceeding rapidly during my junior year. The Soviets beat us by putting the first satellite in space, Sputnik. We watched with great patriotic pride as we sent men into space. We landed men on the moon that summer. We regained ground lost to the Soviets.

I studied calculus with Mr. Kerylow while studying physics with Mr. Morse. Mr. Morse often frustrated me as he tried to get us to derive our own equations. I struggled with it because I was accustomed to being given formulas to memorize. It took some time for me to appreciate how he tried to get us to identify variables in a relationship and then their relative effects on each other. Once, during Mr. Morse's challenge to identify relationships in gravitational acceleration, I recognized the exponential relationship Mr. Kerylow taught us in Calculus. Mr. Morse was surprised and asked how I came up with it. I explained how I learned it in Calculus and he responded, "Oh, your calculus teacher did it for you." I deeply resented any such implication and replied, "No." I gave no input into his future presentations.

Mr. Coté was my French three and four teacher. He was born in France, near Paris. He was nearly blind and had to hold written things extremely close to his eyes but he was fantastic. He got us to start thinking completely in French without having to translate.

Joining any sports was out of the question due to Mom's undependability, outright refusal to transport me, or being too drunk. The school added an eighth period on Fridays so that all students could participate in club activities. This made it possible for me to participate in French Club and Chess Club. In French Club, we raised money and did a two-day field trip to Quebec City, Canada. Mr. Coté chaperoned the trip. He made the experience rememberable. We toured Le Château Frontenac and saw all the splendor of French design. We stayed at boarding houses in the neighborhood, visited local shops, and walked on cobble streets. It was not France but it was the next best thing on this continent. On the way back, we stopped in Montreal to see a performance by *Up with People*. I did not care much for music but very much enjoyed the singing, energy, and message of this traveling group of students from all over the world. They promoted equality and celebration of human diversity.

I took drivers' education during school days. The school paid for it. We got one-quarter credit on our transcript. Buick donated a car. I had no problem with the class, finding it slow and boring like most classes. This was the first time that I had driven a car. I drove many tractors and trucks on the farm, but never a car on the road. The sudden high speed was new to me. Tractors and trucks had a lot of play in the steering wheel. The car had power steering, which I had not experienced. The steering in the car was light and reacted quickly. It also accelerated quickly. I adapted well. Mr. Hall saw a need to spend more time with some classmates, so I did little driving.

I easily passed the written portion of the driver's test. I used the family car, a nineteen fifty-three Buick. It was just one year younger than me. It was heavy and slow. The steering wheel was large. The driver's test was the first time that I drove the car. The instructor commented on how it seemed like a tank. He said I did fine, just slow. He blamed the car. Now, I had a driver's license like my friends, just no car.

I could now drive the hay truck and tractors on the road. Chester and I stayed busy driving trucks late summer and fall as Bob chopped corn silage. The truck I drove was five speed with a two-speed rear end, making ten progressive gears available. It had no door or back window. Some of the fields were rough and steep. Staying in the right position for the tractor was challenging. If I fell behind, I was immediately reprimanded with silage blown through the missing back window and down the back of my neck. It stung, filled my shirt, and was sticky. Sometimes I got stuck. Bob put a chain from the tractor to the front of the truck. He left it there even after I got out of the mud. Now, if I fell behind, I got a jolt from the tractor. Bob also got a jolt. We traversed the side of some steep hills. The truck was top heavy and leaned. It had no seat belt. I kept myself from falling out by jamming my left foot into the inside of the missing door opening. Once, the truck leaned so much that the uphill dual wheels suspended in the air, so the truck could not move. Again, Bob put a chain on it. He failed to assure me when he said the truck would have rolled over if I hit a woodchuck hole on the low side. I felt more comfortable connected to the tractor on steep hills.

Harry worked the tractor with a loader in the trench silo. He spread and packed each load we delivered. The silo was just a large area dug out of a hill. We backed the long distance into it and Harry pointed to where he wanted us to dump our load. It was much more interesting when the silo filled to the top of the back bank. We could drive around it and into it from the high back end. As Harry spread out each load, he carefully assured the silage was evenly packed. If there was a soft spot, our trucks could get stuck. Chester drove the dump truck. Mine emptied with a conveyor from the power take off (PTO). Mine was much more stable as it emptied. Chester's truck once partial tipped when the center of gravity changed as he raised the body. Harry pulled him out. Bob paid us one dollar, sixty cents per hour for this. We made more than many adults. Working for Bob was a major source of my college money.

Mother liked Bob. When the house he rented became available, she decided to move. She liked being close to a working farm and the rent was five dollars per month cheaper. The problem was finding help to move. Uncle Bernie with his truck was not available. He mumbled something about how he was sick of helping us move so much. Bob said that I could use the

International tractor and hay wagon. It was only about a mile, so it worked well.

I knew Mother and Cilla argued often and intensely. I purposefully stayed away from the arguing and screaming. I was surprised when Cilla decided to spend a weekend with Dad. I do not know how she arranged it because we had not seen or heard from Dad for years. As the weekend came to an end, Cilla extended her visit. She eventually just stayed with him.

I came home from being with friends to learn that Gary was in the hospital. He had tried to kill himself by taking a whole bottle of aspirin. He vomited it up, so he was going to be fine. They wanted to observe him. He went to the Concord State Hospital for a few days. A few weeks later, Gary went to live with Dad, too. Cilla graduated from Windsor High School. Gary dropped out. Mother was angry that Dad let Gary drop out but did nothing about it. Or course, she did not tell our social worker and continued to collect all the money as if Cilla and Gary were still living at home.

Home became quieter without Cilla and Gary. Mother started flirting with Frank Kamel and he moved in. I was deeply disturbed by this because Mother and my grandparents always stressed the importance of marriage before living together. Mother was living in sin. She liked Frank because he was about to settle a lawsuit from an injury he sustained while working at Fellows Gear Shaper. He was already collecting disability. Some other workers set off a firecracker next to him. He reacted, crashed into a machine, and injured his neck. I felt that Mother liked Frank because he would be her source of income as we aged out of welfare. My assessment of Frank was someone who was looking for a home with a housekeeper. My opinion got even worse when I overheard him brag about the size of my mother's breasts to his friends.

Mother liked her beer but Frank liked his whiskey. I could easily read my mother's level of intoxication but it was difficult for me to read Frank. He had a high screeching voice and walked awkwardly all the time. I could see no progression of his intoxication. I only knew he was drunk when I found him passed out under the trees on the lawn.

Mother and Frank got part-time work taking care of Bob's veal calves. One day, Bob mentioned to me that he had a problem with how my mother was caring for the calves. She was overfeeding them and using too much bedding. He could not make a profit with what she was doing and overfeeding them would hurt them. He said that he had already spoke to my mother but wanted to mention it to me. He explained, "She was a little under the weather, as you know." I had not heard that phrase before but knew what he was talking about. I could just imagine my mother, who loved animals more than her own kids, going to these extremes in Bob's barn. She was likely singing and dancing as she worked. I told Bob that I would remind her. After he left, I resented that he expected me to correct my mother's bad behavior. I had grown up getting blamed for Gary's misbehavior and being powerless to change it. I was even more powerless to change my mother's behavior. However, I promised Bob. When Mother was sober the next day, I told her that Bob said something about over feeding the veal calves. She said, "I know. He's wrong, but I know." I did not mention it again. Bob eventually found someone else to take care of the calves.

One winter afternoon, Debra left to go to her friend's house a few houses away. Minutes later she returned, crying intensely. She was holding her head and there was blood in her hair. We asked, "What happen?" She replied through her cries, "I don't know. I was in a snowbank." She also complained that one side of her butt hurt. We thought that she must have fallen but it did not seem right. We decided to call the police. On the way to our house, they found a jeep off the road. It appeared that the Jeep operator lost control and slid sideways into my sister, causing the bump to her butt with its back fender. They arrested the driver for driving while intoxicated. Mother brought Debra to the hospital because the cut on her head required stitches.

Debra recovered well. A few days later, Mother received a check from the jeep driver's insurance company. It was more than thirteen hundred dollars. I was puzzled. Mother explained the insurance company came to her and made the offer. She was happy to accept this large amount of money for what she thought was free money. I began to realize that she sold out Debra's remedy for any potential future effects, such as brain damage. Mother was happy. She bought Debra some clothes. She had plenty of money left over for her beer. She and Frank were drunk for days. I stayed away as much as I could.

I managed to work for Bob and continue my job at the hospital. Though I had a driver's license, I still had no car and Mother was unreliable. Gail Prouty, a nurse with whom I worked lived in Charlestown. She was happy to give me a ride to the hospital. She said it was because she wanted my help at work. I was grateful and struggled on how to show my appreciation. We drove across the Cheshire Toll Bridge. They sold tickets in a book. My last week before leaving for college, I bought her one of these. The value of the ride was much greater than this but she wanted me to focus on college. Gail was an adult who appreciated my efforts, which helped motivate me to be successful in college.

I still helped my grandfather on his farm, especially at harvest time. I did not get paid for working for my grandfather. I suspect it is possible he could have given some money to Mother at the end of the season, like before. If he did, she kept it without telling me.

In the spring of my junior year, I took the PSAT (Pre-Scholastic Aptitude Test). It was meant to be practice and an opportunity to expose weaknesses. In the fall of my senior year, I took the SAT. When the results came in, Mr. Livengood, my guidance counselor, called me into the office. He was excited about my math scores. He said that I could get into college and wanted me to begin to apply. I selected Saint Michael's College for several reasons. The first reason was Mr. Livengood recommended it, having just earned his masters' degree there. Another reason was Dartmouth was having many demonstrations, riots, and administrative building take overs. He assured me that I could get in there if I wanted. Each application had a fee, which I had to pay. Dartmouth was four times more expensive than Saint Michael's College. I decided on Saint Michael's College.

The application process began with getting teacher recommendations, college application forms, and applying for scholarships. I was entirely dependent on my guidance counselor. No one in my family had any idea of what I needed to do. They were still telling me that I would have a hard time and assured me that I could quit. I found motivation in that I wanted a different life than the one my family had and intended for me.

I applied to Saint Michael's College in November; the earliest time possible to request early admission. In January, I got the news that I was accepted. Now, my scholarship applications became intense. I checked in with guidance weekly to see what was available. It was a tedious process. Each one had a different application process and a focused essay. I did not learn about whether I would receive most of these scholarships until graduation.

I spent as little time at home as possible and as much time working or with my friends as I could. David had a good part time job at Kiel Lock. He bought a large Chevy Impala that could carry a lot of us. He and I also spent a lot of time together. He had a modern eight track player with much of the popular music. I had no interest in music until he showed me. The school started playing music over the public address system in the cafeteria during lunch. I really liked the Paul McCartney song, *Come and Get It*, when I came over the cafeteria speakers above me. I became much more interested in listening to music.

Richard sometimes had access to the family car but his father charged him six cents per mile, the common mileage reimbursement rate. It significantly limited how much he drove. We all had part time jobs and not a lot of money.

Steve had access to his family's two cars: a Pontiac Firebird and a Pontiac Grand Prix. Both were nice cars. The Grand Prix was fast. It also had positive traction, locking the rear wheels together to provide better traction for acceleration. Normally, if one rear wheel spun, the other did not turn. With positive traction, both back wheels had to spin to get stuck. When both rear wheels spin in slippery weather, the rear end was unstable. This made it easy to make the car slide sideways and spin around, doing donuts. Steve liked to drive down the driveway of a factory with a large parking lot. As he turned in the parking lot, he turned hard and punched the accelerator. The car spun in circles all the way across the parking lot. He laughed as we spun around and around across the parking lot. One night, he challenged himself to do donuts along the entire length of Charlestown's Main Street. David and I followed him, expecting that he would slide off the road. Much to our surprise, he made it. We saw his taillights, head lights, taillights again and again with snow flying from the road, making a cloud.

Chester had a Pinto. It had a four-speed transmission and the largest engine. He liked racing it up the Mount Ascutney Hill Climb, placing well in his category. No one usually rode with Chester. He liked to drink beer. David and I were behind him one night as he drove along Main Street. He seemed to be having trouble getting into the proper gear. Sometimes the engine raced. Other times it almost stalled. He still managed to keep it on the road.

Graduation was not far away when the antiwar demonstrations seemed to increase. Demonstrators were against the "police action" killing of people living halfway around the world in Vietnam. A place where we should have no business. This divided the country with those who demanded unquestioning dedication to these efforts purported to stop the advancement of communism. Tensions grew and the National Guard was often used to control demonstrators. This seemed to make things even worse as National Guard soldiers looked like soldiers of the war demonstrators wanted stopped. An incident occurred between demonstrators and the National Guard at Kent State. Soldiers fired upon the demonstrators, killing four, paralyzing another, and wounded seven others. The nation was in an uproar. Principal Willis decided to lower the school flag to half-mast to honor the dead. Several boys walked out of school. I watched and they walked side-by-side out the parking lot and into the driveway. When they returned the next day, the principal suspended them.

High School Graduation was in the gym. I was surprised that my mother was so willing to attend and she was sober. The process was long and boring. Finally, they came to the awards.

I was disappointed that there was no award for attendance. I had perfect attendance through all junior and high school. They announced a scholarship, then announced that it was awarded to me. I was proud to leave my seat and struggle past my peers sitting in my row then walk up the center aisle to the front. As they announced the winners, my name was called several times. I was pleased but starting to feel embarrassed.

Soon after graduating, Saint Michael's College Financial Assistance Office sent me confirmation of a college grant and matching National Defense Student Loan. I wondered about why they called it a national defense loan. They explained that the government saw value in having educated people to defend the country. Two years later, after Vietnam, they changed it to National Direct Student Loan to remove any perceived connection to preparing for war while retaining the acronym, NDSL. These scholarships, grants, and loans made it possible for me to go to Saint Michael's College. I thought a little about my grandfather and how he said that I was too stupid to go to college. It felt good to have so many people believe in me.

Collateral Damage During the High School Years

As we grew older, we were necessarily more aware of the community around us. Mother intensified her efforts to isolate us with constant reminders that we did not have the money to be like other people. Mother increased her efforts to maintain control over us and limit our interactions with the community. Sometimes, she outright refused to let us do some things like school social events and the sports that Dad encouraged me to try. By isolating us, Mother could better hide her alcoholism. With Dad gone, she dealt her discipline even more harshly. People in the community knew about her drinking, often causing embarrassing times for us. Mother was only successful at hiding it from her parents who did not want to see it.

Our efforts to please Mother were never good enough. Her expectations were unachievable. They were either impossible or elusive. As we nearly achieved her expectation, she changed it. We tried so hard, failed, yet kept trying. We were never good enough for her needs. Conversely, she expected us to fail in school and in the community to keep us within her influence. She accepted no responsibility for her unhappiness and blamed our father and us. Mother said that her kids came first but practiced the opposite. We suffered in intense poverty exacerbated by her alcoholism, diverting much of the little amount of money to support it. Our feelings, desires, concerns, etc. were always second to hers. She shamed us with accusations of being selfish for wanting to satisfy our needs while she satisfied her alcoholism.

We missed many rites of passages, even birthdays. Birthdays were not celebrated and certainly there was no celebration in other achievements in school and work. Getting a driver's license was allowed but not supported. We had to do it on our own, using the family car only to take the road test.

Even our health care was a low priority for Mother. It would cost her nothing. She had no schedule to interrupt, yet she did not bring us for routine medical and dental care unless it was required by the school or the social worker. She no longer bought toothpaste or brushes. She bought little soap, which was unnecessary in the winter months when the pipes froze. We accepted this. When my glasses broke, I was willing to stop wearing them rather than complain and annoy Mother to adequately repair them. I did not have the resources to thoroughly clean them. Wiping them on my shirt only evenly smeared the lenses.

Mother provided food that mostly satisfied her. Never did we have any input into what we wanted to eat. Always, the cheapest alternative was chosen, regardless of nutrition or even spoilage. Our diet was unhealthy and high in fat. Many foods were beyond safe storage times and I suffered food poisoning from her choices. Mother justified her obesity and the growing obesity in her children with comments such as being big boned and meant to be heavy.

We resented the lack of resources and had to be accustomed to going without social activities and other things our peers enjoyed. We became creative and self-sufficient to meet our unmet needs. Even with these efforts, Mother and our grandfather retained low expectations for us. We had mild encouragement to graduate from high school only because my mother had graduated. Gary dropped out of school. The higher education that I sought was discouraged to the point of creating obstacles to it. There was an acceptance and expectation of failure. Failure in the community imprisoned us in Mother's control and service to her.

Mother, in conjunction with my grandfather, created an environment that made it easier to quit. Our greatest resignation was expecting that we could get Mother to stop drinking. We never gave up hoping. Only when Mother engaged us in intense arguments when she was drunk did we have the courage to mention it. Mother responded with intense anger or self-pity, blaming us. We could not join any social groups that may have supported us. Our relief was the times that we could spend with friends.

Cilla and I grew terribly angry about Mother's arbitrary, senseless, and brutal punishments holding us responsible for our younger siblings' misbehaviors. Mother's frequently praising herself for being a great mother weighed heavy on us as we suffered. Mother bestowed a great honor of motherhood upon herself. Cilla and I did not accept her self-proclaimed honor. We wanted to revolt. With little power against her great power over us, we decided that calling her Mom was too much of an honor. We could not deny the fact that she was our mother, so we decided to call her "Mother." Mother never caught on to our minor revolt against her.

Our emotions were denied, being subordinate to Mother's. Mother had wild emotional swings while expecting us to appease her. We were more sensitive to other people's emotions than our own. I twice suppressed my emotions in the loss of a pet. Mother expected me to drown pets that became seriously injured or ill. I was able to violently kill a beloved pet from this emotional conditioning. When intense emotions erupted from one of us, we often overreacted.

I found solace in nature. When I spent time observing nature, I was free from the turmoil at home. I was making sense of the natural around me in contrast to the nonsense of my alcoholic home. When I could not go to nature for solace, I escaped to my daydreams. I preferred to remain quiet and participate minimally in school. An incorrect response would be devasting to my self-esteem. It was better to be quiet than take the risk.

Cilla and Gary escaped Mother's irrational dominance by moving to Dad's house. Mother had successfully poisoned my mind against my father. I was intensely committed to getting into college and depended upon my teachers and guidance counselor. Debra was well conditioned to be Mother's caregiver.

TRANSITIONING TO COLLEGE AND ADULTHOOD

My friends were all adults before graduating from high school. I started college at age seventeen, still a minor legally dependent upon my mother. I had a lot of freedom through the summer, mostly because I just took it. I worked every opportunity I had. I worked for Bob on his farm, haying, cleaning the barns, and many miscellaneous projects. I also worked at the hospital as an orderly. I was building my bank account to help me through college.

No one in my family or among my friends could advise me on what the transition into college would be like. My guidance counselor just told me to study hard. Saint Michael's College was a good college because it had high academic standards and expectations for its students. I received a letter with instructions about what was allowed and not allowed in the dormitories. There were policies on academic performance expectations and academic probation for anyone with an average below C. The registrar sent a list of required courses for each major. A physical and vaccination record were also required.

I also received notice from the Draft Board. I was required to register for the draft. The Vietnam War was still prominently in the news. The instructions described how I could apply for the IIS student deferment. This classification shielded me from the draft while I was in school. It warned that I could be drafted after graduation. If I left college, I was to report it immediately and my status would be changed. Also in the instructions was a requirement to get a doctor's report for anything that might disqualify me for military service. Mother had always told me that my right eye with poor vision would keep me out of the army. I went to Dr. Auten, an ophthalmologist in Claremont, and showed to him the Draft Board's instructions. He examined my sight and said that my vision was good and I could serve in any military branch. In his letter, he recommended military service. He signed it with his credentials as a retired Air Force Lieutenant Colonel. So much for my mother's assurances. To register for the daft, I had to appear at a recruitment station within two weeks of my birthday. The closest one to my home was in Manchester, NH. Since I would be in college at that time, the Burlington, VT. office was the closest.

The day in late August finally came for me to report to college. Saint Michael's College sent detailed directions that were easy to follow. Mother insisted on driving, so that she would remember where it was. Oddly, this would be the only time my mother ever came to Saint Michael's College. After the more than two-hour ride, I saw the campus for the first time. There were signs to the student drop off site. Mother stopped the car at the curb. I took out my suitcase. An upperclassman volunteer met me right away. He explained that I needed to go to a table in the Alliot Student Center to get my dormitory assignment. I turned back to where Mother was standing. She wiped a tear from her eye. This was the first time that I had ever seen my mother cry for me. Then

I thought, she was crying for herself. Only Debra was at home now to take care of her. I went to her and said "Goodbye." There was no hug or kiss offered.

I went into Alliot Student Center and waited in line for my dormitory assignment. It was Ryan Hall on the fourth floor. They gave me a key and a schedule for a meeting with our resident advisory and faculty advisor. When I got to the room, I found that someone's things were already there. Jim returned up a few minutes later. He was from Rutland, VT. The school did well at matching roommates because Jim and I started off well. Unfortunately, he left within a few days. He could not raise the money. I was thinking how nice it was to have a private room but this was against the school's practice. I was transferred to Lyons Hall, on the first floor. I met Bob who had been in the room. He immediately introduced himself as being Scarsdale. He said it like it was some privileged place but that meant nothing to me. I said, "Hello, I am from Charlestown, NH." He responded with a condescending, "Oh, New Hampshire." I asked him what state he was from because I had not heard of any nearby Scarsdale. He replied "New York," as if I should have known. He was a sociology major. The stage was set for conflict.

We met as a group with our faulty advisors. Dr. Klein explained that there were one hundred twenty-two biology majors divided among the four biology faculty members. She explained the required courses and the possible electives to make the forty academic credits required for a major. She pointed out that, due to the fourth credit for lab courses, that fifty-four credits would be required for the major in biology. It also carried an automatic minor in chemistry, but Saint Michael's College did not recognized minors on their degrees. We filled out the forms to register and got our schedules. I had an opening for an elective, so

I decided to take an introductory psychology course. I was hoping to learn something that could help me understand my mother's alcoholism. Dr. Klein told us how to get our books.

Upperclassmen began to arrive and the dormitories filled. There was a big party the first weekend. There was a lot of beer drinking, loud music, and card playing. They were betting money. I was not interested in any of these activities. I spent most of the weekend looking over the thick textbooks and many smaller books for humanities class. I had to sign up for calculus even though I had it in high school. The book looked like things I had already studied, except the logic section.

As the welcome back party progressed into the night, it got louder. I opened the door to check things out and was immediately overwhelmed with smoke. It was not just cigarette smoke. This was my first exposure to marijuana. The smoke grew so thick that I could only distinguish the form of a person at the end of the hallway. The next day, I was alerted to cheers and crashing sounds in the hallway. I opened the door just as a naked person slid by on his back. They had a water fight and someone spread laundry soap on the tile floor. They were having a body surfing competition. I retreated to my room and turned up my radio.

The following morning, I went into the bathroom. The toilet paper rolls were all wet with urine. The showers had all sorts of trash. It discouraged me from using the showers. I had spent months without bathing so skipping showers was acceptable to me. Dorm life was discouraging but I was focused on my studies. As unsettling the dormitory was, it was calm compared to my home experiences. It was predictable chaos. I had no reason to fear for my safety. Certainly, there was nothing as dangerous as riding in a car with my intoxicated mother.

Studies went at a much faster pace than in high school. I rarely daydreamed. I struggled with trying to keep notes. Dr. Klein had warned us that keeping good notes was critical to our success. I tried to just take as much notes as I could and would worry about organizing them later. I found that rewriting my notes in the evening worked best for me. I could compare my notes to my readings in the textbooks. It was another strange adjustment for me to be able to write in my textbooks. I underlined key vocabulary in red and the definitions in blue. I added information such as word definitions in the margins. After organizing, reviewing, and studying some more, I came to a point where I felt a conceptual understanding. Perhaps my life of making sense of nonsense assisted me to find sense in the topics I was studying.

I struggled in chemistry more than I expected. The instructor, Mr. Michaels, seemed poorly organized for our large lecture hall filled with students. He did silly things like drawing a martini glass on the board, calling it a beaker. Whenever someone had an obvious arm or leg injury, he accused them of falling off a bar stool. Most faculty members were expected to have or be working on their doctorate. He had a master's degree and the rumor was that he was not working on his doctorate as the school required of its instructors. He left mid semester and Dr. Grady took over. I liked Dr. Grady much better. He explained chemistry concepts well. I participated more in his lectures than I did all through high school. I was well-prepared and confident in my responses to his questions.

Whenever we took a test or submitted a report, we could find our grades posted outside the instructor's office. There was a list organized by our student number. I was not doing as well as I had hoped until I compared myself to the other students' grades.

Many were failing badly. I was in the top ten percent but scoring grades of C. I needed an A.

There were a nice individual study desks in our dorm rooms but it was mostly impossible to study in the noisy dorm in the evening. I went to the library and found a place in the science section that I liked. Another benefit was that the library bathrooms were much cleaner. On weeknights, I studied until ten o'clock. On weekends, I stayed until the library closed at two o'clock in the morning. The dorm was usually quieting down by now. There was a sharp contrast in being a science major compared to other majors like my roommate's sociology. Science classes always started early and we had labs in the afternoon. Other majors could find late morning or all afternoon classes. Rooming with someone who partied until late disturbed my sleep time.

I felt very alone in college. My college peers had widely varied connections to their home and families. Some parents called into the dorm at scheduled times. Some parents regularly came to visit and take their student out to lunch or dinner. Many received an allowance. Some of my peers' parents took them skiing. I realized much of what my mother said about how other people can do things that we could not was true.

I felt homesick and tried to keep a connection to home. There were pay phones in the student center. I gathered up some change and called. These calls provided little satisfaction. I found myself trying to judge how drunk Mother was as I spoke with her. I only confirmed that nothing changed. I worried about it getting worse because I was there to mitigate Mother's recklessness.

There were times that I felt very depressed. These were times when I did not do so well on a test and was arguing with my roommate. I started going for walks on weekends. I remembered an earlier personal belief. If anyone can do it, I can. I just need to be sufficiently motivated. Burlington had a regular bus service and the cost was low, but I benefitted more by walking. I often walked around Burlington observing the nice, clean city. The physical activity and change of scenery improved my mood.

I found the federal building where I needed to register for the draft during one of my walks. I had an afternoon free of classes or labs. I brought my birth certificate, driver's license, social security card, and school identification card. I needed the school identification card to show why I was not registering with Burlington office and to apply for the IIS deferment. It was easy to do. Now I was required to carry my draft card. So many people were burning theirs. The penalties for doing this was explained well. It was punishable with fines or imprisonment or both. Though I worried about going to war, I would never burn my draft card.

I took the Vermont Transit bus home for Thanksgiving that was always celebrated at Pop and Grandma's farm with the whole family. Pop challenged me to wrist wrestling as he often did. I almost beat him. This was the last time that he asked. Pop offered all the adults a shot of brandy. Mother rejected it at first, then accepted it. I knew that this was a trigger for her. I could not read Frank and his connection to alcohol. I made plans to visit with my friends to avoid Mother's certain intoxication after the family party. I headed back to college on the following Sunday.

After a few days, I received a letter from Cilla who was still living with Dad. This was a surprise as she never wrote to me. She wrote to me because she was certain that our mother would never tell me. She learned from Debra that Frank had been arrested for driving while intoxicated. He blamed the police officer for being overzealous. I was not surprised and a little pleased about Frank's arrest. I did not like him.

I finished the semester. We were required to leave campus and I had plans to work over the semester break, so I went home. It was a few days before Christmas. Bob had immediate work for Chester and me to clean the barns. After he paid me, I got my savings book to make a deposit. I was shocked when I opened it. I could not believe what I was seeing. I had over eight hundred dollars but it showed a little over eight dollars. It showed multiple withdrawals of ten or fifteen dollars at a time and over many days. Sometimes twice in one day. I knew that this was the amount of money that Mother needed to buy three six-packs of beer. I stood looking at it. There was also a two hundred twenty-five-dollar withdrawal soon after Thanksgiving. I could not believe it. My legs were feeling weak because I needed two hundred dollars to return to school. I sat down and tried to process how a mother, who claimed to place her children first, could do such a thing. As much as I hated the things that my mother did, I just could not have foreseen this.

I confronted my mother with more anger than I have ever felt towards anyone or thing. She was sober, sitting in her favorite chair and staring at the floor. I asked her, "How could you do this!?" She did not have an answer. I asked her about the two hundred twenty-five-dollar withdrawal. She explained that was to repay Frenchie, the store owner. When Frank got arrested for driving while intoxicated late at night, Frenchie was willing to loan her the cash but had to be repaid the next morning. She thought that I would not mind. This would be true if she replaced it. Instead, it was followed with draining my account in less than a month. She liked the word piss to describe my father, specifically piss up a rope and piss hole in the snow. She literally pissed away many months of my hard work. I believed that she purposefully planned to make it impossible for me to return to college. She wanted to cause and take advantage of my failure of school. I demanded that she repay me right away, knowing full well that she could not. I said that I must have the two hundred and twenty-five dollars at a minimum. I warned her that I was considering going to the police. She said that she would talk to Frank. She returned with assurance that Frank's disability check was about that much and I could have it. I was partially pleased that I would be able to return to college but still angry in that it felt like he was doing me a favor by returning money that she stole from me made necessary by his poor judgement.

I thought about how I could prevent this from happening again. I told my mother that I was going to the bank to take her name off my account. I thought about just doing it and letting her be denied by the bank, then thought that they would probably still let her, knowing that she is my mother and she would lie about my permission. I was an adult now and did not have to have her name on it. It would put me in a difficult position because I would not be able to transfer money into my checking account from college if I needed it. I met with Gary Gray at the bank. He explained to me that they have a new Now Account. It is a checking account that paid interest. It was perfect. I closed both my savings and checking accounts and opened the Now Account. I told my mother when it was completed. She said, "It's just as well, then I won't be tempted anymore." I worked all I could over the month-long break and managed to build my account back to four hundred dollars. My mother never repaid the rest of the money.

My relationship with my mother suffered irreparable harm. I did not want to ever come home again. I was in a difficult position because college required us to leave campus during semester breaks. I would have gone to stay with my grandparents except Aunt Alice and my cousins were staying there. Aunt Alice was divorcing Uncle Beau. I was trapped into having to maintain a relationship with my mother that I did not want.

COLLATERAL DAMAGES

My alcoholic mother conditioned my siblings and me to fail to maintain control and indenture us to serve her. This was reinforced by my maternal grandfather, who was not an alcoholic. My great grandfather, who I never met, was an alcoholic. Though alcoholism skips generations, the effects are prevalent across generations.

My family conditioned me to be a mediocre student and accept menial work as a profession. My grandfather conditioned me to be reliant upon him with failure by design. I rarely met his illusive standards and expectations. He repeatedly told me how stupid I was because I could not even hoe weeds properly. I tried hard to please him. I failed only in trying to make sense and consistency with his ever-changing expectations. My mother reminded me that school would become more difficult as I progressed, a signal that she expected my grades to be lower. These lower expectations would keep me close to home to serve my alcoholic mother and my demanding grandfather on his farm.

My mother had parentified my older sister and me. She wanted me to control my younger brother and serve her needs in maintaining the home. Cilla and I were only seven and six years old when we were left to care for Gary and Debra, who were only four and two years old, while she was incapacitated in her drunken state. At an incredibly young age, I maintained the fire in the woodstove, our only source of heat. I mowed the lawn, cared for animals, shoveled the snow from the driveway, did laundry, prepared meals, and many more things. My grandfather similarly reinforced responsibility at an early age. I started driving the farm tractor under supervision at eight years old. By ten years of age, I operated the tractor doing complex farm chores entirely alone.

I remained willing to meet the high standards my mother and grandfather set. I grew frustrated with the constantly changing directions but never gave up. My tenacity was more to avoid prolonged negative verbal assaults than to please them. I was accustomed to their lack of praise for my extraordinary effort. Like the simple thing my father did, taking a step back as I swam to him, I could never reach the target. Never able to achieve the goal, it became easier for me to accept a family culture of failure, never being good enough. Gary accepted this fate. It motivated me to succeed despite them.

The alcoholic's needs dominated our entire family. Money was scarce most of the time. Mother was ultraconservative on such things as food and transportation and ignored such things as clothing to have more money to support her beer habit. Attending any after school activities was out of the question. She did not have the gas money. We also feared she would be drunk, forget about us, or risk a car accident. Mother did not even bother to take us to the dentist until it was required by the state social worker. Our vaccinations were done because we had to bring proof to the school. When my glasses broke, adhesive tape was the only option. It was easier to struggle without glasses than to keep the broken glasses in proper position. Significant injuries, even a pitchfork through Debra's foot, was first treated with home remedies. The cut on my chin obviously needed medical attention yet I was conditioned to understand that it was of lesser importance to my mother's conversation with the neighbor. I had a serious ear infection that was entirely untreated, leaving a permanent scar. Surprisingly, there was no loss of hearing.

We were conditioned to accept certain things as absolute. For instance, priests represented the goodness as God's representatives and must always be trusted. Police could always be trusted to protect the public. Teachers were always right. Our social standing was predetermined and cannot be changed. As I grew older and learned more, I began to question these. Uncle Pat crushed my concept of priests' motives to serve. Our police chief botched the murder investigation of my classmate and was even a suspect. A game warden degraded me for a safely firing my rifle. Teachers' criticism was often personal. I strived with all my effort to please the impossible to please. I learned to question the motives of people who attempted to influence me and gained strength to refuse the stereotype placed upon me.

I learned to trust very few people. Mrs. Hronek genuinely cared for my future and made the extra effort. She had earned my trust over the course of two years with her very dynamic and encouraging math instruction. Similarly, I learned to distrust people beginning with my mother. Cilla and I often disagreed but we still had each other to process the insanity around us. When she could no longer tolerate the constant hateful criticism from our mother, Cilla went to live with our father. I felt a bit deserted as she abruptly left to join our mother's described enemy. Cilla's leaving helped me to reevaluate all the evil things Mother said about our father. He could not have been so evil and irresponsible if he accepted Cilla and later Gary into his home with his new family.

For me, empty praise was as hurtful as harsh criticism. I was alerted to praise telling me how good I was because it was followed by a harsh demand. "You are such a good boy because you will…" I benefitted by praise when I earned it. Praising me for simple things was demeaning. I knew that I could do better. If the person who praised freely and abundantly did not know that I could do better, she or he did not really care about me.

My sister, Cilla, and I struggled one day to remember the happy times. We acknowledged that they were few. As we started identifying some, we realized that most were when my father was around.

I became self-reliant. I heard "You can do anything" from many teachers and the media. My family proved that was not true. Higher class people with the support of their families could do anything. I found an internal thought that encouraged me best. "If anyone can do it, I can." If it is humanly possible, I could prove all those who told me I could not do it were wrong. I relied on this inner encouraging voice whenever I felt discouraged. I also evaluated the benefit of overcoming a challenging situation with the effort required. I accepted abandoning the challenge when I realized that I lacked the motivation, not the ability. I readily abandoned things that seem to have a greater physical or emotional cost than benefit.

I made short-term and long-term plans. Short term plans included schoolwork and projects. Long-term plans included my college education and professional career. Many of the short-term plans supported the long-term plans. I assessed resources and limitations. For instance, all my friends had cars. I saved my money for college. My plans were deliberate and interconnected.

When something did not go as planned, it disrupted everything. Changes outside of my control were very frustrating. The most disruptive influence in my life was my mother's alcoholism. I needed a firm base from which to secure my plans. The solid base I needed was always in turmoil.

Fortunately, I had some good friends in high school. Amazingly, with as many times we moved, we managed to stay in the same school district through junior high and high school. Examining outcomes in my mother's family, I realized all three of Pop and Grandma's children's marriages ended in divorce. Alcohol and, with Uncle Bernie, marijuana were prevalent. My alcoholic great grandfather's alcoholism is the root of collateral damage that spanned several generations. He also had a failed marriage. The alcoholism skipped Pop's generation and landed squarely on their children. My mother and Uncle Bernie were alcoholics. Aunt Alice married one.

As I grew older, I gained more control over my life. However, I suffered some deep physical and emotional wounds. I have some permanent effects of physical abuse and neglect. I must explain to the doctor the scar on my eardrum with every physical. I suffer with declining dental health from the neglect during my childhood. Most notable and forever challenging is the damage to my vision. The blow to the top of my head from my angry mother caused the brain damage that affects my right eye. My eyes do not work together. I mostly ignore the sight in my right eye as it drifts up and away from my focus. I often just close the eye to stop conflicting messages so I can concentrate better. An interesting physical effect is that I feel no pain when someone pulls my hair. It was my victory over one of my mother's impulsive and brutal punishments. I learned to turn off the pain. I only felt the annoying strain in my neck muscles.

Self-esteem and emotion regulation were more difficult to understand and control. I found it helpful to convince myself that I could do anything so long as I had the motivation. All my life my mother and grandmother told me how I should feel. Grandma's guidance was based on her rigid Catholic beliefs. She identified what would cause someone to go to heaven or hell. There seemed to be many more things that would cause one to go to hell. Mother's emotional guidance was more centered around her and isolating the family. She disseminated brutal consequences for violations of her expectations. The kneeling in the corner was intended to make us think about what we did wrong. There was no explanations or discussion. All it did was fuel my hatred of her involvement in my life. As we grew older, Mother moved away from physical punishment to more of her dramatic emotional response while disregarding our emotional needs. We guarded her emotional well-being to avoid her wrath. Emotions were something that I kept to myself and mostly suppressed. We heard many times, "Stop crying or I will give you something to cry about." When we perceived justice when a sibling was rightfully punished, Mother would say, "Wipe that smirk off your face before I do." Mother was the important victim requiring the greatest sympathy. She was stuck with four kids. Only she was allowed feel sorry for herself and cry. We were expected to appreciate everything she did for us. My self-esteem suffered with the devaluation of my emotions by the adult family members.

For me, trust and ethics are inseparable. An alcoholic makes many unkept promises. They are little things such as a treat for performing some task on behalf of the alcoholic. The alcoholic often does not deliver the treat. When questioned, excuses can be simply that there is not enough money and she will provide it later, which never happens. The sobered alcoholic may viciously respond scornfully because we are being selfish. These simple broken promises erode at the conceptual development of right and wrong. The adult can make a promise and later deny the rightful reward.

An alcoholic's life is a life of lies. The greatest denial is the alcoholism. Other lies are ones she tells herself and repeats to her children, "You have it better than I had it." The alcoholic's repetition of the lie somehow makes it true. The alcoholic tells great and small lies to people in authority. Mother lied to her own parents about her drinking. She deceived the welfare lady. She even deceived the local store owners by buying subsequent six packs of her beer from different stores. Her most serious lie was trying to accuse the subject of her shunned sexual advance of trying to abduct my sister.

Science and math became my strength. In math, there were rules that did not change. The numbers were true as you followed the rules. I could be consistently right. Science was about facts. Most facts are easily measurable. Some involve a certain interpretation, but it always followed a process. Facts do not change. How you look at them can. I found a means to make sense of my crazy world. English grammar has rules, but there were too many exceptions. History was wide open for interpretations and teachers encouraged it. I had great difficulty with this relaxed structure. A portion of my world was described by math and science and provided stability. The remainder of my world was in constant turmoil and flux. My world around my mother also fell into two categories. One was when she was sober. The other was when she was drunk.

I had power and control over my math and science world. I accepted that I had little power and control over the remainder. It was easy for me to give up on things in the world of flux. My math and science mind could not make sense of the craziness in the flux world. I avoided most things in the flux world when I could not understand them. I escaped into my daydream world where I had absolute control. My dreamworld was based on science concepts.

I recognized how some things triggered my coping skills. When alcohol is present, I immediately become very guarded. I intensely seek additional information on the people consuming it. Why are they drinking? How much have they drunk? I seek ways to limit my involvement based on my observations, then escape.

Supermoms and the statement "My kids come first" and describe their great mothering skills are triggers for me. The worst supermom trigger shares physical and behavioral characteristics with my mother. Large, overweight women who sit and direct their kids on what and how to do things. I respect those mothers who get up, show their children how to do things, and use kind words of praise. To me, a child's needs are obviously a priority. Stating it leads me to suspect that the kids' needs are not always the priority. Supermoms describe their great attributes as a mother. Honorable parents focus on the child's accomplishments.

Another trigger for me is when someone takes advantage of another. I remember how my mother was so happy to receive extra money in change from the grocer. She did not care that the clerk would have to make up the difference. Mom would say, "It's her fault for not counting right." School bullies also bothered me. I had little power to stand up to them, being one of the youngest during the early school years. Even after I grew larger than the bully, I continued to be prevented from standing up for myself for fear of punishment from school officials. I suffered in silence.

Humans seek order and symmetry to feel safe. When events are in logical sequence and circumstance, they are predictable. Rules and expectations are consistent. They apply in minor and major circumstances. Forgiveness for rule violations is earned with reasonable restitution. In an alcoholic dominated home, there is no consistency. The unpredictability feeds insecurity for all household members, including the alcoholic. Cilla and I benefitted from the order and symmetry in my grandparents' home during the summers. I found more security at school and especially with certain teachers and topics.

Transitioning to adulthood and college was not enough to escape the effects of my mother's alcoholism through my childhood. It was hard for me to focus on my studies while worrying about what was going on at home. With Cilla and Gary living with Dad, only Debra was at home. As futile as it was most of the time, we were perhaps the only check on Mother's bizarre behavior when she was drunk. Debra lacked the minimal recognition we were able to muster. The most overwhelming realization of Mother's profound effects upon me was when I discovered that she depleted my bank account, preventing me from returning to school. I managed to rally funds and protections so that I was able to return to college. I had to defend myself against my mother's efforts to sabotage my future. Her actions left a deep, irreparable harm to my relationship to her. I still needed a place to go when college was not in session. I remained trapped in a lifestyle with no immediate escape. I hated my mother. I loved my mother. How can two strong and opposing emotions exist simultaneously?

An alcoholic who has stopped drinking is still an alcoholic. We describe him or her as an alcoholic in recovery. While recovering, the alcoholic is hoping to put her or his life back together, recreating some normalcy. The people harmed by this alcoholic are his or her collateral damage. These people are always in recovery. We might have never had experienced any normalcy and never will. We are the collaterally damaged persons who are forever in recovery, seeking that elusive normal life.

I sometimes ponder this analogy when I do the laundry. You cannot put your pants on with one leg inside out. You can put part of one leg on properly. This is the part that people see. What they do not see is your efforts to put that inside out leg on. You might try twisting the waist and slipping your second leg in, but you can only pull your pants part way up. You might try to insert you leg into the bottom end of the inside out leg. Again, you can only pull it part way up. Lastly, you might try turning one leg inside out while wearing it. Again, you will not get the leg fully inside out. Indeed, you might cause great pain to your groin trying any of these techniques. Collaterally damaged children of alcoholics keep trying to put their pants on with one leg inside out, unable to admit that it is impossible. We can easily fix our pants and put them on properly. We cannot fully correct the inside out damage the alcoholic caused to our lives. We can adjust, compensate, and even find motivation from it.

CPSIA information can be obtained
at www.ICGtesting.com
Printed in the USA
LVHW012210050821
694387LV00008B/369